Dear Grandma & Papa (or Grampy, Gramps, Grandpapa etc)

Because you didn't have enough to read already we thought you would like a book. Thank you for the wonderful example you have set and continue to set for us. Our thoughts and prayers go with you as you begin your second mission.

We love you.

Sincerely Greg, Emily and the boys.

The
INFINITE
ATONEMENT

The INFINITE ATONEMENT

TAD R. CALLISTER

DESERET BOOK

SALT LAKE CITY, UTAH

Visit us at DeseretBook.com

First printing in hardbound 2000
First printing in leatherbound 2006

Library of Congress Cataloging-in-Publication Data

Callister, Tad R., 1945–
   The infinite atonement / Tad R. Callister.
      p.   cm.
   Includes bibliographical references.
   ISBN-10 1-57345-623-3 (hardbound)
   ISBN-13 978-1-57345-623-4 (hardbound)
   ISBN-10 1-59038-671-X (leatherbound)
   ISBN-13 978-1-59038-671-2 (leatherbound)
   1. Jesus Christ—Mormon interpretations. 2. Atonement. I. Title.
BX8643.A85 C35   2000
2322'.3—dc21   99-055571

Printed in the United States of America
Edwards Brothers Inc., Ann Arbor, MI

47 48

CONTENTS

ACKNOWLEDGMENTS

To each of the following I express my profound gratitude for their candid, but ever-so-helpful comments and support:

To my wife, Kathy, and to each of our children (and their spouses)—namely Kenneth and Angela Dalebout, Richard and Heather Callister, Nathan and Bethany Callister, Robert and Rebecca Thompson, Jeremy Callister, and Jared Callister—for their patience and for their willingness to tell me not only what I wanted to hear, but what I needed to know. They were an invaluable support system who not only encouraged me but also made many helpful contributions along the way.

To my secretary, Julie McLaren, who for eighteen years typed multiple manuscripts, researched, discussed many issues with me, made repeated constructive comments about style and substance, and encouraged me from beginning to end.

To my brother Douglas L. Callister, whose doctrinal background is extensive and who helped me refine and temper my thinking and judgment on many critical and difficult doctrinal issues.

To Howard and Joyce Swainston, who courageously suggested that I read the manuscript aloud in the presence of others—and then who patiently and painstakingly participated in that very process. They frequently made significant contributions, drawing from their broad cultural and spiritual backgrounds.

To each of the following who carefully reviewed the manuscript and contributed much through their probing and insightful comments: Joseph Bentley, Stephen R. Callister, Stephen M. D'Arc, Cathie Humphries, Ty Jamison, Paul A. Manwaring, Thomas M. Pearson, and John S. Welch.

To Randall Pixton of Deseret Book Company for the dignified cover and interior designs; to Tonya Rae Facemyer and Laurie C. Cook for their professional typography; to Jay Parry for his meticulous review, uncanny editorial skills, and sensitivity to teaching the atoning doctrine with purity.

FOREWORD

—◦◦◦—

Some things simply matter more than others. Even some doctrines, though interesting and even fun to discuss, must take a
back seat to more fundamental and foundational doctrines. It is
just so with the Atonement of Jesus Christ. The Atonement is the
central act of human history, the pivotal point in all time, the
doctrine of doctrines. Everything we do and everything we teach
should somehow be anchored to the Atonement. Elder Boyd K.
Packer testified: "Truth, glorious truth, proclaims there is . . . a
Mediator. . . . Through Him mercy can be fully extended to each
of us without offending the eternal law of justice. This truth," he
continued, "is the very root of Christian doctrine. You may know
much about the gospel as it branches out from there, but if you
only know the branches and those branches do not touch that
root, if they have been cut free from that truth, there will be no
life nor substance nor redemption in them" (Conference Report,
April 1977, 80).

This is no doubt why the Prophet Joseph Smith spoke of the
resurrection and Atonement as the fundamental principles of our
religion, with "all other things which pertain to our religion" as
appendages (*Teachings of the Prophet Joseph Smith,* 121). An
appendage is something extra, something ancillary, something
attached to the body. Such remarkable doctrines as the premortal

and postmortal existences of man, salvation for the dead, and the knowledge of various degrees of glory hereafter—such doctrines add vitality and substance to our knowledge of the Father's plan and provide answers to age-old questions in the religious world, but they have meaning for us only because of the mediation and Atonement of Jesus Christ.

Because of this, because the Atonement is at the heart and core of all we do, it is vital that we study it, understand it, and apply it. Elder Bruce R. McConkie offered the following sobering counsel: "Now, the atonement of Christ is the most basic and fundamental doctrine of the gospel, and it is the least understood of all our revealed truths. Many of us have a superficial knowledge and rely upon the Lord and his goodness to see us through the trials and perils of life. But if we are to have faith like Enoch and Elijah we must believe what they believed, know what they knew, and live as they lived. May I invite you to join with me in gaining a sound and sure knowledge of the Atonement. We must cast aside the philosophies of men and the wisdom of the wise and hearken to that Spirit which is given to us to guide us into all truth. We must search the scriptures, accepting them as the mind and will and voice of the Lord and the very power of God unto salvation" (Conference Report, April 1985, 11).

Fortunately, there is not an isolated chapter in holy writ to which we turn in order to learn all that we need to know about the Atonement. Wisely, the Lord has spoken often and regularly with his covenant spokesmen concerning this central verity, and thus the doctrinal refrain of redemption in Christ runs throughout the whole of scripture. While Lehi and Jacob offer a sublime treatment of the Atonement, we must also turn to John and Paul and Peter and Benjamin and Alma and Amulek and Isaiah to learn particulars. The Atonement is the burden of all scripture.

Because there is such need to focus our hearts and minds on this central message, I was delighted to discover a book like the present work that focuses so clearly and speaks so forcefully of the Atonement. In organizing and writing this volume, Tad Callister is to be commended for a significant labor, in fact what must have been for him a great labor of love. I find this book to be one of the most complete treatments of the Atonement that I know of anywhere. The flow of the book is systematic and orderly, the writing crisp and penetrating, and the doctrine sound and solid. He has been true to the intent of the ancient seers and particularly loyal to the underlying message of the Book of Mormon and the prophets of the Restoration, without which we would be extremely limited in our knowledge of the Atonement.

It is not easy to strike the delicate balance between a work that is intellectually enlarging and spiritually strengthening, to create something that provides an even deeper reason for the hope within us (1 Peter 3:15). Every once in a while a book comes along that does just that—that stretches the mind and soothes and settles the heart. Brother Callister's work has done that for me. My initial reading of the book found me in deep reflection on a particular doctrinal matter, and within minutes I was busily cross-referencing selected passages whose connection to one another I had not seen before.

After instructing the Nephites (and us as readers of the Book of Mormon) about the need to be reconciled to God through Christ, Jacob inquired: "And now, beloved, marvel not that I tell you these things; for why not speak of the atonement of Christ, and attain to a perfect knowledge of him, as to attain to the knowledge of a resurrection and the world to come?" (Jacob 4:12). Indeed, why not? To be sure, coming to a perfect knowledge of Christ and the Atonement is a lofty goal, one that we probably will not fully reach in this life. But we are called upon in mortality to pursue the course that leads to it, and that course involves searching the scriptures, reading and pondering the teachings of the prophets, and receiving divine direction and insight from that God who delights to honor those who serve him in righteousness and truth (D&C 76:5).

The scriptures. The prophets. Personal revelation. These are the principal tools by which we build our house of faith. And we are assisted in the building process through seeking out of the best books words of wisdom. We thereby "seek learning, even by study

and also by faith" (D&C 88:118). I trust that the reader will conclude, as I have, that this book is worthy of repeated study, first
because it is so well written, but, more important, because it
addresses a subject, *the* subject, that is of everlasting import to
every son and daughter of God.

ROBERT L. MILLET

Dean of Religious Education and
Professor of Ancient Scripture,
Brigham Young University

CHAPTER 1

WHAT IS THE SIGNIFICANCE OF THE ATONEMENT?

———— ∽∞∾ ————

A DOCTRINE FOR ALL SEASONS

A person studying the Atonement is somewhat like the man who retreats to his mountain cabin to enjoy the scenery. If he looks out the window to the east, he will see the snow-capped peaks of the Rockies; but if he fails to examine the view on the west, he will miss the crimson-streaked sunset on the horizon; if he neglects the scene to the north, he will never see the shimmering emerald lake; and if he bypasses the window on the south, he will fail to witness the wild flowers in all their brilliant glory, dancing in the gentle mountain breeze. Beauty besets him in every direction. So it is with the Atonement. Regardless of our vantage point, it is glorious to behold. Every principle underlying it, every consequence flowing from it rewards our intellect, animates our emotions, and enlivens our spirit. It is a doctrine for all seasons.

An attempt to master this doctrine requires an immersion of all our senses, all our feelings, and all our intellect. Given the opportunity, the Atonement will invade each of the human passions and faculties, and in so doing will invite an exhaustion of each in order to more fully grasp its meaning. Those who have refined their cultural sensitivities will approach the Atonement with a more heart-felt empathy for the tenderness and compassion it represents. Those who have sacrificed their lives in service will stand in even greater awe of him who sacrificed his all. Those who have perfected the powers of reason will probe with even deeper insight into the "whys" and "hows," not just the consequences of this intensely sublime doctrine. And those whose spirits are pure and lives are clean will feel a closer kinship to him whose life they have but in small measure mirrored.

The Atonement is not a doctrine that lends itself to some singular approach, like a universal formula. It must be felt, not just "figured"; internalized, not just analyzed. The pursuit of this doctrine requires the total person, for the Atonement of Jesus Christ is the most supernal, mind-expanding, passionate doctrine this world or universe will ever know.

THE MOST IMPORTANT EVENT IN HISTORY

The final week of the Savior's mortal ministry had arrived. For four thousand years prophets had preached and prophesied of the events that would culminate in this particular week. All events in history, memorable as they had been or would yet be, paled in comparison to this moment. This was the focal point of all history.

He who had created worlds without number was about to enter a quiet, secluded garden, a humble plot of ground in his vast cosmic universe. There was no fanfare, no pressing throng to witness the most profound event his creations would ever know. This was a moment so sacred, so sublime, that no human eye could fully pierce, no human mind could fully comprehend its transcending importance. Only three other mortals—Peter, James and John—would be near, and even their witness would be tempered by the twilight and shrouded by sleep.

The appointed hour was at hand. The Son of God stood alone

in all his majestic power against all the artillery of the Evil One. Here was divine love in its consummate expression battling diabolic evil in its cruelest proportions. This was the place and the time for the atonement of Jesus Christ.

If a survey were taken of history's most significant events, common answers might include the harnessing of fire, the discovery of America, the splitting of the atom, landing on the moon, or the invention of the computer. Each is a wondrous event, but absent the backdrop of the Atonement each is of but transitory importance—no more than a shooting star illuminating the sky for a brief moment, and then vanishing into the night. The Atonement gives purpose and potency to every event in history. President Gordon B. Hinckley spoke of its relationship to other events in world history: "When all is said and done, when all of history is examined, when the deepest depths of the human mind have been explored, there is nothing so wonderful, so majestic, so tremendous as this act of grace."[1] This was not just another great event in the chronicles of history. It was, as Hugh Nibley observed, "the one supreme reality of our life upon this earth!"[2]

The prophet Alma shared this belief. He had stepped down as chief judge so he might fully devote his time to the ministry. With prophetic vision he looked down the stream of time and saw "many things to come" (Alma 7:7), and then concluded, "there is one thing which is of more importance than they all— for behold, the time is not far distant that the Redeemer liveth and cometh among his people" (Alma 7:7). Elder Bruce R. McConkie added his testimony to that of Alma: "The most transcendent event in his entire eternal existence, the most glorious single happening from creation's dawn to eternity's endless continuance, the crowning work of his infinite goodness—such took place in a garden called Gethsemane."[3]

All other events, doctrines, and principles are subservient to and appendages of that godly act. That is what the Prophet Joseph taught: "The fundamental principles of our religion are the testimony of the Apostles and Prophets, concerning Jesus Christ, that He died, was buried, and rose again the third day, and ascended into heaven; and all other things which pertain to our religion are only appendages to it."[4]

Lehi knew of the Atonement's preeminent status among gospel principles. Sensing the end was near at hand, he delivered his final sermon to his sons, and in so doing laid out in masterful simplicity the essence of the Fall and Atonement. He then concluded, "I have spoken these few words unto you all, my sons, in the last days of my probation; and I have chosen the good part" (2 Nephi 2:30).

The "good part" of the gospel and, indeed, of all history is the Savior and his atoning sacrifice. The Atonement of Jesus Christ outweighs, surpasses, and transcends every other mortal event, every new discovery, and every acquisition of knowledge, for without the Atonement all else in life is meaningless.

Elder McConkie pays fitting tribute to this noblest of all deeds: "Nothing in the entire plan of salvation compares in any way in importance with that most transcendent of all events, the atoning sacrifice of our Lord. *It is the most important single thing that has ever occurred in the entire history of created things;* it is the rock foundation upon which the gospel and all other things rest."[5] That being the case, one would think that all the world would anxiously turn to the Savior. Unfortunately, that has not been the case. The Savior observed, "I . . . came unto mine own, and mine own received me not" (D&C 6:21). Nephi foresaw this deplorable state of affairs: "The world, because of their iniquity, shall judge him to be a thing of naught" (1 Nephi 19:9). What a tragic observation. It is serious indeed to reject the Savior, but to ignore him, to snub him, to consider him "a thing of naught" is most displeasing to the Lord. There is no mistake about his position on this subject: "I would thou wert cold or hot. So then because thou are lukewarm . . . I will spue thee out of my mouth" (Revelation 3:15–16).

In striking contrast to the room-temperature saints so abhorred by the Lord, Nephi spoke of his people's passion to "talk of Christ . . . rejoice in Christ . . . preach of Christ . . . prophesy of Christ . . . that our children may know to what source they may look for a remission of their sins" (2 Nephi 25:26). Such rejoicing was prompted by their absolute trust in Christ's future Atonement. They knew it was the only event in history that could save them, and thus, for this reason—the redemption of man—the Savior would make his entry into mortality.

The Savior's earthly experience can be conveniently divided into three categories, namely his message, his ministry, and his mission. Only the events associated with his mission, however, required his personal appearance, and thus, his mission, the atoning sacrifice, became the compelling reason for his condescension.

HIS MESSAGE

The Savior's message, meaning the gospel of Jesus Christ, had been preached before the meridian of time and would yet be preached again. From the lips of Adam the pristine gospel truths had been declared millennia before the Savior's ministry. The Lord made it clear that "the Gospel began to be preached, from the beginning" (Moses 5:58). Enoch, Noah, and Abraham also preached the gospel in their dispensations. In post-meridian times the Prophet Joseph would restore the gospel in its fulness, for, as promised to him by the Lord, "This generation shall have my word through you" (D&C 5:10).

Certainly it was a great blessing to have the Savior personally preach his gospel message, but that was not the essential reason for which he came. Others have been his spokesmen, both before and after his mortal advent. Of these spokesmen the Lord declared, "Whether by mine own voice or by the voice of my servants, it is the same" (D&C 1:38). The Savior's message was essential to our salvation, but his personal exposition of it was not. President J. Reuben Clark Jr. gave this caution:

"Brethren, it is all right to speak of the Savior and the beauty of his doctrines, and the beauty of the truth. But remember, and this is the thing I wish you . . . [to] always carry with you, the Savior is to be looked at as the Messiah, the Redeemer of the world. His teachings were ancillary and auxiliary to that great fact."[6]

HIS MINISTRY

The Savior's ministry included the working of miracles, but Enoch, Moses, Elijah, and others had performed similar wonders before his birth. Peter, Paul, and others would perform like miracles after his ascension.

Among the miracles performed by the Savior was his mastery over the elements of nature. Who is not struck when he reads of the Savior's confrontation with the tempest on the Sea of Galilee? The winds had whipped up in a frenzied fury. The waves thrashed against the small fishing vessel with reckless abandon. All hope seemed to be lost. "Master," they said, "carest thou not that we perish?" Then Jesus arose, and with a voice that pierced the troubled elements, cried out, "Peace, be still." In response, those inexorable forces of nature, those forces that seemingly know no restraint, calmed in humble submission. So overwhelming was this display of power that even his disciples cried out, "What manner of man is this, that even the wind and the sea obey him?" (Mark 4:38–39, 41).

The Savior's mastery of nature and the elements was not unique to him, however. Acting with divine power, Joshua bid the sun to stand still and it was done. At Moses' inspired command the Red Sea parted. Upon the spoken word of Enoch the mountains moved, the rivers changed their course, and the earth trembled. Did such power over the elements cease after the meridian of time? Mormon asked a similar question: "Have miracles ceased because Christ hath ascended into heaven?" Then came the unequivocal response, "Behold I say unto you, Nay" (Moroni 7:27, 29). The Savior promised the believer of future generations, "greater works than these shall he do" (John 14:12).

The Savior raised the dead on multiple occasions, but he was not alone in this extraordinary feat. The scriptures record that Elijah raised the widow's son (1 Kings 17:20–22). Peter and Paul restored the dead to life (Acts 9:39–41; 20:9–13). Joseph Smith spoke to Elijah Fordham on his deathbed, "Brother Fordham, in the name of Jesus Christ, arise and walk." History recounts that

Brother Fordham then leaped from his bed in instantaneous recovery.[7] Certainly the powers over death were not restricted to the mortal ministry of the Savior alone.

The Savior had the power to supersede the laws of gravity—he walked upon the water; but this was not a first. Had not Elisha, centuries before, caused an iron axe-head to float so it might be retrieved for the grieved borrower (2 Kings 6:5–6)?

Have not the healing of the blind, the lame, the leper all occurred in other dispensations? The power underlying every miracle performed by the Savior has been present in every dispensation of the gospel, and rightfully so. One of the signs of the true church is to have the same power, gifts, and miracles as existed in the primitive church.

The Savior's ministry included the performance of sacred ordinances (JST, John 4:1–4), as well as miracles, but did not his apostles also baptize, give the gift of the Holy Ghost, and perform every other essential gospel ordinance? The Lord's mortal ministry left us with a wonderful legacy of compassionate deeds, miracles, and priesthood ordinances, but such acts were not confined to his ministry alone.

HIS MISSION

While others could preach the Savior's message and even perform a ministry of miracles and priesthood ordinances, only he could accomplish that divinely appointed mission, namely the redemption of the world. No proxies, no substitutes, no surrogates, not even heaven-sent angels or prophets would or could do. The Atonement required the life and power of a perfect being. He was the sole candidate, the only "name under heaven . . . whereby we must be saved" (Acts 4:12). This is the prime reason he came to the earth: "Behold, I have come unto the world to bring redemption unto the world, to save the world from sin" (3 Nephi 9:21; see also D&C 49:5; 76:40–42).[8] Matthew, quoting the mortal Messiah, recorded the same truth, "The Son of man is come to save that which was lost" (Matthew 18:11; see also Mormon 7:6–7). As important as were his personal message and ministry, they were secondary to his mission—the atoning sacrifice.

THE HEART OF THE GOSPEL

The Atonement is not just a prime teaching of the gospel; it is the heart of the gospel. It infuses life into every doctrine, every principle, and every ordinance, transforming what might otherwise be a lofty but nonetheless lifeless ideal, to a vibrant spiritual truth. So essential is the Atonement to a purposeful life that on occasion it is referred to as "the gospel." While expounding to the Nephites the Savior confirmed this: "This is the gospel . . . that I came into the world to do the will of my Father. . . . And my Father sent me that I might be lifted up upon the cross" (3 Nephi 27:13–14). This same doctrine was audibly declared from the heavens to the Prophet Joseph: "This is the gospel, the glad tidings . . . that he came into the world, even Jesus, to be crucified for the world, and to bear the sins of the world" (D&C 76:40–41). The LDS Bible Dictionary[9] defines the gospel as "good news" and then adds, "The good news is that Jesus Christ has made a perfect atonement."[10]

In a more expansive sense, the gospel is referred to as all those principles and ordinances that comprise the plan of salvation (see D&C 39:6). Even when used in this latter sense, however, we must remember that those principles and ordinances have life and efficacy only because of the Savior's atoning sacrifice. That is exactly what Enoch taught: "This is the plan of salvation unto all men, through the blood of mine Only Begotten" (Moses 6:62). The Atonement is the lifeblood that quickens every gospel precept. It is, as President Gordon B. Hinckley said, "the keystone in the arch of the great plan."[11] Without it all else collapses.

No doctrine supersedes or even approaches the Atonement in importance. It is the grandest miracle to have ever occurred. C. S. Lewis observed that if one takes away the miracles attributed to Buddhism, there would be "no loss" to the religion. If all miracles were eliminated from Islam, he adds, "nothing essential would be altered." Then this striking observation: "But you cannot possibly do that with Christianity, because the Christian story is precisely the story of one grand miracle, the Christian assertion" that Christ came "into human nature, descended into His own universe, and rose again, bringing Nature up with Him. It is precisely one great miracle. If you take that away there is nothing specifically Christian left."[12]

The Atonement is, as Elder McConkie observed, "the center and core and heart of revealed religion."[13] It is indeed the keystone of Christianity and the foundation of a spiritual life. It is the beacon light for a benighted world. It is the fountain from which all hopes spring. Any theology, any philosophy, any doctrine that teaches contrary to the Atonement is built on sand. Brigham Young taught: "The moment the atonement of the Savior is done away, that moment, at one sweep, the hopes of salvation entertained by the Christian world are destroyed, the foundation of their faith is taken away, and there is nothing left for them to stand upon."[14] The Atonement is our singular hope for a meaningful life.

NOTES

1. Hinckley, *Teachings of Gordon B. Hinckley,* 28. (Note: Full references to all footnotes are found in the bibliography.)
2. Nibley, *Of All Things,* 6.
3. McConkie, *Promised Messiah,* 2.
4. Smith, *Teachings of the Prophet Joseph Smith,* 121.
5. McConkie, *Mormon Doctrine,* 60; emphasis added.
6. Clark, *Selected Papers,* 187.
7. Pratt, *Autobiography of Parley P. Pratt,* 254.
8. President Joseph F. Smith spoke of another reason Christ came to earth: "Christ came not only to atone for the sins of the world, but to set an example before all men and to establish the standard of God's perfection, of God's law, and of obedience to the Father." (Smith, *Gospel Doctrine,* 270). This is consistent with the observation of Peter: "For even hereunto were ye called: because Christ also suffered for us, leaving us an example, that ye should follow his steps" (1 Peter 2:21).

9. The Bible Dictionary prepared by The Church of Jesus Christ of Latter-day Saints and published with the LDS edition of the Bible is referred to throughout this work as the LDS Bible Dictionary.

10. LDS Bible Dictionary, 682.

11. Hinckley, *Teachings of Gordon B. Hinckley,* 30.

12. Lewis, *Grand Miracle,* 55.

13. McConkie, *New Witness,* 81.

14. *Journal of Discourses,* 14:41.

CHAPTER 2

WHY STUDY THE ATONEMENT?

———— ⊷⊷ ————

KNOWLEDGE LEADS TO SALVATION

If the Atonement is the foundation of our faith (and it is), then no one should be content with a casual acquaintance of this doctrine. Instead, the Atonement should be paramount in our intellectual and spiritual pursuits. President John Taylor, who fervently pondered the complexities of the Atonement, observed: "There must be some reason why [Christ] was allowed to suffer and to endure; why it was necessary that he should give up his life a sacrifice for the sins of the world. . . . In these reasons we and all the world are intimately concerned; there is something of great importance in all this to us. *The whys and wherefores of these great events are pregnant with importance to us all.*"[1]

Lehi understood the need to both explore and teach the doctrine of the Atonement. While counseling his son Jacob he said, "How great the importance to make these things [the Atonement] known unto the inhabitants of the earth, that they may know that there is no flesh that can dwell in the presence of God, save it be through the merits, and mercy, and grace of the Holy Messiah" (2 Nephi 2:8). Jacob caught the vision of this counsel, for while preaching to his people he thoughtfully asked, "Why not speak of the atonement of Christ, and attain to a perfect knowledge of him . . . ?" (Jacob 4:12). The Prophet Joseph spoke of the depths we must plumb to acquire this "perfect knowledge":

"The things of God are of deep import; and time, and experience, and careful and ponderous and solemn thoughts can only find them out. Thy mind, O man! . . . must stretch as high as the utmost heavens, and search into and contemplate the darkest abyss, and the broad expanse of eternity—thou must commune with God."[2]

B. H. Roberts, one of the prominent scholars of the Church, made reference to "the difficult doctrine of atonement."[3] After intense study he wrote: "By deeper delving into the subject, my intellect also gives its full and complete assent to the soundness of the philosophy and the absolute necessity for the atonement of Jesus Christ. . . . I account it for myself a new conversion, an intellectual conversion, to the atonement of Jesus Christ; and I have been rejoicing in it of late, exceedingly."[4]

For Elder Roberts, such intense study of the Atonement proved to be both a mind-expanding and soul-stretching experience. The intellectual and spiritual blended in wonderful harmony.

King Benjamin knew that our study of the Atonement was not meant solely as an intellectual exercise to satisfy our mental curiosities, nor was it a doctrine to be comprehended only by an elite few. It was critical to our salvation. His last sermon so states: "I say unto you, if ye have come to a knowledge of the goodness of God, and his matchless power, . . . and also, the atonement which has been prepared from the foundation of the world, . . . and should be diligent in keeping his commandments . . . I say, that this is the man who receiveth salvation" (Mosiah 4:6–7). There is no escaping it—our salvation is predicated upon both an understanding and acceptance of Christ's atoning sacrifice.

A MISUNDERSTOOD DOCTRINE

It seems paradoxical that the very doctrine that is essential to our salvation is also one of the least understood doctrines in the

Christian world. The misunderstandings, confusion, and doctrinal heresies associated with this foundational doctrine and its precursor, the Fall, are rampant. The following are examples of such misconceptions taught by many in the Christian world today:[5]

1. Adam and Eve would have had children in the Garden of Eden if they had been allowed to remain.

2. Adam and Eve were not in a state of innocence in the Garden, but rather were experiencing unparalleled joy.

3. The Fall was not part of God's master plan, but rather a tragic step backwards. It was a stumbling block, not a stepping stone in man's eternal journey.

4. If Adam had not fallen, all of Adam's children would have been born in a state of bliss, to live "happily ever after" in Edenic conditions.

5. Because of the Fall, all infants are tainted with original sin.

6. Grace alone can save (i.e., exalt) us, regardless of any works on our part.

7. The physical resurrection of the Savior was merely symbolic; we will be resurrected as spirits without the "limitations" of a physical body.

8. The Atonement does not have the power to transform us into gods; in fact, such a thought is blasphemous.

Each of the foregoing doctrinal assertions is false. They are not minor issues, but major theological points that strike at the doctrinal core of the Atonement. Without a correct understanding of them one will "end up" with many misconceptions of this central Christian teaching. Fortunately, the truth about each of these doctrinal points is taught in the Book of Mormon,[6] with additional support from modern scriptures. (Each of these doctrines is discussed in detail in later chapters.)

There are also many key points of the Atonement that are not incorrectly taught by other religions—they simply are not taught at all. For example, which other religions discuss not only Christ's taking upon himself all sins, but likewise his assumption of all pains, infirmities, and sicknesses inherent in the mortal experience? Who else preaches of the Atonement's power to reach those who have no law or of its retroactive effect upon the saints of premeridian times? Who speaks of its power to transcend the grave and redeem spirits in the postmortal realm? Who else discusses the Atonement's infinite implications as referred to by the Book of Mormon prophets? Ironically, the answers to these questions are not to be found in what many call "mainstream" Christianity, but rather in the restored Church of Jesus Christ. President Ezra Taft Benson taught:

"Much of the Christian world today rejects the divinity of the Savior. They question His miraculous birth, His perfect life, and the reality of His glorious resurrection. The Book of Mormon teaches in plain and unmistakable terms about the truth of all of those. It also provides the most complete explanation of the doctrine of the Atonement. Truly, this divinely inspired book is a keystone in bearing witness to the world that Jesus is the Christ."[7]

Some years ago I had dinner with a retired judge. In the course of our conversation we found ourselves focusing on the Book of Mormon. At one point he made this bewildering statement: "I've read the Book of Mormon and there's nothing new in it that's not already in the Bible." I was dumbfounded. It was obvious that he either had not read the Book of Mormon, or he did not understand it. If it were not for the Book of Mormon, we would fall victim to many of the misconceptions about the Fall and the Atonement, as discussed above, simply because the Bible, as inspired as it is, has had "many parts which are plain and most precious" deleted from its original contents. Nephi prophesied, however, that in the last days "other books" would restore "the plain and precious things which have been taken away from [the Bible]" (1 Nephi 13:39, 40). Fortunately, the Book of Mormon has come to our rescue. It clarifies certain doctrinal points that are ambiguous in the Bible, confirms others, and even more importantly, fills in many of the gaps and voids that are glaringly apparent. As Elder Jeffrey R. Holland has said: "Much of this doctrine [of the Atonement] has been lost or expunged from the biblical records. It is therefore of great consequence that the Book of

Mormon prophets taught that doctrine in detail and with clarity."[8]

Sometimes it is difficult for us as members of the Church to distinguish between our beliefs in the Atonement and those of the rest of the Christian world. Many of us grow up thinking that what we know and believe about this central doctrine is also what the world knows and believes, but it is not so. Without modern scriptures, particularly the Book of Mormon, it is extremely difficult, if not impossible, to grasp many of the basic tenets of the Atonement. Almost two thousand years of Bible interpretation and the varied conclusions arrived at by many in the Christian world should be ample evidence of the need for additional scriptural insight.

For many, the beautiful and deep doctrine of the Atonement is summarily dismissed and placed on the back shelf with the facile response, "Just believe and be saved." Why such an approach? Perhaps Hugh Nibley best articulates the reason:

"So cool has been the reception of the message [of the Atonement] that through the centuries, while heated controversy and debate have raged over evolution, atheism, the sacraments, the Trinity, authority, predestination, faith and works, and so on, there has been no argument or discussion at all about the meaning of the Atonement. Why were there no debates or pronouncements in the synods? People either do not care enough or do not know enough even to argue about it. For the doctrine of the Atonement is far too complicated to have the appeal of a world religion."[9]

Satan has been successful in diverting much of the Christian world's attention from the one doctrine that can save us, the Atonement of Jesus Christ, to the ancillary doctrines that have meaning only because they draw their sustenance from this redeeming event. Like a skilled magician, Satan's every move is to divert our attention and dilute our focus from the primary object at hand, namely Christ's atoning sacrifice, in hopes we will turn exclusively to doctrines of secondary and far lesser import.

His diversionary tactics have been, and will be, of such global proportions that John tragically exclaimed, "Satan . . . deceiveth the whole world" (Revelation 12:9; see also D&C 10:63). After all the sleight of hand ceases and the smoke clears, it is still Jesus Christ, his Atonement, and our obedience to him that saves us— nothing else can do it.

A SOURCE OF FAITH AND MOTIVATION

Some might wonder what difference it makes whether or not they understand the Atonement, as long as they believe and accept its consequences. Such a need is illustrated by an experience of Florence Chadwick, as shared by Sterling W. Sill. It was July 4, 1952. Chadwick, who had previously swum the English Channel, now attempted the twenty-one-mile swim from the southern California mainland to Catalina Island. The water was a freezing 48 degrees. The fog was thick and visibility almost nil. Finally, only a half mile from her destination, she became discouraged and quit. The next day reporters clamored around her asking why she had quit—had it been the cold water or the distance. It proved to be neither. She responded, "I was licked by the fog." She then recalled a similar experience while swimming the English Channel. Evidently the fog was likewise engulfing. She was exhausted. As she was about to reach out for her father's hand in the nearby boat, he pointed to the shore. She raised her head out of the water just long enough to see the land ahead. With that new vision, she pressed on and became the first woman to conquer the English Channel.[10]

That story teaches a magnificent principle: with increased vision can come increased motivation. So it is with the Atonement. As our vision of the Atonement is enhanced, our motivation to embrace its full effects is proportionately increased. President Howard W. Hunter gave this promise: "As we come to understand His mission and the atonement which He wrought, we will desire to live more like Him."[11] The divine consequences of so studying were disclosed by Elder Neal A. Maxwell: "The more we know of Jesus' Atonement, the more we will humbly and gladly glorify Him, His Atonement, and His character."[12] Finally, Elder Bruce R. McConkie shared his testimony of the need for this spiritual pursuit in our lives:

"The atonement of Christ is the most basic and fundamental doctrine of the gospel, and it is the least understood of all our revealed truths. Many of us have a superficial knowledge and rely upon the Lord and his goodness to see us through the trials and perils of life. But if we are to have faith like that of Enoch and Elijah, we must believe what they believed, know what they knew, and live as they lived.

"May I invite you to join with me in gaining a sound and sure knowledge of the Atonement."[13]

Every attempt to reflect upon the Atonement, to study it, to embrace it, to express appreciation for it, however small or feeble it may be, will kindle the fires of faith and work its miracle towards a more Christlike life. It is an inescapable consequence of so doing. We become like those things we habitually love and admire. And thus, as we study Christ's life and live his teachings, we become more like him.

NOTES

1. *Journal of Discourses,* 10:115–16; emphasis added.
2. Smith, *Teachings of the Prophet Joseph Smith,* 137.
3. Madsen, "The Meaning of Christ," 277.
4. Conference Report, Apr. 1911, 59.
5. See Smith, *Religious Truths Defined,* 99, 353, and 365 for a summary of various Christian misstatements on the Fall and Atonement; see also Roberts, *The Truth, The Way, The Life,* 345–48, 428; and Smith, *Way to Perfection,* 35.
6. The correct answers are taught, among other places, as follows:

First misconception:	2 Nephi 2:23; Moses 5:11
Second misconception:	2 Nephi 2:22–23
Third misconception:	2 Nephi 2; Alma 42
Fourth misconception:	2 Nephi 2:22–23
Fifth misconception:	Moroni 8

Sixth misconception:	2 Nephi 25:23
Seventh misconception:	Alma 40:23; 3 Nephi 11:13–17
Eighth misconception:	3 Nephi 12:48; 27:27; Moroni 10:30–33.

7. Benson, *Witness and a Warning,* 18.

8. Holland, *Christ and the New Covenant,* 199.

9. Nibley, *Approaching Zion,* 600–601.

10. Conference Report, April 1955, 117.

11. Hunter, "Speeches of President Hunter," 7.

12. Maxwell, "Enduring Well," 10.

13. McConkie, *New Witness,* xv.

Chapter 3

Can We Fully Comprehend the Atonement?

⎯⎯ ⊶⊷⊷ ⎯⎯

RECEIVING KNOWLEDGE UPON KNOWLEDGE

As we study the Atonement, can we master its intricacies and details? Can we know the whys and hows as well as we know the consequences? Elder James E. Talmage shed light on our inability to fully comprehend this doctrine:

"All the details of the glorious plan, by which the salvation of the human family is assured, may not lie within the understanding of man; but man has learned, even from his futile attempts to fathom the primary causes of the phenomena of nature, that his powers of comprehension are limited; and he will admit, that to deny an effect because of his inability to elucidate its cause would be to forfeit his claims as an observing and reasoning being.

"Simple as is the plan of redemption in its general features, it is confessedly a mystery in detail to the finite mind." [1]

Our inability to "know it all," however, does not absolve the need (nor should it diminish our desire) to know what is "knowable." Perhaps by so exhausting the knowable, we push and probe and occasionally even penetrate the infinite. The Prophet Joseph was our exemplar in this regard. He was the "master asker." His queries triggered the First Vision, the Word of Wisdom, the revelation on celestial marriage, the vision on the three degrees of glory, and in truth, almost every other notable revelation in this dispensation. He exploded the parameters of divine knowledge because he righteously asked. He was empirical proof of the divine invitation, "If thou shalt ask, thou shalt receive revelation upon revelation, knowledge upon knowledge, that thou mayest know the mysteries and peaceable things" (D&C 42:61; see also 1 Nephi 10:19; D&C 6:7; 11:7).

It was this same spiritual process of inquiry that allowed Nephi to see and understand the vision his father had witnessed concerning the tree of life. Is it any wonder that Nephi became frustrated with his brothers when he learned of their disputations concerning Lehi's dream? He asked of them the soul-searching question, "Have ye inquired of the Lord?" Their answer was most disappointing: "We have not; for the Lord maketh no such thing known unto us." Nephi was not about to let this answer stand. Speaking for the Lord, he responded with the correct principle that unlocks the door to divine knowledge: "If ye will not harden your hearts, and ask me [God] in faith . . . with diligence in keeping my commandments, surely these things shall be made known unto you" (1 Nephi 15:8, 9, 11). The Lord made this reassuring promise to all those who diligently search for truth: "If thou wilt inquire, thou shalt know mysteries which are great and marvelous" (D&C 6:11).

One might consider the consequences if President Joseph F. Smith had not inquired concerning the spirits beyond the veil. Or what if President Spencer W. Kimball had not sought revelation concerning extending the priesthood to all worthy male members? If those good men had not righteously ventured out, seeking more, the glorious truths they received would have remained unrevealed in the celestial realms. As long as there is truth to be known and righteous men who ask, the Lord can and will, in his due course, pour "down knowledge from heaven upon the heads of the Latter-day Saints" (D&C 121:33). The possibilities for future revelation seem limitless, as foretold by the Lord:

"To them will I reveal all mysteries, yea, all the hidden mysteries of my kingdom from days of old, and for ages to come. . . . Yea, even the wonders of eternity shall they know. . . . For by my Spirit will I enlighten them, and by my power will I make known unto them the secrets of my will—yea, even those things which eye has not seen, nor ear heard, nor yet entered into the heart of man" (D&C 76:7–8, 10; see also Articles of Faith 1:9).

Following that promise the Lord opened his heavenly treasures and poured out priceless gems concerning the resurrection and degrees of eternal glory in what many consider to be the most expansive revelation given in this dispensation. No doubt heavenly doors will continue to open, and divine treasures will yield up their sacred gems in response to honest men and women who earnestly and humbly seek the greater light. It is such souls who will be privileged to "understand in their hearts" (3 Nephi 19:33), as well as in their minds, the deep doctrine and purifying passion of the Atonement.

NO GENERATION SHOULD KNOW MORE

With the completion of the LDS edition of the King James Bible in 1979, a new era of gospel scholarship commenced. As a result, the current generation is discovering truths, insights, and additional confirmations unknown to many of its forefathers—not because the current generation is necessarily more righteous, nor because it has greater intellect, but because it has better tools. The most knowledgeable farmer with a horse and plow is no match for an equally proficient farmer with a high-tech tractor at his command. The mathematician with a slide rule is no challenge to his colleague with a high-speed computer. A Galileo with a hand-held telescope will never discover the universe like a Galileo with the most advanced telescope at his disposal. The Lord must expect much more of us in gospel scholarship than he did of previous generations, because we have so much more at our disposal.

Elder Boyd K. Packer observed: "The older generation has been raised without them [the LDS edition of scriptures], but there is another generation growing up. The revelations will be opened to them as to no previous generation in the history of the world. . . . They will develop a gospel scholarship beyond that which their forebears could achieve."[2]

Nephi saw our day and prophesied that the believers "shall come to the knowledge of their Redeemer and the very points of his doctrine, that they may know how to come unto him and be saved" (1 Nephi 15:14). While it is true for the time being that we "cannot bear all things," it is also true that the Lord has given us this consoling hope: "Be of good cheer, for I will lead you along" (D&C 78:18). If we will be patient and let the Lord lead us along in our gospel studies, we might ultimately become recipients of that glorious promise, "The day shall come when you shall comprehend even God, being quickened in him and by him" (D&C 88:49).

The following chapters are intended to draw upon the reservoir of spiritual tools with which the Lord has blessed us in this generation and thus assist us in our pursuit of exhausting the "knowable" and, on occasion, perhaps scratching the surface of what now seems to be the infinite. By so doing, may we increase our devotion to and appreciation for the Atoning One, and ultimately "come unto him and be saved" (1 Nephi 15:14).

NOTES

1. Talmage, *Articles of Faith*, 76–77; emphasis added.
2. Packer, *Let Not Your Heart Be Troubled*, 9.

CHAPTER 4

WHAT ARE THE PURPOSES OF THE ATONEMENT?

⊶∞⊷

THREE PURPOSES

What is the Atonement of Jesus Christ? It is, in short, that *suffering* endured, that *power* displayed, and that *love* manifested by the Savior in three principal locations, namely, the Garden of Gethsemane, the cross of Calvary, and the tomb of Arimathaea. In a larger sense, the Atonement commenced when the Savior made that selfless offer in the premortal council, "Here am I, send me" (Abraham 3:27), and continues without end as he "bring[s] to pass the immortality and eternal life of man" (Moses 1:39).

There are at least three principal purposes of the Atonement:

First: To restore all that was lost by the fall of Adam. This was done by (1) bringing about the resurrection for *all* men,[1] thus overcoming physical death (see 1 Corinthians 15:21–22); and (2) restoring *all* men to the presence of God for the purpose of being judged, thus overcoming what the scriptures call a first spiritual death (see Helaman 14:16; D&C 29:41). Both of these deaths were imposed upon all men because of Adam; both of these deaths were overcome for all men through Christ.

Second: To provide for the possibility of repentance so that men might be cleansed from their individual sins and by so doing overcome what the scriptures call a second spiritual death (see Helaman 14:18).

Third: To provide the power necessary to exalt us to the status of a god (see D&C 76:69).

These three purposes are designed to help us permanently return to God's presence and become like Him.

TO BECOME "AT ONE" WITH GOD AND LIKE GOD

The word *atonement* as used in the scriptures generally refers to the events centered in Gethsemane, Calvary, and the tomb—or to sacrifices that were a "type" of such events. The events in these three locations constitute the mainspring of the Savior's mission. Some have suggested that the structure of this word also helps us to understand the prime purpose underlying these holy events, namely, to achieve a *one*-ness with God.

The word *atonement* is not Greek or Latin, but rather has its origins in the English language. Hugh Nibley explains that the structure of the word "really does mean, when we write it out, at-*one*-ment, denoting both a state of being 'at one' with another and the process by which that end is achieved."[2] Further insight into the meaning of the word is offered by Elder James E. Talmage: "The structure of the word in its present form is suggestive of the true meaning; it is literally *at-one-ment,* 'denoting reconciliation, or the bringing into agreement of those who have been estranged.'"[3] Stephen Robinson made a similar observation: "*Atonement* means taking two things that have become separated, estranged, or incompatible, like a perfect God and an imperfect me or you, and bringing them together again, thus making the two be 'at one.'"[4] A corollary thought is shared in the LDS Bible Dictionary: "The word [*atonement*] describes the setting 'at one' of those who have been estranged, and denotes the reconciliation of man to God."[5] Jacob focused on such a oneness when he admonished his brethren to "be reconciled unto him [God] through the atonement of Christ" (Jacob 4:11; see also 2 Chronicles 29:24). The literal meaning of the word *atonement* is further explained by Hugh Nibley: "There is not a word among those translated as 'atonement' that does not plainly indicate the return to a former state or condition; one rejoins the family, returns to the Father, becomes united, reconciled, embracing and sitting down happily with others after a sad separation."[6]

Accordingly, one purpose of the Atonement, as denoted by the structure of the word, is to help us become at one *with* God in the sense that we can physically live in his presence. The Atonement provides a means by which we can reconcile with God and return to our native home. Hugh Nibley spoke of this divine reunion: "The law leads us back home; the at-*one*-ment takes place when we get there."[7]

Our mortal lives are a constant struggle between choosing a oneness with God or a oneness with the world. To assist us in this pursuit, Christ "gave himself for our sins, that he might deliver us from this present evil world" (Galatians 1:4). He wants to bring us to the safety of his home. That is why the Savior pled, "Father, I will that they also, whom thou hast given me, be with me where I am" (John 17:24). The Savior promised the faithful that "where my Father and I am, there ye shall be also" (D&C 98:18). This is the *redemptive* quality of the Atonement—to so *cleanse* our lives that we are worthy to dwell with God eternally, for "no unclean thing can dwell with God" (1 Nephi 10:21; see also D&C 25:15). That is the glorious condition Eliza R. Snow sought, as revealed in her concluding verse of "O My Father":

> *Then, at length, when I've completed*
> *All you sent me forth to do,*
> *With your mutual approbation*
> *Let me come and dwell with you.*[8]

There is another purpose of the Atonement, however, as denoted by the structure of the word. It is to help us become at one *with* God in the sense that we are *like* him. This is the *exalting* quality—to become so *perfected* in our lives that not only do we live with God, but we become like him. This is the ultimate oneness. Oneness is not only a matter of geography, but of identity. The issue is not just where we live, but what we become. To live with God does not assure us we will be like him. All who live in the celestial kingdom dwell with God, but only those who are exalted become as he is. The objective of the Atonement is not just to cleanse us, but to so transform our lives and our way of thinking and acting that we become like God. Hugh Nibley spoke of this oneness:

"It should be clear what kind of *oneness* is meant by the Atonement—it is being received in a close embrace of the prodigal son, expressing not only forgiveness but oneness of heart and mind that amounts to identity, like a literal family identity as John sets it forth so vividly in chapters 14 through 17 of his Gospel."[9]

Near the conclusion of the Savior's mission he prayed for all those who believed on him. He prayed that "they all may be one; as thou, Father, art in me, and I in thee, that they also may be one in us" (John 17:21; see also D&C 35:2). He affirmed that "the glory which thou gavest me I have given them; that they may be one, even as we are one" (John 17:22). Finally he pled, "that they may be made perfect in one" (John 17:23). This is the ultimate in oneness, to be as God is.

If there had been no Atonement of Jesus Christ, there would have been a terrifying oneness—a negative atonement so to speak—a living with and becoming like the Evil One. Jacob spoke the somber truth when he said we would "remain with the father of lies" and worse yet, we would "become like unto him" (2 Nephi 9:9). Simply stated, we would be at one with Satan in location and at one with him in likeness. Such a terrifying thought helps put the Atonement in perspective. Without it, all is lost. With it, all may be gained. However bleak or desperate our condition may seem, however dark and ominous the skies may appear, Mormon gave the reassuring answer: "Behold I say unto you that ye shall have hope through the atonement of Christ" (Moroni 7:41). Because of the Savior we can be reconciled with God; we can be one again.

The ability of man to be at one with God in both location and in likeness is possible only because the Savior first became at one with man in location, through his mortal birth, and at one with man in likeness, through his assumption of man's frailties—without ever abandoning his godlike character. Paul observed that the Savior became "*like* unto his brethren" (Hebrews 2:17; emphasis added). There was something in the Savior's descent that made possible man's ascent.

A PHYSICAL SYMBOL OF THE ATONEMENT

This reconciliation between God and man is figuratively and literally symbolized by an embrace. Lehi alluded to this in his dying sermon to his sons: "The Lord hath redeemed my soul from hell; I have beheld his glory, and I am encircled about eternally in the arms of his love" (2 Nephi 1:15). The Doctrine and Covenants suggests the same imagery: "Be faithful and diligent in keeping the commandments of God, and I will encircle thee in the arms of my love" (D&C 6:20). Amulek preached in like fashion: "Mercy can satisfy the demands of justice, and encircles them in the arms of safety" (Alma 34:16). What a beautiful metaphor. What child does not feel safety in the arms of his kind and loving father? What peace, what warmth, what reassurance, to know that in his arms he is safe from crime, anger, rejection, loneliness, and all the ills of this world.

Isaiah spoke of those tender moments when the Lord would "gather the lambs with his arm, and carry them in his bosom" (Isaiah 40:11). Elder Orson F. Whitney experienced such a glorious moment when he saw a marvelous manifestation of the Savior. In his dream, he said, "I ran [to meet Him] . . . , fell at his feet, clasped Him around the knees, and begged Him to take me with him. I shall never forget the kind and gentle manner in which He stooped, raised me up, *and embraced me*. It was so vivid, so real. I felt the very warmth of his body, as He held me in his arms."[10] Who would not long for that warmth, that embrace?

Who among us will be safely encircled in those arms of love? Are there a chosen few reserved for this honor? Alma lets it be known there is no exclusionary policy: "Behold, he sendeth an invitation unto all men, for the arms of mercy are extended towards them" (Alma 5:33; see also 2 Nephi 26:25–33). That is what the Savior told the Nephites at the time of his appearance: "Behold, mine arm of mercy is extended towards you, and whosoever will come, him will I receive" (3 Nephi 9:14). Such an invitation was not for a brief moment alone, but for our entire probationary period. Nephi understood: "I [the Lord] will be merciful unto them, . . . for mine arm is lengthened out all the day long" (2 Nephi 28:32; see also 3 Nephi 10:6). Even in God's moments of anger, his arms are stretched out still, anxiously enticing the repentant soul.

The Savior spoke to Enoch of that glorious day of reconciliation for the righteous when He said, "We will receive them into our bosom, and they shall see us; and we will fall upon their necks, and they shall fall upon our necks, and we will kiss each other" (Moses 7:63). It is hard to visualize a more glorious reunion than that.

In retrospect, Mormon agonized over the inevitable fate of the fast-decaying Nephite civilization: "O ye fair ones, how could ye have rejected that Jesus, who stood with open arms to receive you!" (Mormon 6:17). It was almost more than he could bear. If they had only repented "they might have been clasped in the arms of Jesus" (Mormon 5:11); they might have been "encircled about with the matchless bounty of his love" (Alma 26:15).

Elder Neal A. Maxwell suggests that the prime reason the Savior personally acts as the gatekeeper of the celestial kingdom is not to exclude people, but to personally welcome and embrace those who have made it back home. It is a touching, intimate thought, expressed as follows:

"If there is any imagery upon which I would focus as I close, it is two scriptures from the Book of Mormon. The one in which we are reminded that Jesus himself is the gatekeeper and that 'he employeth no servant there.' (2 Nephi 9:41.) . . . I will tell you . . . out of the conviction of my soul . . . what I think the major reason is [why he 'employeth no servant there'], as contained in another Book of Mormon scripture which says he waits for you 'with open arms.' (Mormon 6:17.) That's why he's there! He waits for you 'with open arms.' That imagery is too powerful to brush aside. . . . It is imagery that should work itself into the very center core of one's mind—a rendezvous impending, a moment in time and space, the likes of which there is none other. And that rendezvous is a reality. I certify that to you. He does wait for us with open arms, because his love of us is perfect."[11]

Contemplate for a moment the magnetic pull when a little child sees her father on bended knee with arms extended. The invitation is irresistible. The reaction to return is automatic. There is no intellectual analysis. It is like reaching for a blanket in cold weather, turning on the light in a dark room. Some things are not mind-driven, but heart-prompted. These are natural yearnings of the soul—the need for warmth, light, and love. Likewise, our Father in Heaven is extending his arms with the intent to entice us home. How irresistible those arms are to those who seek his warmth, his light, and his love. He invites us to the day of reconciliation, the return to our true home, the day of reunification with our primeval family; he invites us to run to his arms and bask in his embrace. This was the Lord's promise to the children of Israel: "I will redeem you with a stretched out arm. . . . And I will take you to me for a people, and I will be to you a God" (Exodus 6:6–7).

THE NEED TO UNDERSTAND THE FALL

The structure of the word *atonement* gives us insight into its purpose. Likewise, dictionary definitions are helpful. Such definitions tell us that *atonement* means "to redeem," "to reconcile," "to ransom," "to pay one's dues," "to make amends."[12] But for what? The answer—for the fall of Adam and for the "fall" of each person who sins. The fall of Adam necessitated the Atonement. Accordingly, we cannot hope to understand the Atonement without first understanding the Fall. These two doctrines are inextricably bound. In this regard Elder Bruce R. McConkie commented: "Our Lord's infinite and eternal atonement . . . rests on two foundations. One is the fall of Adam; the other is Christ's divine Sonship."[13] President Benson taught a related truth: "No one adequately and properly knows why he needs Christ until he understands and accepts the doctrine of the Fall and its effect upon all mankind."[14] To attempt a mastery of the Atonement without first comprehending the Fall would be tantamount to confronting geometry without a grasp of basic algebraic principles. It would be a futile and frustrating pursuit, hence the need to first study the Fall.

NOTES

1. Chapter 16 explains in greater detail why the resurrection is part of the Atonement.
2. Nibley, *Approaching Zion,* 556.
3. Talmage, *Articles of Faith,* 75.
4. Robinson, *Believing Christ,* 7.
5. LDS Bible Dictionary, 617.
6. Nibley, *Approaching Zion,* 581.
7. Nibley, *Approaching Zion,* 578. Such return, however, is by no means guaranteed. Elder Joseph Fielding Smith gave this caution: "We often hear the word *atonement* defined as being 'at-one-ment' with God. That is a very small part of it. In fact, *the great majority of mankind never becomes one with God, although they receive the atonement.* 'Because strait is the gate, and narrow is the way, which leadeth unto life, and few there be that find it'" (Smith, *Doctrines of Salvation,* 1:125).
8. Snow, "O My Father," in *Hymns,* no. 292.
9. Nibley, *Approaching Zion,* 567–68.
10. Whitney, *Through Memory's Halls,* 83; emphasis added.
11. Maxwell, "But a Few Days," 7.
12. *Roget's 21st Century Thesaurus,* s.v. "atone."
13. McConkie, *New Witness,* 110.
14. Benson, *Witness and a Warning,* 33.

CHAPTER 5

THE FALL OF ADAM

―∞∞―

THE CONDITIONS BEFORE THE FALL

While Adam and Eve lived in the Garden of Eden, they found themselves subject to four basic conditions—two positive and two negative.[1] First, they were immortal,[2] not subject to pain, disease, or death. Speaking of the tree of knowledge of good and evil, God said, "In the day that thou eatest thereof thou shalt surely die" (Genesis 2:17), implying that in the interim, until such an event should occur, Adam and Eve would enjoy a state of immortality. This was a positive.

Second, Adam and Eve walked and talked in the presence of God. This was also a positive. The Prophet Joseph spoke of those glorious days when "God conversed with him [Adam] face to face. In his presence he was permitted to stand, and from his own mouth he was permitted to receive instruction. He heard his [God's] voice, walked before him and gazed upon his glory, while intelligence burst upon his understanding."[3]

Parley P. Pratt had a similar vision of the Garden: "He [Adam] stood in the presence of his Maker, conversed with him face to face, and gazed upon his glory, without a dimming veil between. O reader, contemplate for a moment this beautiful creation, with peace and plenty: the earth teeming with harmless animals, . . .

the air swarming with delightful birds whose never-ceasing notes filled the air with varied melody; . . . while legions of angels encamped round about him and joined their glad voices in grateful songs of praise and shouts of joy. Neither sigh nor groan was heard through the vast expanse; neither were there sorrow, fear, pain, weeping, sickness, nor death; neither contentions, wars, nor bloodshed; but peace crowned the seasons as they rolled, and life, joy, and love reigned over all God's works."[4]

It is hard to imagine a more idyllic setting in which to reside. Adam and Eve were spiritually alive, basking in the presence of our divine Father.

Unlike the first two conditions, the third was a negative. Adam and Eve were in a state of innocence, without a full knowledge of good and evil, and thus unable to experience a fulness of joy. Lehi describes this condition: "And all things which were created must have remained in the same state in which they were after they were created; and they must have remained forever, and had no end. . . . Wherefore they would have remained in a state of innocence, having no joy, for they knew no misery; doing no good, for they knew no sin" (2 Nephi 2:22–23). This was an obstacle to their individual development and progression. Without a complete knowledge of good and evil, Adam and Eve could not exercise the full moral agency that was necessary to bring them to godhood. John Fiske, a Harvard philosopher, grasped this dilemma:

"Clearly, for strong and resolute men and women an Eden would be but a fool's paradise. How could anything fit to be called *character* have ever been produced there? . . . We can at least begin to realize distinctly that unless our eyes had been opened at some time, so that we might come to know the good and the evil, we should never have become fashioned in God's image. We should have been the denizens of a world of puppets, where neither morality nor religion could have found place or meaning."[5]

Professor Fiske understood the transient nature of the Garden in God's plan. Eden was a way-station, not a destination. It was a temporary resting spot in the journey of life. One could not expect to become like God in the Garden of Eden any more than one could expect to drive from Los Angeles to New York while in neutral. Except for the tree of knowledge of good and evil, there were no challenges, no temptations, and no obstacles in that quasi-heavenly setting. Accordingly, there could be no progression. They were temporarily stuck in a world of spiritual sterility.

Lehi spoke of those creations that might be placed in a state where no opposition existed: "Wherefore, it must needs have been created for a thing of naught; wherefore there would have been no purpose in the end of its creation" (2 Nephi 2:12).

The fourth condition was likewise negative. As long as they remained in this garden state, Adam and Eve would have no children (2 Nephi 2:23), no joy in a posterity. What a devastating drawback. Under these conditions they could not obey the divine command to multiply and replenish the earth, which was the foremost design and object of their married life. This condition, if allowed to remain, would have completely negated the reasons the sons of God shouted for joy in premortal times. A continuation of this condition would literally defeat the plan of salvation.

THE CONDITIONS AFTER THE FALL

When Adam and Eve transgressed they were cast out of the Garden. Accordingly, the phrase "the fall of Adam" is used for at least two reasons: first, to describe Adam and Eve's fall from the Father's physical presence, and second, to describe their fall from the state of immortal to mortal beings.[6] Such terminology was used by Alma when describing the consequences of partaking of the forbidden fruit: "We see that Adam did fall" (Alma 12:22; see also 2 Nephi 9:6; Alma 42:6). Elder Talmage confirms that the Fall was a result of partaking of the forbidden fruit and not a consequence of some other act: "Here, let me say, that therein consisted the fall—the eating of things unfit, . . . and I take this occasion to raise my voice against the false interpretation of scripture, which . . . is referred to in a hushed and half-secret way, that the fall of man consisted in some offense against the laws of chastity and of virtue. Such a doctrine is an abomination."[7]

What conditions would Adam and Eve now encounter as fallen beings? Ironically, those four conditions that existed prior to the Fall reversed themselves. The positives became negatives, and the negatives became positives.

First, they were no longer immortal. God had decreed: "In the day that thou eatest thereof thou shalt surely die" (Genesis 2:17). It is interesting to note that Adam, who lived just short of one thousand years, died in one "day" in the Lord's time (2 Peter 3:8; Abraham 3:4). When that promise of death was spoken, the earth was still subject to "the Lord's time, which was after the time of Kolob" (Abraham 5:13). The literalness of God's promise is apparent when we consider a historical account of Edward Stevenson, who quoted the Prophet Joseph as follows: "Father Adam began his work and finished what was to be done in his time, living to be one thousand years old with the exception of about six months. Truly the Bible gives Methuselah the credit of being the oldest but the Prophet Joseph had it revealed to him otherwise. It is only an error of man in translating the record."[8] In the Lord's timetable, Adam died in the same "day" he partook of the fruit, just as God had decreed.

When Adam and Eve partook of the fruit, the seeds of death were planted in their veins and we, their children, inherited their mortal nature. As a result, Adam's race was subjected to physical death, pain, disease, and all the ailments of humanity. Immortality became mortality, and a positive condition became a temporary negative in the eternal plan.

Second, Adam and Eve's transgression resulted in their being cast out from God's presence, which separation from God is spiritual death. The concluding lines of John Milton's *Paradise Lost* capture this heartrending moment of expulsion:

> *The world was all before them, where to choose*
> *Their place of rest, and Providence their guide;*
> *They, hand in hand, with wandering steps and slow,*
> *Through Eden took their solitary way.*[9]

The Doctrine and Covenants describes Adam's fate as follows:

"I, the Lord God, caused that he should be cast out from the Garden of Eden, from my presence, because of his transgression, wherein he became spiritually dead" (D&C 29:41). Jacob describes this spiritual death, triggered by the Fall, as being "cut off from the presence of the Lord" (2 Nephi 9:6; see also Helaman 14:16). No longer did Adam and Eve walk and talk with God. They were now separated from his companionship. Milton poetically dramatizes Adam's tragic lament, as our first parent contemplates the thought of being "cast out" from the presence of the Holy One:

> Therefore to his great bidding I submit.
> This most afflicts me, that, departing hence,
> As from his face I shall be hid, deprived
> His blessed countenance; here I could frequent,
> With worship, place by place where he vouchsafed
> Presence Divine, and to my sons relate,
> "On this mount he appeared; under this tree
> Stood visible; among these pines his voice
> I heard; here with him at this fountain talked."[10]

Adam and Eve were quick to learn the harsh consequences of the Fall: "I [the Lord] will greatly multiply thy sorrow" and "cursed shall be the ground for thy sake" (Moses 4:22–23). For the first time there would be thorns and thistles to prick them and wild animals to threaten them. No longer would Adam leisurely pick the fruit of the Garden's endless supply, for the Lord decreed, "By the sweat of thy face shalt thou eat bread" (Moses 4:25).

After the expulsion, the Lord spoke to Adam and Eve "from the way toward the Garden of Eden," to which Moses then adds, "and they saw him not; for they were shut out from his presence" (Moses 5:4). To be shut out from the presence of God was not to lose all communication with him; that would defeat the plan of salvation. Rather, it was to be cast out from his physical presence, leaving all other forms of communication open. Such physical separation, caused by the Fall, seems to have been triggered by dual, compelling forces: first, the eternal law that prohibits a fallen mortal being from standing in the presence of God,[11] for no "natural man [can] abide the presence of God" (D&C 67:12), and second, the inherent drive of the transgressor to spiritually retreat from that which is holy. Moses was so ashamed of his disobedience that he "hid his face from the Lord" (JST, Exodus 4:26). Peter pleaded before the Savior, "Depart from me; for I am a sinful man" (Luke 5:8). It was as though King Benjamin were reading the spirit of every errant man when he commented, "The demands of divine justice do awaken his immortal soul to a lively sense of his own guilt, which doth cause him to shrink from the presence of the Lord" (Mosiah 2:38).

Adam and Eve may have been so shrinking when they sought to "hide themselves from the presence of the Lord" (Moses 4:14). Their hiding seems to be much more than an issue of modesty. Elder Talmage so concludes: "They hid themselves; for they had awakened to the fact that there was something vile about them, something unseemingly [sic], something unclean, and they hid themselves."[12] How uncomfortable it must have been for them to stand in the presence of that Holy One who had "breathed" into them the breath of life, who had provided both sustenance and setting, and who had required of them but one restraint, which restraint they had now broken.

It is difficult to fully understand why God gave seemingly conflicting commands in the Garden. Some people feel that the "command" not to partake of the fruit of the tree of knowledge of good and evil was more a warning than a commandment, and thus, Adam and Eve purposefully "disobeyed" a lower law in order to fulfill a higher one.[13]

The scriptures suggest, however, that Eve was at least partially deceived. This "conflict" of commandments seemed to be a necessary part of the grand plan, so that man would not later claim that God forced him to accept the awesome responsibility of mortality. Man had already made the decision to accept earth-life in premortal times, but that was done without the vantage point of terrestrial glasses. Now, Adam and Eve, as the designated representatives of the human race, would confirm that decision from their earthly abode. After their fall, they could not blame God for their mortal travails. He had not mandated their choice. Rather, in apparent opposition to God's command, they and they alone, had chosen to proceed. Perhaps in this way God brought "about his eternal purposes" for he said "[there] must needs be that there was an opposition; even the forbidden fruit in opposition to the tree of life" (2 Nephi 2:15).

In response to God's inquiry as to what Eve had done, she replied, "The serpent beguiled me, and I did eat" (Moses 4:19; see also Genesis 3:13; 2 Corinthians 11:3). In the LDS edition of the Bible, the chapter heading to Genesis 3 reads, "The Serpent (Lucifer) deceives Eve." Paul made a similar observation: "Adam was not deceived, but the woman being deceived was in the transgression" (1 Timothy 2:14). The Doctrine and Covenants tells us "that the devil tempted Adam, and he partook of the forbidden fruit and transgressed the commandment, wherein he became subject to the will of the devil, because he yielded unto temptation" (D&C 29:40).

If Adam and Eve had partaken with "full" knowledge of obeying a higher law, as some would suggest, one wonders why the scriptures would have used words and phrases such as "beguiled," "deceived," "yielded" and even "spiritually dead" (D&C 29:41), to describe their Edenic conduct and subsequent state of affairs. One also wonders how they could have "full" knowledge when they lived in a state of innocence, knowing neither good nor evil. In that state of innocence, it would not have been possible for them to completely comprehend which choice was good and which was evil. One further wonders why Adam, upon responding to the Lord's question, "Hast thou eaten of the tree whereof I commanded thee that thou shouldst not eat . . . ?" (Moses 4:17), would shift the "blame" or responsibility to Eve, and likewise, she would further shift the "blame" to the Serpent (Moses 4:18–19). If they had proceeded with a full or even partial knowledge of the consequences, this would have been an appropriate moment to respond: "We knowingly broke the lesser law in order to keep a higher one. We understand there will be some harsh consequences for the moment, but in the eternal scale of things, it will be a blessing, not a curse to us and our posterity." This would have been a time not of blame, but of explanation as to why the choice had been made.

One might ask: "But what if Adam and Eve had not transgressed? What if they never had yielded and partaken of the forbidden fruit, regardless of their length of stay in the Garden? Would God's plan be frustrated?" Of course, the answer is no. God's work is never frustrated (see D&C 3:3). Certainly God with his omniscience knew that Adam and Eve, of their own agency, would partake. Nonetheless, Elder Talmage responds to the hypothetical questions posed above: "If it can be supposed that our first parents had not fallen surely some other means would have been employed to initiate the condition of mortality on earth."[14]

We do not know all the conditions under which Adam and Eve made that fateful, yet wonderful choice of mortality. Whatever the underlying motivation may have been, we can hold fast to two fundamental truths. First, Adam and Eve are to be commended, not condemned. Someday we will know the full stature of their nobility. If they consciously partook of the fruit, sufficiently understanding the consequences, we honor them. If they partook in innocence or were partially deceived, and thereafter learned the plan of salvation because of their obedience and faithfulness, which plan they thereafter taught with love and diligence to their posterity, then, again, we honor them. Speaking of the Fall, Brigham Young explained: "It was all in the economy of heaven, . . . it is all right. We should never blame Mother Eve, not the least."[15] In that spirit, the scriptures refer to her as "our glorious Mother Eve" (D&C 138:39). Elder Talmage added his witness: "Our first parents were pure and noble, and when we pass behind the veil we shall perhaps learn something of their high estate."[16]

The second truth to be learned is that the Fall was part of God's master plan; it was not an afterthought to address some unexpected action on the part of our first parents. While speaking of the Fall, Lehi commented, "All things have been done in the wisdom of him who knoweth all things" (2 Nephi 2:24). President John Taylor taught: "Was it known that man would fall? Yes. We are clearly told that it was understood that man should fall."[17] The LDS Bible Dictionary adds: "The fall was no surprise to the Lord. It was a necessary step in the progress of man."[18]

The time would come when Adam and Eve would rejoice in their decision, but at the moment of expulsion they knew only thorns, thistles, and sweat. Day after day Adam offered sacrifices without knowing why, without fully understanding the plan of salvation. After "many days" (Moses 5:6), meaning after Adam and Eve had begotten sons and daughters and they in turn had begotten "sons and daughters" (Moses 5:3), an angel came and offered these words of consummate comfort: "As thou hast fallen thou mayest be redeemed, and all mankind, even as many as will." Adam was overjoyed. He "blessed God" and "began to prophesy" and declared "in this life I shall have joy." No doubt he quickly ran to share the good news with Eve, who "heard all these things and was glad." It was at this later date, not at the moment they were driven from the Garden, that Eve, with newfound insight, declared, "Were it not for our transgression we never should have had seed, and never should have known good and evil, and the joy of our redemption" (Moses 5:9–11).

Perhaps, like a woman in labor, Adam and Eve were hopeful the end result of the Fall would be glorious, but the time immediately following their expulsion was one of pain and travail. The Savior spoke to his disciples of a similar moment. During the final week of his mortal ministry he prophesied of his impending crucifixion and departure. He knew they would "be sorrowful" at his separation, but he also promised that in due time their "sorrow [would] be turned into joy" (John 16:20). So it would be with Adam and Eve. The words of the psalmist are ever so applicable: "Weeping may endure for a night, but joy cometh in the morning" (Psalm 30:5).

Our finite minds cannot remotely grasp the enormity of the Fall and its overwhelming consequences. Adam and Eve had enjoyed a heavenly association in God's physical presence.

Melvin J. Ballard, who was privileged for a brief moment to dream of being in that presence, recounts:

"If I shall live to be a million years old, I shall never forget that smile. He [the Savior] took me into his arms and kissed me, pressed me to his bosom, and blessed me, until the marrow of my bones seemed to melt! . . . The feeling that I had in the presence of him who hath all things in his hands, to have his love, his affection, and his blessing was such that if I ever can receive that of which I had but a foretaste, I would give all that I am, all that I ever hope to be, to feel what I then felt!"[19]

David, who knew the pangs of separation, sang, "In thy presence is fulness of joy; at thy right hand there are pleasures for evermore" (Psalms 16:11). Later he pled, "Cast me not away from thy presence" (Psalms 51:11). There is a certain sociality in the presence of God that manifests itself in a fulness of joy. Elder Ballard experienced it; David yearned for it; and Cain forfeited it. Upon learning he had been "driven . . . from the face of the Lord," Cain cried out, "My punishment is greater than I can bear" (Moses 5:38–39). Even Cain in his depraved condition shuddered at the thought of banishment from God, that one being who had shed forth warmth and love, even for him.

To be cast from the presence of the Holy One is estrangement of the worst kind. It is to take from us that which means most—our sense of belonging to the divine family. It is to strip us of security and self-worth in one fatal blow. It is like tearing the suckling babe from her mother's bosom, sending the wayward child to his room, or sentencing the incorrigible to solitary confinement. It is akin to restricting our communication with a loved one to the telephone; the lines can be clear, the conversation frequent, but the happiness that comes from being in another's physical presence is missing. John understood this principle, for when writing to the saints he said, "I would not write with paper and ink: but I trust to come unto you, *and speak face to face, that our joy may be full*" (2 John 1:12; emphasis added). This privilege Adam and Eve were now denied, for they had fallen from God's presence.

Not only had Adam and Eve fallen, but now their entire posterity would be relegated to a similar fate, to be born and raised estranged from the presence of God, a form of spiritual death. Such a universal condemnation was observed by Alma: "By his fall, all mankind became a lost and fallen people" (Alma 12:22).

Two of the consequences of the Fall were negatives, namely physical and spiritual death. But there was also good news. The two previous negatives of the Garden became positives. Adam and Eve were now blessed with a knowledge of good and evil, and appropriately so, for they had partaken of the tree of knowledge of good and evil. This enabled them to "[become] as Gods, knowing good from evil" (Alma 12:31). Satan had told a half-truth: "Ye shall not surely die [this was the falsehood]" but "in the day ye eat thereof, then your eyes shall be opened, and ye shall be as gods, knowing good and evil" (Genesis 3:4–5; see also Alma 42:3). The latter portion of Satan's promise was true. At least eventually, they did become like God in their understanding of good and evil; innocence was exchanged for knowledge; and the potential for joy became a reality. A negative became a glorious positive in the eternal scheme.

In addition, Adam and Eve's mortal bodies could now procreate and fulfill the divine command to multiply and replenish the earth.[20] Lehi wrote, "Adam fell that men might be" (2 Nephi 2:25; see also Moses 6:48), or in the words of Eve, one of the best witnesses of all, "Were it not for our transgression we never should have had seed" (Moses 5:11). Thus with the Fall the human race was born. All of this was consistent with God's master plan.

The Fall was not a tragic step backward; to the contrary, it was a painful but nonetheless giant step forward in our eternal journey. It was the springboard to our ascent.

NOTES

1. The word *negative* as used here is not intended to suggest that anything in God's plan was inappropriate, but rather that the conditions in the Garden of Eden and thereafter resulting from the Fall would have been a bar to our eternal progress had these conditions been allowed to

permanently remain. For each of these conditions, however, God had prepared a remedy.

2. The word *immortal* is used in this context to mean that Adam and Eve could live indefinitely; it is not intended to imply that they possessed the same bodies as immortal resurrected beings receive.

3. Smith, *Lectures on Faith,* 13.

4. Pratt, *Key to the Science of Theology and Voice of Warning,* 85.

5. Fiske, *Studies in Religion,* 252, 266, in Roberts, *The Truth, The Way, The Life,* 349.

6. Elder Talmage wrote: "Their [Adam and Eve's] change from the un-mortal to the mortal state is called the *Fall*" (Talmage, *Sunday Night Talks,* 63).

7. Talmage, *Essential James E. Talmage,* 109. Elder Joseph Fielding Smith taught: "The transgression of Adam did *not* involve sex sin as some falsely believe and teach. Adam and Eve were married by the Lord while they were yet immortal beings in the Garden of Eden" (Smith, *Doctrines of Salvation,* 1:114–15).

8. Joseph Grant Stevenson, "The Life of Edward Stevenson," master's thesis (Provo, Utah: Brigham Young University, 1955), 73; in Matthews, *"A Plainer Translation,"* 85.

9. Milton, *Paradise Lost,* 343.

10. Ibid., 308.

11. Of course, certain mortals have stood in the presence of God, such as Joseph Smith, but only (1) for limited periods of time and (2) after their mortal bodies were transfigured for such purpose. After Moses saw God, he explained that if he had not been transfigured he "should have withered and died in his presence" (Moses 1:11).

12. Talmage, *Essential James E. Talmage,* 111.

13. Elder John A. Widtsoe expressed this feeling: "It [the instruction that Adam could choose for himself] really converts the command into a warning, as much as if to say, if you do this thing, you will bring upon yourself a certain punishment; but do it if you choose." Elder Widtsoe further suggests that "the gospel had been taught [Adam and Eve] during their sojourn in the Garden of Eden. They could not have been left in complete ignorance of the purpose of their creation" (Widtsoe, *Evidences and Reconciliations,* 193–94). Joseph Fielding Smith had similar feelings: "Now this is the way I interpret that: The Lord said to Adam, here is the tree of the knowledge of good and evil. If you want to stay here, then you cannot eat of that fruit. If you want to stay here, then I forbid you to eat it. But you may act for yourself, and you may eat of it if you want to. And if you eat it, you will die." ("Fall—Atonement—Resurrection—Sacrament," in Church Educational System, *Charge to Religious Educators,* 124.)

14. Talmage, *Sunday Night Talks,* 69. See, however, 2 Nephi 2:22–23.

15. *Journal of Discourses,* 13:145.
16. Talmage, *Essential James E. Talmage,* 110.
17. Taylor, *Gospel Kingdom,* 97.
18. LDS Bible Dictionary, 670.
19. Hinckley, *Sermons and Missionary Services of Melvin J. Ballard,* 156.
20. The accounts of the Garden in the canonized scriptures suggest that Eve did not receive her name until after she and Adam had partaken of the forbidden fruit. When Eve was first created, Adam decreed that "she shall be called Woman" (Genesis 2:23; Moses 3:23; Abraham 5:17). Any dialogue in the Garden between Eve, and either God or Satan, conspicuously deletes any reference to the name of Eve. Instead, she is referred to as "the woman," or the wife of Adam. There is a single reference by Moses to the name of Eve, but not in the context of any actual dialogue. He was merely referring to the woman, whom with hindsight he knew to be Eve. After the transgression in the Garden, the Lord announced the manner in which Eve should conceive: "In sorrow thou shalt bring forth children" (Genesis 3:16; Moses 4:22). Then, just as the future parents of all mortals were about to be expelled from their garden home, Adam called "his wife's name Eve; because she was the mother of all living" (Genesis 3:20; Moses 4:26). Moses revealed that this appellation was of the Lord's choosing, "For thus have I, the Lord God, called the first of all women, which are many" (Moses 4:26).

The timing of Eve's "naming" is important because it seems to confirm that she could not become the mother of the human race until after the effects of the forbidden fruit coursed through her veins. This is consistent with other scriptural accounts. In other words, she was not called Eve until she was capable of being Eve (i.e., the mother of all living).

CHAPTER 6

THE RELATIONSHIP BETWEEN THE FALL AND THE ATONEMENT

—⟨∞⟩—

THE ATONEMENT RECTIFIES THE FALL

How could the negatives of the Fall, namely physical and spiritual death, be corrected, amended, and reconciled in the eternal scheme? Of what value was a posterity or godly knowledge if men and women were doomed to remain in the grave, separated from the presence of their God? There was no solution without a Redeemer—someone who would atone, redeem, reconcile, and make amends for these negative conditions. Lehi states it simply and succinctly: "The Messiah cometh in the fulness of time, that he may redeem the children of men from the fall" (2 Nephi 2:26). Lehi understood that the Fall was not without its remedy, for he declared, "The way is prepared from the fall of man, and salvation is free" (2 Nephi 2:4).

The Atonement, Elder Talmage taught, became "a necessary sequel of the transgression of Adam."[1] Moroni clearly explained this sequential necessity: "By Adam came the fall of man. And because of the fall of man came Jesus Christ, . . . and because of Jesus Christ came the redemption of man" (Mormon 9:12). Alma spent considerable time discussing the consequences of the Fall and then declared, "It was expedient that mankind should be reclaimed from this spiritual death" (Alma 42:9). The Atonement was that means of reclamation.

But how was it done? By means of an infinite and eternal sacrifice. As Elder Bruce R. McConkie said, "In some way, incomprehensible to us, Gethsemane, the cross, and the empty tomb join into one grand and eternal drama, in the course of which Jesus abolishes death, and out of which comes immortality for all and eternal life for the righteous."[2]

OVERCOMING PHYSICAL DEATH AND THE FIRST SPIRITUAL DEATH FOR ALL

If asked, "What are the consequences of the Atonement?" many people respond, "It overcame physical death for all men and spiritual death for those who repent." While that answer is correct as far as it goes, it is incomplete. The Fall brought about physical death and, in addition, one type of spiritual death to all men. This was caused by our first parents' transgression in the Garden, known by the world as "original sin." All men physically die because of Adam's transgression. There is no escape from this consequence. Likewise, all men will be resurrected because of Christ. There is no exception to this remedy. Physical death, however, is not the only universal consequence of the Fall. As another consequence of Adam's transgression, all men are born in a setting outside God's physical presence. This separation is known in the scriptures as the *first* spiritual death (see Helaman 14:16–18; D&C 29:41). It is an estrangement from God caused by Adam.

There is also a *second* spiritual death. It is a separation from God caused by our individual sins.

Each form of spiritual death has its cure. The Atonement corrects the first spiritual death for all men without any effort on their own, and understandably so, for they in no way were its cause. The Atonement corrects the second spiritual death on an individual basis for those who repent, since each of us who has sinned must individually contribute to our own redemption, "For we know that it is by grace that we are saved, after all we can do" (2 Nephi 25:23).

The universal effects of the first spiritual death were externally imposed by Adam and externally corrected by Christ for all mankind. Paul taught, "For as in Adam all die, even so in Christ shall all be made alive" (1 Corinthians 15:22). Robert J. Matthews points out that many do not understand these words of Paul. "Most think it only pertains to the death of the body and the resurrection of the body. In truth, Paul's statement covers both physical death and spiritual death,"[3] meaning the first spiritual death brought about by Adam. Brother Matthews then offers this helpful explanation:

"There is a prevailing idea that although the resurrection is free, only those who repent and obey the gospel will ever return to the presence of God. Those who adhere to this idea, however, seem to have missed a very essential point and fundamental concept of the Atonement, and that is that Jesus Christ has redeemed all mankind from *all* the consequences of the fall of Adam.

"The scriptures teach that every person, saint or sinner, will return to the presence of God after the resurrection. It may be only a temporary reunion in his presence, but justice requires that all that was lost in Adam be restored in Jesus Christ. Every person will return to God's presence, behold his face, and be judged for his own works. Then, those who have obeyed the gospel will be able to stay in his presence, while all others will have to be shut out of his presence a second time and will thus die what is called a second spiritual death."[4]

The scriptures teach that "no unclean thing can dwell with God" (1 Nephi 10:21). This does not mean, however, that we will not return to God's presence temporarily for judgment purposes—for in fact each individual will. It simply means we cannot "dwell" or remain in the presence of God on a permanent basis or "be received into the kingdom of God" (Alma 7:21) if we are unclean. In the same verse in which Nephi states that the unclean cannot "dwell with God," he also teaches that the unclean will be brought "before the judgment-seat of God" (1 Nephi 10:21). Lehi clearly taught that all men, even the wicked, will return to God's presence:

"Because of the intercession for all, all men come unto God; where-fore, they stand in the presence of him, to be judged of him according to the truth and holiness which is in him" (2 Nephi 2:10; see also Alma 33:22). Jacob, who learned so much about the Atonement from his father, also spoke of this temporary reunion, even for the wicked: "Wo unto all those who die in their sins; for they shall return to God, and behold his face, and remain in their sins" (2 Nephi 9:38). Jacob then prophesied that those who reject the prophets will stand "with shame and awful guilt before the bar of God" (Jacob 6:9; see also Mormon 9:5).

Alma makes it clear that the return to God's presence is no optional program, no joyous reunion for the wicked, for "we would fain be glad if we could command the rocks and the mountains to fall upon us to hide us from his presence." As if this were not enough, his description adds to the terror of the moment: "We must come forth and stand before him in his glory, and in his power, and in his might, majesty, and dominion, and acknowledge to our everlasting shame that all his judgments are just" (Alma 12:14–15). This will be the day of reckoning when "the judgments of God . . . stare them in the face" (Helaman 4:23).

Amulek warned that at the fateful moment of our judgment we will "have a bright recollection of all our guilt" (Alma 11:43). Jacob knew that we would have "a perfect knowledge of all our guilt, and our uncleanness" (2 Nephi 9:14), and Alma foresaw that we would have "a perfect remembrance" (Alma 5:18) of all our wicked deeds. What a sobering thought. It was such a frightening reality that confronted Alma: "Yea, I did remember all my sins and iniquities, . . . and in fine so great had been my iniquities, that the very thought of coming into the presence of my God did rack my soul with inexpressible horror" (Alma 36:13–14). So terrifying was the prospect of this encounter with the Holy One that Alma longed for banishment and extinction rather than "be brought to stand in the presence of my God" (Alma 36:15).

Then a miracle occurred. In the midst of Alma's suffering he recalled his father speaking of the Savior and his atoning sacrifice "for the sins of the world" (Alma 36:17). The very thought of the

Savior was a balm to his wounded soul and frenzied mind, so much so that he exclaimed, "I was harrowed up by the memory of my sins no more" (Alma 36:19). He then saw "God sitting upon his throne" and in a stunning spiritual turnabout his "soul did long to be there" (Alma 36:22). He, who earlier had sought banishment from God's presence and extinction of his soul, now yearned for life everlasting in God's presence.

The scriptures are clear on this point: whether pleasant or unpleasant, there will be a reunion for all men before their Maker.

In summary, the Atonement was intended to restore all that was lost by the Fall, including the resurrection and a return to God's presence regardless of our state of righteousness. Alma explains, "The atonement bringeth to pass the resurrection of the dead; and the resurrection of the dead bringeth back men into the presence of God; and thus they are restored into his presence, to be judged according to their works" (Alma 42:23). This return to God's presence overcame the first spiritual death triggered by Adam, and thus, all that was lost by the Fall was equally restored by the Atonement. As Amulek so beautifully taught, "This restoration shall come to all" (Alma 11:44). In some cases, this restoration is temporarily accelerated. Due to the faith of the brother of Jared, the Lord promised him, "Because thou knowest these things *ye are redeemed from the fall;* therefore ye are brought back into my presence; therefore I show myself unto you" (Ether 3:13; emphasis added).

There is nothing anyone can do to reject these saving powers of the Atonement. They will descend upon every man "in spite of himself,"[5] as observed by Joseph F. Smith. There is no one to whom they do not apply, whether saint or sinner. These blessings are guaranteed—in fact, they are compulsory upon all men. Thus all men are saved from physical death and the first spiritual death.

OVERCOMING THE SECOND
SPIRITUAL DEATH FOR THE REPENTANT

The second spiritual death is brought about by our individual sins. It is separate and apart from Adam's original transgression, though it is not unrelated. It results in a permanent separation from God's presence, unless we avail ourselves of repentance before the judgment day. Samuel the Lamanite explained the difference between what the scriptures call the first death and the second death. In so doing, Samuel spoke of the Savior's death as that death which "bringeth to pass the resurrection, and redeemeth all mankind from the first death—that spiritual death; for all mankind, by the fall of Adam being cut off from the presence of the Lord, are considered as dead." This Lamanite prophet then taught that the resurrection brought all men "back into the presence of the Lord," thus saving them from the first death. He then declared the fate of those who fail to repent: "Whosoever repenteth the same is not hewn down and cast into the fire; but whosoever repenteth not is hewn down and cast into the fire; and there cometh upon them again a spiritual death, yea, a second death, for they are cut off again as to things pertaining to righteousness" (Helaman 14:16–18; see also Alma 12:16; Mormon 9:13–14).

"Original sin" per se was not inherited by mankind, but its universal effects were inherited. There is a substantial difference in the consequences. Joseph Smith made this distinction: "We believe that men will be punished for their own sins, and not for Adam's transgression" (Second Article of Faith). This is absolutely correct in the eternal sense. The consequences of "original sin" are temporary, since they were remedied by the Savior on an unconditional basis. The consequences of individual sin, however, are permanent, unless we repent. Hence the Atonement provides unconditional redemption from "original sin," but conditional redemption from individual sin.[6] The scriptures clearly teach that the Atonement automatically rectifies all the effects of Adam's transgressions, without any action on our part, and, in addition, redeems each of us from our individual sins, if we will but repent.

A SUMMARY OF THE FALL AND ATONEMENT

The Atonement, as it relates to the Fall, was the price paid by the Savior to (1) overcome physical death for all men,

(2) overcome the first spiritual death (or separation from God caused by Adam) for all men, and (3) overcome the second spiritual death (caused by our individual sins) for those who are willing to repent. Following is a chart that summarizes the consequences of the Fall and Atonement. It is not intended to be all-inclusive, but it may be helpful in giving an overall perspective to these interrelated events.

Before the Fall	After the Fall	After the Atonement
1. Immortality (+) Genesis 2:17	1. Mortality (-) Genesis 2:17 (a) man (b) plants and animals (c) earth	1. Resurrection (+) (unconditional for all) 1 Corinthians 15:20–22
2. Lived in God's presence (+) Genesis 3:8 Moses 4:14	2. Spiritual Death (-) (a) First spiritual death (born outside God's presence) D&C 29:41 2 Nephi 9:6 Helaman 14:16 (b) Second spiritual death (separated from God because of individual sin) 1 Nephi 10:6 Alma 12:16; 42:9	2. Overcame Spiritual Death (+) (a) Unconditional, because all men return to God's presence for judgment purposes 2 Nephi 2:10 2 Nephi 9:38 Alma 12:15; 42:23 Helaman 14:15–18 Mormon 9:12–14 (b) Conditional, because second spiritual death is overcome only if we repent Helaman 14:15–18 Moroni 9:12–14
3. Innocent (-) 2 Nephi 2:22–23	3. Knowledge of good and evil (+) Genesis 3:5 Alma 42:3	3. Unlimited knowledge of good and evil for the exalted (+) John 14:26
4. Childless (-) 2 Nephi 2:23	4. Children (+) 2 Nephi 2:25 Moses 5:11	4. Children forever for the exalted (+) D&C 132:19

WHAT DOES IT MEAN TO BE SAVED
BY THE ATONEMENT?

To be "saved" by the Atonement has multiple connotations. In much of the Christian world, the term "saved" is used as though it had some singular, universal meaning. The truth is that it does not. In a religious sense the word "saved" means to be rescued from some evil thing or negative consequence. Joseph Smith defined it as follows: "Salvation means a man's being placed beyond the power of all his enemies."[7] Following are four ways in which the word "saved" or "salvation" is used in a religious context:

First, all men, even the sons of perdition, will be resurrected and thus be saved from physical death. Paul taught this truth: "For as in Adam all die, even so in Christ shall all be made alive" (1 Corinthians 15:22).[8] Amulek taught similarly: "All shall be raised from this temporal death" (Alma 11:42; see also Alma 11:41). In this sense all men are saved.

Second, all men, except the sons of perdition, will be saved in yet another way, namely, they will be resurrected with a glorified body and be assigned to a kingdom of glory over which one or more of the members of the Godhood will preside (D&C 76:71, 77, 86). In this respect, all such men will be rescued from the power and dominion of Satan. While those who inherit the telestial kingdom "shall not be redeemed from the devil until the last resurrection" (D&C 76:85), they shall, nonetheless, in due course be saved from his clutches. This is what the Lord was referring to when he said that he "saves all the works of his hands, except those sons of perdition" who "shall go away into everlasting punishment . . . to reign with the devil and his angels in eternity" (D&C 76:43–44). Accordingly, the sons of perdition are "the only ones who shall not be redeemed in the due time of the Lord" (D&C 76:38). Everyone else inherits a kingdom of glory and is saved from Satan's rule.

Third, most Christians use the term saved to mean they are guaranteed a life of bliss forever in the presence of God. Such a usage would equate most closely, but certainly not perfectly, with our concept of the celestial kingdom. Those who inherit the celestial kingdom, but not the highest level of exaltation, are saved in the sense they are not banished from the Father's presence. Such saints "remain separately and singly, without exaltation, in their saved condition, to all eternity" (D&C 132:17). They are not saved, however, from all forms of damnation (i. e., the inability to progress). They cannot have eternal seed, and they cannot become like God. Accordingly, they are saved only in a limited sense.

Fourth, to be saved in the fullest sense means to be exalted. This means that someone is not only rescued from physical death, Satan, and banishment from the Father's presence, but in addition is saved from every form of damnation. In other words, there is absolutely nothing that can stop this person's progress. He or she may have eternal increase, create worlds without number, and become like God (D&C 132:19–20, 37; see also chapter 21). After speaking of Abraham's exalted status as a god, the Lord said, "Enter ye into my law and ye shall be saved" (D&C 132:32; see also 2 Nephi 25:23). Referring to exaltation, Elder McConkie taught: "With few exceptions this is the salvation of which the scriptures speak."[9] In this sense, the Atonement of Jesus Christ not only saves us from the effects of the Fall, but in addition endows us with those powers necessary to save us from every weakness, every ignorance, and every obstacle that might otherwise hinder or prevent our progress in some way. This is the ultimate salvation, referred to in the scriptures as exaltation. This is the crowning aim of the Atonement.

NOTES

1. Talmage, *Articles of Faith,* 75.
2. McConkie, *Mortal Messiah,* 4:224.
3. Matthews, *A Bible!,* 260, 262.
4. Ibid., 262.
5. Smith, *Gospel Doctrine,* 69.

6. Orson Pratt helps us understand the difference between unconditional redemption and conditional redemption:

"Universal redemption from the effects of *original sin,* has nothing to do with redemption from our *personal sins;* for the original sin of Adam and the personal sins of his children, are two different things. . . .

"The children of Adam had no agency in the transgression of their first parents, and therefore, they are not required to exercise any agency in their redemption from its penalty. . . .

"*Conditional redemption* is also universal in its nature; it is offered to all but not received by all; . . . its benefits can be obtained only through faith, repentance, baptism, the laying on of hands, and obedience to all other requirements of the gospel.

"*Unconditional redemption* is a gift forced upon mankind which they cannot reject, though they were disposed. Not so with conditional redemption; it can be received or rejected according to the will of the creature. . . .

". . . *Both are the gifts of free grace.* . . . The redemption of the one is *compulsory;* the reception of the other is *voluntary.* Man cannot, by any possible act, prevent his redemption from the fall; but he can utterly refuse and prevent his redemption from the penalty of his own sins" (*Millennial Star,* 12:69; quoted in Smith, *Doctrines of Salvation,* 2:9–10).

7. Smith, *Teachings of the Prophet Joseph Smith,* 301.

8. The sons of perdition will be resurrected, but they will come forth with unglorified bodies, destined to "rise to the damnation of their own filthiness" (Smith, *Teachings of the Prophet Joseph Smith,* 361). The *Encyclopedia of Mormonism* gives this additional insight: "It has been suggested that in the absence of the life-sustaining powers of God's Spirit, sons of perdition will eventually become disorganized and return to 'native element' (*JD,* 1:349–52; 5:271; 7:358–59). However, scripture declares that 'the soul can never die' (Alma 12:20). . . . The ultimate fate of sons of perdition will be made known only to those who are partakers thereof and will not be definitely revealed until the last judgment (D&C 29:27–30; 43:33; 76:43–48; *TPJS,* 24)" (*Encyclopedia of Mormonism,* s.v. "Sons of Perdition," 3:1391–92). See also 2 Ne. 1:22.

9. McConkie, *Mormon Doctrine,* 670.

CHAPTER 7

THE CONSEQUENCES IF THERE HAD BEEN NO ATONEMENT

————— ∞∞∞ —————

A LIFE WITHOUT HOPE

One Sunday morning our teenaged son stood with two other priests to administer the sacrament, as they had done on many prior occasions. They pulled back the white cloth, but to their dismay there was no bread. One of them slipped out to the preparation room in hopes some could be found. There was none. Finally our troubled son made his way to the bishop and shared the concern with him. A wise bishop then stood, explained the situation to the congregation, and asked, "How would it be if the sacrament table were empty today because there were no atonement?" I have thought of that often—what would it be like if there were no bread because there had been no crucifixion, no water because there had been no shedding of blood? If there had been no Atonement, what would the consequences be to us? Of course, the question is now moot, but it does put in perspective our total dependence on the Lord. To ask and answer this question only heightens our awareness of, and appreciation for, the Savior. What might have been, even for the "righteous," if there had been no atoning sacrifice, stirs the very depths of human emotion.

First, there would be no resurrection, or as suggested in the explicit language of Jacob: "This flesh must have laid down to rot and to crumble to its mother earth, to rise no more" (2 Nephi 9:7).

Second, our spirits would become subject to the devil. He would have "all power over you" and "seal you his" (Alma 34:35). In fact we would become like him, even "angels to a devil" (2 Nephi 9:9).

Third, we would be "shut out from the presence of our God" (2 Nephi 9:9), to remain forever with the father of lies.

Fourth, we would "endure a never-ending torment" (Mosiah 2:39).

Fifth, we would be without hope, for "if Christ be not risen, then is our preaching vain, and your faith is also vain. . . . If in this life only we have hope in Christ, we are of all men most miserable" (1 Corinthians 15:14, 19). The poet, John Fletcher, captures the desperate lot of the individual who inherits Lucifer's life:

> And when he falls, he falls like Lucifer,
> Never to hope again.[1]

Dante spoke of that same fate when he discovered these lines inscribed on the gates of hell: "ABANDON HOPE, ALL YE WHO ENTER HERE!"[2] Without the Atonement, Macbeth's fatalistic outlook on life would have been tragically correct; it would be a play without a purpose:

> Life's but a walking shadow, a poor player
> That struts and frets his hour upon the stage
> And then is heard no more. It is a tale
> Told by an idiot, full of sound and fury,
> Signifying nothing.[3]

Life would signify nothing without Christ's redemptive act. The Book of Mormon prophets taught this truth frequently and forcefully. Abinadi prophesied that without the redemption "all mankind . . . would have been endlessly lost" (Mosiah 16:4; see also Mosiah 15:19). Amulek taught with unerring clarity that without an atonement all mankind "must unavoidably perish" (Alma 34:9). Alma, who had tasted of the pains of hell, taught in his discourse to Corianton that the souls of all men would be miserable, "being cut off from the presence of the Lord" (Alma 42:11). Perhaps no prophet knew better than Alma the "exquisite and so bitter . . . pains" (Alma 36:21) of being cut off from the presence of the Holy One. Lehi taught Jacob, "There is no flesh that can dwell in the presence of God, save it be through the merits, and mercy, and grace of the Holy Messiah" (2 Nephi 2:8).

The Book of Mormon prophets foresaw the tragic consequences that would naturally flow if there had been no atoning sacrifice. So did the modern prophets. Brigham Young taught that no kingdom of glory, not even the least, can be obtained without the Atonement: "[The Latter-day Saints] believe that Jesus is the Savior of the world; they believe that all who attain to any glory whatever, in any kingdom, will do so because Jesus has purchased it by his atonement."[4]

If there had been no Atonement the possibility for any kingdom of glory, let alone godhood and exaltation, would have been an idle dream and the resurrection but a futile hope. Shakespeare's Ophelia must have felt this, for in her melancholy she sighed:

I would give you some violets,
but they withered all when my father died.[5]

On one occasion I was asked to speak at a graveside service for a fine man who had passed away. Prior to the service, I met with the family at the mortuary. It was obvious from those in attendance that the deceased was greatly loved and missed. For a few moments, as the family gathered round the casket, I tried to offer some words of counsel and comfort. We then had a word of prayer and all departed for the graveside service. I lingered long enough, however, to see the bereaved widow walk over to the casket for the last time, gently kiss her beloved companion's forehead, and say, "Goodbye, darling, I love you." How senseless life would be if that goodbye were forever. Yet such would be the case without the Savior.

If there had been no Atonement, the rising of every sun would be a reminder that for us it would one day rise no more, that for each of us death would claim its victory, and the grave would have its sting. Every death would be a tragedy, and every birth but a tragedy in embryo. The culmination of love between husbands and wives, fathers and sons, mothers and daughters would perish in the grave, to rise no more. Without the Atonement, futility would replace purpose, hopelessness would be exchanged for hope, and misery would be traded for happiness. If there were no Atonement, Elder Marion G. Romney declared, "The whole purpose for the creation of earth and our living upon it would fail."[6] President David O. McKay quotes James L. Gordon in this regard: "A cathedral without windows, a face without eyes, a field without flowers, an alphabet without vowels, a continent without rivers, a night without stars, and a sky without a sun—these would not be so sad as a . . . soul without Christ."[7] The contemplation of such a world as this would be the most despairing thought that could ever darken the mind or sadden the heart of man. But fortunately, there is a Christ, and there was an Atonement, and it is infinite for all mankind.

NOTES

1. Fletcher, "Henry VIII," in Cook, *Famous Poems,* 44.
2. Dante, *Divine Comedy,* 5.
3. Shakespeare, *Macbeth,* 5.5.24–28.
4. *Journal of Discourses,* 13:328.
5. Shakespeare, *Hamlet,* 4.5.183–85.
6. Conference Report, Oct. 1953, 34.
7. Conference Report, Oct. 1952, 12.

CHAPTER 8

THE INFINITE NATURE OF THE ATONEMENT

———— ∞ ————

INFINITE IN A MULTIPLICITY OF WAYS

What do the Book of Mormon prophets mean when they refer to an "infinite atonement"? Jacob taught, "It must needs be an infinite atonement—save it should be an infinite atonement this corruption could not put on incorruption" (2 Nephi 9:7). Nephi prophesied that the Atonement would be "infinite for all mankind" (2 Nephi 25:16). And Amulek similarly taught, "It must be an infinite and eternal sacrifice. . . . Therefore there can be nothing which is short of an infinite atonement which will suffice for the sins of the world" (Alma 34:10, 12). Again and again, the key word is "infinite."

The phrase "infinite atonement" or "infinite sacrifice" may refer to an atonement or sacrifice by a God, a being who is infinite in knowledge, power, and glory. Amulek makes that connection when he observes that the "great and last sacrifice will be the Son of God, yea, infinite and eternal" (Alma 34:14). Accordingly, the Atonement is "infinite" because its source is "infinite."

But the Atonement is infinite in other ways as well. B. H. Roberts, in referring to the use of the phrase "infinite atonement" by the Nephite prophets, comments, "I think they sought to express the idea of the sufficiency of it; its completeness; the universality and power of it to restore all that was lost, both spiritual and physical, as well as to express the rank and dignity of him who would make the Atonement."[1] Nephi was referring to the effects of the Atonement, rather than its source, when he observed, "The atonement . . . is infinite for all mankind" (2 Nephi 25:16). The word *infinite,* as used in this context, may refer to an atonement that is infinite in its scope and coverage, or to an atonement that simultaneously applies retroactively and prospectively, oblivious to constraints and measurements of time. It may refer to a sacrifice that has no bounds, no outer limits, no final extremities as to the suffering that would be endured. It may refer to an atonement that applies to all God's creations, past, present, and future, and thus is infinite in its application, duration, and effect. Elder McConkie seems to support all these views: "When the prophets speak of an *infinite* atonement, they mean just that. Its effects cover all men, the earth itself and all forms of life thereon, and reach out into the endless expanses of eternity."[2]

The Atonement seems infinite, as so designated by the Book of Mormon prophets, for at least the following eight reasons, as further discussed in chapters 9 to 23:

First, as Elder Maxwell has suggested, it is "infinite in the *divineness* of the one sacrificed."[3] The title of that stirring song, "O Divine Redeemer," is an apt reminder that he who brought about the Atonement is the consummate expression of godliness.

Second, it is infinite in *power.* The Savior went from grace to grace until he "received all power, both in heaven and on earth" (D&C 93:17).

Third, the Atonement is infinite in *time.* It applies retroactively and prospectively through time immemorial.

Fourth, it is infinite in *coverage.* It applies to all God's creations and all forms of life thereon. Elder Maxwell called it "infinite . . . in the *comprehensiveness* of its coverage."[4]

Fifth, it is infinite in *depth.* It is infinite not only in who it covers, but in what it covers. "The Son of Man hath descended below them all" (D&C 122:8).

Sixth, it is infinite in the degree of *suffering* endured by the Redeemer. It was that suffering that caused "even God, the greatest of all, to tremble because of pain, and to bleed at every pore" (D&C 19:18).

Seventh, it is infinite in *love*. The words of the hymn "He Died! The Great Redeemer Died" are a powerful reminder of his boundless love:

> *Here's love and grief beyond degree;*
> *The Lord of glory died for men.*[5]

Eighth, it is infinite in the *blessings* it bestows. The blessings of the Atonement extend far beyond its well-known triumph over physical and spiritual death. Some of these blessings overlap; some complement and supplement each other; but in the aggregate the effect of this event so blesses our lives in a multiplicity of ways, both known and yet to be discovered, that it might appropriately be said to be infinite in its blessing nature.

NOTES

1. Roberts, *Seventy's Course in Theology*, Fourth Year, 95.
2. McConkie, *Mormon Doctrine*, 64.
3. Maxwell, *Not My Will, But Thine*, 51; emphasis added.
4. Ibid., 51.
5. Isaac Watts, "He Died! The Great Redeemer Died," in *Hymns*, no. 192.

CHAPTER 9

INFINITE IN DIVINENESS OF THE CHOSEN ONE

※

INFINITE IN GODLY TRAITS

The Atonement is infinite in the divineness of the One who was sacrificed. The scriptures refer to the Savior as that "God in heaven, who is infinite and eternal" (D&C 20:17; see also D&C 20:28). He possesses every worthwhile passion and godly attribute in unbounded measure, hence the reference to his infinite nature.

Clearly Christ "has all power, all wisdom, and all understanding; he comprehendeth all things" (Alma 26:35), and hence is omniscient. Jacob confirmed this truth: "There is not anything save he knows it" (2 Nephi 9:20). He has mastered each and every law. He is polylingual; there is no such thing as a foreign language to him. He knows the cure for every virus, every disease, and every ailment. He has created worlds without number. Nothing escapes his grasp. As David declared, "His understanding is infinite" (Psalm 147:5). Elder McConkie referred to the link between the Savior's infinite knowledge and his chosen status when he said, "By obedience and devotion to the truth he attained that pinnacle of intelligence which ranked him as a God, as the Lord

Omnipotent, while yet in his pre-existent state . . . and he was then chosen to work out the infinite and eternal atonement."[1]

Just as there are no limits to the Savior's omniscience, there are no limits to his love and power (John 3:16; 15:13; Ephesians 3:19; D&C 132:20). John Greenleaf Whittier wrote these insightful lines:

> *I walk with bare, hushed feet the ground*
> *Ye tread with boldness shod;*
> *I dare not fix with mete and bound*
> *The love and power of God. . . .*
> *I know not where His islands lift*
> *Their fronded palms in air;*
> *I only know I cannot drift*
> *Beyond His love and care.*[2]

One wonders if Milton almost pierced the veil when he wrote lines of equal vision:

> *Beyond compare the Son of God was seen*
> *Most glorious; in him all his Father shone*
> *Substantially expressed; and in his face*
> *Divine compassion visibly appeared,*
> *Love without end, and without measure grace.*[3]

Man's needs, however onerous they may be, will never exhaust God's love. His supply is boundless.

Not only does God possess infinite love and power, but he also possesses "infinite goodness" (2 Nephi 1:10; Mosiah 5:3; Helaman 12:1; Moroni 8:3); he demonstrates "infinite mercy" (Mosiah 28:4; see also 1 Chronicles 16:34); and he is filled with "infinite . . . grace" (Moroni 8:3). So all-encompassing and far-reaching are the Lord's virtues that the Prophet Joseph enumerated certain of those divine qualities in his dedicatory prayer at the Kirtland Temple. The Prophet Joseph referred to the Savior as that being who is "enthroned, with glory, honor, power, majesty, might, dominion, truth, justice, judgment, mercy," and then, perhaps sensing the futility of listing God's virtues ad infinitum, concluded by describing him as possessing "an *infinity of fulness,* from everlasting to everlasting" (D&C 109:77; emphasis added). The Book of Mormon prophets also recognized the Savior's divine qualities. President Ezra Taft Benson noted that the Savior was "given over one hundred different names in the Book of Mormon." He then observed, "Those names have a particular significance in describing His divine nature."[4] In poetic fashion Isaiah drew from that vast reservoir of names to write, "His name shall be called Wonderful, Counsellor, The mighty God, The everlasting Father, The Prince of Peace" (Isaiah 9:6). He was all of that and more.

Amulek preached that the "great and last sacrifice will be . . . infinite and eternal" because it "will be the Son of God" (Alma 34:14). Accordingly, it is proper to refer to the Atonement as infinite because it expresses the nature and character of him who made that wondrous sacrifice.

THE CONDESCENSION OF GOD

Years ago my wife and I traveled to the Holy Land. As we ascended Shepherd's Field, we overlooked the quaint little town of Bethlehem. It was as though time stood still. We tried to imagine the scene two thousand years earlier with no paved roads, no running water, no electricity, no shopping malls. Life was reduced to its simplest terms: rude shelters to protect one from the elements, a central well from which to draw water, transportation by foot or donkey or horse. The days were spent plowing the field, tending the sheep, or selling a few simple items of merchandise. It was hard to believe we were viewing the place where a God was born.

As one envisions this scene, he grasps for a fleeting moment but the smallest understanding of what the scriptures call "the condescension of God" (1 Nephi 11:16, 26; see also 2 Nephi 9:53).[5] The word *condescension* comes from the Latin roots *con* and *descendere,* meaning *to descend with.* The Savior's descent to humanity was personally announced by the Savior to Nephi on that first "Christmas Eve": "Behold, the time is at hand . . . on the morrow come I into the world" (3 Nephi 1:13). Oh, the magnitude of that sacrifice, that condescension! That night, God the Son traded his heavenly home with all its celestial adornments for a mortal abode with all its primitive trappings. He, "the King of heaven" (Alma 5:50), "the Lord Omnipotent who reigneth" (Mosiah 3:5), left a throne to inherit a manger. He exchanged the dominion of a god for the dependence of a babe. He gave up wealth, power, dominion, and the fulness of his glory—for what?—for taunting, mocking, humiliation, and subjection. It was a trade of unparalleled dimension, a condescension of incredible proportions, a descent of incalculable depth. And so, the great Jehovah, creator of worlds without number, infinite in virtue and power, made his entry into this world in swaddling clothes and a manger.

A TRAIL OF GODHOOD

Be that as it may, no one could mask his godhood. One might clothe his spirit with flesh and blood, wrap him in mortal garb, draw the veil of forgetfulness across his mind, but no one, absolutely no one, could rob him of his divinely inherited traits. They could not be buried in his mortal frame. They could not be silenced. Every moment of every day his godly attributes were etching themselves on his outer shell. They manifested themselves in every smile, every glance, every spoken word. Godliness exuded itself in every thought, every action, and every deed. In but thirty-three years he left a streaming trail of godhood that none but a spiritual corpse could deny. Sermon after sermon, miracle after miracle, kindness after kindness testified of his divine origin.

It was these transcendent qualities that caused the people of Galilee to be astonished at his doctrine. As Christ concluded the Sermon on the Mount, the scriptures record, "He taught them as one having authority, and not as the scribes" (Matthew 7:29). It was such celestial traits that compelled the spiritually enlightened to gravitate to him. "Follow me," he said (Matthew 4:19), and men would drop their nets, leave their life-sought vocations, and follow him. It was this divine radiance that caused the wicked to shrink from his presence as he, one man—no, one God—drove them from the temple, when vice in all its ugly horror retreated from virtue in all its mighty splendor. Is it any wonder that this Jesus, crowned in thorns, draped in purple robe, scourged and scorned, should have Pilate say of him, "Behold the man!" (John 19:5).

One wonders about his emerging godhood, as he grew from infancy to boyhood, and boyhood to manhood. What were his feelings? What was it like to be a God among mortals? With whom did he discuss his burdens? True, the bodies of other men walked by his side, but none was his intellectual and spiritual equal. None could see and feel and understand as he saw and felt and understood. What was it like for Christ to walk the dusty trails of his own creation, to see his divine works through mortal eyes? When did he come to know that the birds that sang music to his ears, the flowers that scented the air, the hills and valleys on which he loved to run and play, the sunsets and stars upon which he longed to gaze and ponder were his creations? He was their designer, their architect, their framer—yes, their very creator.

We do not know with exactness when Christ became aware of his divine mission, but a consciousness of his godhood was emerging at an early age. With every breath of every day his divine qualities were manifesting themselves until his mortal frame was immersed in godliness. Then came the time of his appointed mission. All that could be remembered had been recalled; all the powers that could be summoned had been retrieved. The designated hour had arrived. The long anticipated moment of confrontation was here. Godhood and evil had traveled their diverse roads. Christ was ready to save his children; ironically, they "sought how they might kill him" (Luke 22:2). This was the showdown—the climax. It was focused on the power of the Infinite One versus the power of the Evil One.

NOTES

1. McConkie, *Mormon Doctrine,* 129.
2. Whittier, "The Eternal Goodness," in Cook, *Famous Poems,* 113, 115.
3. Milton, *Paradise Lost,* 95–96.
4. Benson, *Witness and a Warning,* 53.
5. This discussion is not intended to suggest that this phrase does not also have other interpretations.

CHAPTER 10

INFINITE IN POWER

⸻ ∞ ⸻

POWER IS PROPORTIONAL TO
ONE'S DIVINE ATTRIBUTES

Why was it essential that the Atonement be performed by Jesus, who is "infinite and eternal" (Alma 34:14)? Because the Atonement required power, incredible power, even infinite power. It required power to resurrect the dead, power to conquer spiritual death, and power to exalt an ordinary person to the status of a god. Such power could be exercised only by a being who was infinite, meaning a being who possessed all divine virtues in unlimited measure, and was therefore a God. In the Savior's great intercessory prayer, he alluded to the power the Father had given him: "Thou hast given [me] power over all flesh" (John 17:2). Pilate did not understand this. He thought he had "power to crucify" and "power to release," but the Savior quickly corrected him: "Thou couldest have no power at all against me, except it were given thee from above" (John 19:10–11).

Certainly Satan has his power for the moment, his hour of darkness, but when the end comes, the Savior, the fountain of all power, will "put down all rule and all authority and power" (1 Corinthians 15:24). The Savior will exercise his power, far superior to what he has allowed Satan to momentarily possess, "even to the destroying of Satan and his works at the end of the world" (D&C 19:3). Accordingly, the Savior has that infinite power required to perform the Atonement, born out of divine virtues manifested in infinite measure. So all-encompassing is the power possessed by the Savior that Alma taught, "He has all power to save every man" (Alma 12:15; see also Alma 9:28). King Benjamin recognized the presence of that power even in premortal times: "For behold, the time cometh . . . that with power, the Lord Omnipotent who reigneth . . . shall come down from heaven among the children of men" (Mosiah 3:5). Milton acknowledged the power of Jehovah: "Great are thy works, Jehovah, infinite thy power; what thought can measure thee, or tongue relate thee?"[1]

It should be no surprise that as we become more godlike we become more powerful. Knowledge brings power; purity brings power; love brings power. The acquisition of each divine trait brings power. Power and godhood are directly related. Paul spoke of this truth when he wrote of Jesus as possessing a "fulness of the Godhead bodily" and then added, that he "is the head of all principality and power" (Colossians 2:9–10; see also 1 Chronicles 29:12, Psalm 66:7). The Savior's life is a confirmation of this truth. He went from grace to grace until he received a fulness of the Father and then "he received all power, both in heaven and on earth" (D&C 93:17; see also 1 Nephi 1:14; Alma 26:35; D&C 100:1).

Speaking of those who may become gods, the Lord declared: "Then shall they be above all, because all things are subject unto them. Then shall they be gods, because they have all power" (D&C 132:20). The Savior was infinite in his godly attributes. This meant he had infinite power and with that power he could perform an infinite atonement.

In the world of physics, there is a law of thermodynamics known as the law of entropy. It suggests that the universe, left to itself, would constantly move toward a state of disorder. Stephen W. Hawking, the noted mathematician, described this law in layman's terms: "It is a matter of common experience that disorder will tend to increase if things are left to themselves. (One has only to stop making repairs around the house to see that!)" He then amplifies as follows:

"The explanation that is usually given as to why we don't see broken cups gathering themselves together off the floor and jumping back onto the table is that it is forbidden by the second law of thermodynamics. This says that in any closed system disorder, or entropy, always increases with time. In other words, it is a form of Murphy's law: Things always tend to go wrong! An intact cup on the table is a state of high order, but a broken cup on the floor is a disordered state. One can go readily from the cup on the table in the past to the broken cup on the floor in the future, but not the other way round."[2]

This disorder, or condition of progressive randomness, would proceed uninterrupted unless there were an intelligent, powerful force in the universe that could somehow reverse this natural course. John Taylor spoke of such an intelligent force:

"These laws [which govern the universe] are under the surveillance and control of the great Law-giver, who manages, controls, and directs all these worlds. If it were not the case, they would move through space in wild confusion, and system would rush against system, and worlds upon worlds would be destroyed, together with their inhabitants."[3]

Certainly the creation was an awesome demonstration of these reversing powers. The Atonement was another such manifestation. Again and again in the scriptures the Atonement is referred to as power. With the possible exception of the word *love,* it seems to be the single most repeated word used to describe the atoning process. Such power was a natural outgrowth of the Savior's infinite nature. Just as happiness cannot be acquired independent of obedience to God's laws, so power cannot be permanently acquired independent of developing divine virtues. You cannot have one without the other. They are inseparably connected.

AN EXERCISE AND ACQUISITION OF POWER

The Atonement was both an exercise of power and an acquisition of power. One of the ironies of life is that we acquire love as we give it away; we increase in knowledge as we dispense what we have. And so it is with certain powers. As we exercise power in righteousness, we acquire more power. As we exercise power in unrighteousness, we lose even more than we "gave away." It is but a reflection of the parable of the talents.

The Savior exercised power as he endured the consequence of sin, withstood pain, and eventually relinquished his life. Moroni cautioned, "Deny not the power of God; for he worketh by power" (Moroni 10:7). The exercise of those powers necessary to endure the sufferings of all mankind may in turn have opened the door to the additional powers needed to resurrect, to redeem, and to exalt. The celestial chorus will one day sing, "Worthy is the Lamb *that was slain to receive power*" (Revelation 5:12; emphasis added). Note the reference to the future receipt of power. The Lamb seems to receive new power after he is slain. The scriptures make it clear that the Savior could not have resurrected man if he had not first died. Paul made reference to this necessary sequence when he observed that "through death he might destroy him that had the power of death, that is, the devil" (Hebrews 2:14). Alma alluded to this same causal connection: "He will take upon him death"—why?—"that he may loose the bands of death" (Alma 7:12). Later he would preach, "The death of Christ shall loose the bands of this temporal death" (Alma 11:42). Each of these prophets taught that the death of the Savior was a necessary prerequisite to the resurrection of man. Out of the death of One was born the power of everlasting life for all. The Savior also taught this principle: "Except a corn of wheat fall into the ground and die, it abideth alone: *but if it die, it bringeth forth much fruit*" (John 12:24; emphasis added).

One might wonder, could the Savior redeem us from spiritual death if he had not first suffered the consequences of our sins? Or, could he exalt an ordinary individual if he had not first internalized the woes of mortals? On one hand, the Atonement was an exercise of incredible power, enabling Christ *to endure* the total human plight. On the other hand, the atoning process was the acquisition and then the manifestation of incredible power *to overcome* that plight, as demonstrated by the power to resurrect, to redeem, and to exalt. Could it be that the exercise of the power to endure was essential to the acquisition of the power to overcome? Was the latter power born out of the former? In any case, the awesome power to both endure and overcome was a direct consequence and reflection of the Savior's infinite nature.

NOTES

1. Milton, *Paradise Lost*, 213.
2. Hawking, *Brief History of Time*, 144–45.
3. Taylor, *Gospel Kingdom*, 67–68.

CHAPTER 11

INFINITE IN TIME

———— ✺ ————

MORTALS WHO PREDATE THE SAVIOR'S SACRIFICE

The Atonement was clearly efficacious for mortal men who lived after the Savior's ordeal in the Garden and on the cross. But what of mortals who lived before the Savior or even further back in time to spirits of the premortal realm? Does the Atonement reach that far? Is it infinite in time both retroactively and prospectively?

Does the Atonement apply retroactively to mortals who predated his sacrifice? In other words, could the people of the Old Testament repent and be cleansed of their sins before the Savior's mission had been performed? The answer is yes. The headnote to Alma 39 reads in part, "Christ's redemption is retroactive in saving the faithful who preceded it." Paul taught that the gospel was "preached before . . . unto Abraham" (Galatians 3:8). Faith, repentance, and baptism were taught in every dispensation of the gospel commencing with Adam. This is what the scriptures mean when they say, "The Gospel began to be preached, from the beginning" (Moses 5:58; see also D&C 20:25–26).

Without the retroactive effect of the Savior's Atonement, the teaching of gospel principles and the performance of related ordinances in Old Testament times would have been futile acts. The

Lord made this unconditional declaration concerning the brother of Jared, who predated the Savior's Atonement by about twenty-two hundred years: "Because thou knowest these things ye are redeemed from the fall" (Ether 3:13). King Benjamin put to rest any question about the retroactive nature of the Atonement in his magnificent discourse: "Whosoever should believe that Christ should come, the same might receive remission of their sins, and rejoice with exceedingly great joy, *even as though he had already come among them*" (Mosiah 3:13; emphasis added). Then King Benjamin confirmed the timelessness of the Atonement when he testified that men shall be damned unless they "believe that salvation *was, and is, and is to come,* in and through the atoning blood of Christ" (Mosiah 3:18; emphasis added). But how could that be? How could God retroactively extend the blessings of the Atonement before the purchase price was paid? Would this not violate the principles of justice? What if the Savior chose not to proceed? What if no blood were ever shed?

The principle of retroactive credit should not seem foreign to us today. In fact, it is an everyday occurrence. On a daily basis we buy merchandise with our credit cards and then pay for it *after* the fruits have been enjoyed. As we prove dependable and timely in making our payments the amount of our credit increases. Once we have proven creditworthy, companies will even solicit our credit with fervor. They know certain people can always be counted on to pay the bill.

How much more so it was with the Savior. Over long eons of time in the premortal realm he proved faithful and dependable and honorable in every commitment, every responsibility, and every charge. The scriptures tell us that "from eternity to eternity he is the same" (D&C 76:4).[1] He never deviated from the mark, never slacked in his performance, never shrank from his word. He kept every command with exactness; he discharged every duty with precision; he was "not slack concerning his promise" (2 Peter 3:9). His promises were "immutable and unchangeable" (D&C 104:2). As a result, his spiritual credit was rapidly escalating until it was pure gold, even infinite in value. That is why the laws of justice could recognize the benefits of the Atonement *before* the purchase price was ever paid, because his promise, his pledge, his credit was "good for it," and everyone who honored their first estate knew it.

In the premortal council the Savior covenanted with the Father to perform the Atonement. John Taylor wrote, "A covenant was entered into between Him and His Father, in which He agreed to atone for the sins of the world,"[2] and hence he became known as "the Lamb slain from the foundation of the world" (Revelation 13:8; see also Moses 7:47). The Gospel of Philip, one of the Nag Hammadi books, suggests similarly: "It was not only when he appeared that he voluntarily laid down his life, but he voluntarily laid down his life from the very day the world came into being. Then he came forth in order to take it, *since it had been given as a pledge.*"[3] Based on that pledge or covenant we had faith in him. Based on that covenant the Father could promise remission of sins prior to the atoning sacrifice because he "knew" his Son would not fail. The issue was not that he could not break his covenant, but rather, that he would not. In rhetorical fashion, the Savior reminds us of that truth: "Who am I," he asks, "that have promised and have not fulfilled?" (D&C 58:31; see also Numbers 23:19). Solomon acknowledged that the Lord "hath not failed one word of all his good promise, which he promised by the hand of Moses" (1 Kings 8:56; see also Deuteronomy 7:8). Abraham was yet another witness: "There is nothing that the Lord thy God shall take in his heart to do but what he will do it" (Abraham 3:17). It should not be surprising that Nehemiah referred to him as the "God, who keepest covenant" (Nehemiah 9:32). Any question about the underlying integrity of the Lord's promises was answered when he declared anciently, "I will *never* break my covenant with you" (Judges 2:1; emphasis added).

In *A Christmas Carol,* Charles Dickens addresses the importance of fulfilling promises, as seen in his portrayal of Scrooge. After a life of parsimony, Scrooge's heart is finally softened by the spirit of Christmas. He promises Bob Cratchit a raise; he promises to assist

Cratchit's struggling family—in fact, he promises to begin that very afternoon. And then this magnificent tribute to Scrooge: "[He] was better than his word. He did it all, and infinitely more."[4] In such a spirit the Savior did it all; he kept his word; he performed an infinite atonement.

Consider for a moment the binding nature of an oath in Old Testament and Book of Mormon times. Now elevate that to the covenant of God, who is "bound" (D&C 82:10) when he so covenants, and who "never doth vary from that which he hath said" (Mosiah 2:22). Speaking of the oath and covenant of the priesthood, the Lord declared, "All those who receive the priesthood, receive this oath and covenant of my Father, which *he cannot break*" (D&C 84:40; emphasis added).

If a God "cannot break" a covenant, then why could not the laws of justice recognize the effects of a covenant prior to its performance? B. H. Roberts believed this to be the case: "The effects of the Atonement were realized by the ancient saints previous to the coming of Christ to earth and hence previous to his actually making the Atonement; but that was because the Atonement for man's sins, the satisfaction to Justice, had been pre-determined upon [by means of a covenant], and this fact gave virtue to their faith, repentance and obedience to ordinances of the Gospel."[5]

It may have been that such a covenant helped sustain the Savior in the Garden when all his apparent spiritual and physical energies had been exhausted, when there was "nothing left" to combat the Evil One and sin itself but the pure covenant to atone. How many such covenants have lifted men to loftier heights, conferred upon them added strength, and generated new-found reservoirs of resistance when all else seemed to collapse around them? So it may have been that, in some way, this covenant satisfied the laws of justice for those who lived before the Atonement was performed, and, in addition, helped to sustain the Savior in his hour of greatest need.

PREMORTAL SPIRITS

Once the retroactive nature of the Atonement has been established, the next logical question is, "How far back does it extend?" Does the Atonement retreat into the premortal realm of spirits? Does it need to? It is apparent that premortal spirits possessed moral agency with the capability of making choices. Joseph Fielding Smith made that clear when he declared:

"God gave his children their free agency even in the spirit world, by which the individual spirits had the privilege, just as men have here, of choosing the good and rejecting the evil, or partaking of the evil to suffer the consequences of their sins. Because of this, some even there were more faithful than others in keeping the commandments of the Lord."[6]

On another occasion he spoke in like manner: *"The spirits of men were not equal. They may have had an equal start,* and we know they were all innocent in the beginning; but the right of free agency which was given to them enabled some to outstrip others, and thus, through the eons of immortal existence, to become more intelligent, more faithful, for they were free to act for themselves, to think for themselves, to receive the truth or rebel against it."[7]

Alma described a premortal spirit as "being left to choose good or evil" (Alma 13:3), and thus possessing the power to sin. The Savior's disciples believed that a person had power to sin in premortality, as evidenced by their inquiry of the Savior, "Master, who did sin, this man, or his parents, that he was born blind?" (John 9:2). One-third of the premortal spirits committed such a serious sin in giving allegiance to Lucifer that they were cast out from the presence of God (D&C 29:36; Revelation 12:4). Peter explained that "God spared not the angels that sinned, but cast them down to hell" (2 Peter 2:4). This was not an innocent transgression, but open rebellion against God, led by the Evil One who "sinneth from the beginning" (1 John 3:8). This third part of the heavenly hosts chose Satan over God "because of their agency" (D&C 29:36). The two-thirds that remained were not all equal in their allegiance and obedience to God. At their spiritual birth they were "on the same standing with their brethren" (Alma 13:5), but through the laws of agency each spirit advanced at his own rate so that only some became "noble and great ones" (Abraham 3:22).

All premortal spirits commenced their spirit sojourn innocent (i.e., meaning free from sin), but all such spirits lost their innocence through individual sin. Some sin was of such a serious nature that it triggered expulsion from heaven. Cain, who was not expelled, must nonetheless have seriously sinned in the premortal realm because the Lord decreed, "Thou shalt be called Perdition; for *thou wast also before* the world" (Moses 5:24; emphasis added). Elder McConkie wrote, "Though he was a rebel and an associate of Lucifer in pre-existence, and though he was a liar from the beginning whose name was *Perdition, Cain* managed to attain the privilege of mortal birth."[8]

Such concepts as agency, expulsion, and foreordination, all of which were present in the premortal life, imply a choice and opportunity to obey or to sin. If there were no sin after Satan was expelled, then we must assume that the remaining two-thirds either lived in a state of innocence or were perfect—neither of which is consistent with the premortal conditions of agency and foreordination. Obviously if we lived in a state of innocence or perfection, there would be no spiritual distinction among spirits and, therefore, no reason to label only some as "noble and great ones," and yet another as "Perdition." Likewise there would be no reason to designate some, but not all, as "rulers" or as "chosen" or as "good" (Abraham 3:22–23) if all were either innocent or perfect. Both the scriptures and the powers of reason lead us to the inevitable conclusion that sin was present in premortal times. Joseph Fielding Smith Jr. so concluded: "The picture is complete. Man could sin before his mortal birth."[9]

Some might inquire, however, "How does such a concept reconcile with the scripture that says 'no unclean thing can dwell with God'?" (1 Nephi 10:21; see also 1 Nephi 15:33). A careful reading of this and related scriptures will reveal that the word "dwell" as used in this context refers to a permanent or eternal condition that exists *after* men are brought "before the judgment-seat of God" (1 Nephi 10:21; see also 3 Nephi 27:19; Mormon 7:7; D&C 76:62). Dwelling, in this sense, is a future condition. Until the judgment occurs there seems to be no scriptural prohibition against imperfect beings temporarily residing in God's presence. In fact, the scriptures make it clear that sinners did indeed temporarily live in God's presence in premortal times, as evidenced by Satan's rebellion and the subsequent war in heaven. We know that all men, even the wicked, will return to God's presence for judgment purposes and "behold his face" (2 Nephi 9:38). Even Paul, on his way to persecute the saints of Damascus, stood in the presence of the resurrected Lord (Acts 9:3–6, 17). Furthermore, the glorified Savior "dwelt" among the righteous, but still imperfect, Nephites who experienced his coming. To them he preached, "Repent of your sins" (3 Nephi 9:13; see also 3 Nephi 11:23, 37). Accordingly, it does not seem scripturally inconsistent that God in premortal times would allow his imperfect children to temporarily reside in his presence while he taught and nurtured and prepared them for the day of their mortal testing. Here they "received their first lessons in the world of spirits" (D&C 138:56). Eliza R. Snow wrote of these times in her beloved hymn, "O My Father":

> *In thy holy habitation,*
> *Did my spirit once reside?*
> *In my first primeval childhood,*
> *Was I nurtured near thy side?*[10]

If faithful, these spirit children would one day return to the father of us all, and then permanently live (i.e., dwell) with Him—"worlds without end" (D&C 76:112).

Assuming we did sin in premortality, how could our premortal sins be "washed away" so we could be born innocent? Perhaps the Savior's infinite Atonement also encompassed this phase of our eternal journey and thus provided the necessary cleansing. Orson Pratt believed and taught such doctrine: "We see no impropriety in Jesus offering Himself as an acceptable offering and sacrifice before the Father to atone for the sins of His brethren, committed, *not only in the second, but also in the first estate.*"[11] Robert J. Matthews quotes Orson Pratt and then adds, "He is not speaking the doctrine of the Church but what he says is clear and consistent and reasonable and I believe it."[12] The Doctrine and Covenants seems to confirm this belief: "Every spirit of man was innocent in the beginning [referring to our spirit birth]; and *God having redeemed man from the fall* [referring to the Atonement], *men became again, in their infant state* [referring to mortal birth], *innocent before God"* (D&C 93:38; emphasis added).

We began our spirit existence in an innocent state, meaning we were pure and free from sin.[13] Evidently, through the Atonement of Jesus Christ and his redeeming powers, we were likewise born innocent into mortality—untainted and unstained from our premortal sins. While it would be premature to reach a definite conclusion before further revelation is received, it seems that the Atonement stretched far enough back to encompass *all* our sins, including, if necessary, our premortal life. In such a way it would apply retroactively with infinite effect.

POSTMORTAL SPIRITS

The consequences of the Atonement are no less effective prospectively. The redeeming powers of the Savior stretch forward to reach the spirits of the dead just as readily as they stretched back to our premortal life.

On October 3, 1918, President Joseph F. Smith sat in his room pondering the scriptures and reflecting on the great atoning sacrifice of the Savior. He was impressed with Peter's account of the Savior's visit to the dead (1 Peter 3:18–20; 4:6). While so meditating, the eyes of his "understanding were opened" (D&C 138:11) and he saw the hosts of the dead of whom Peter spoke. He perceived that the Savior organized his missionary forces and sent them forth to preach the gospel to those who had not yet heard its glorious truths. In unmistakable language, President

Smith reports that the redemption and its effects were taught to those earth-departed spirits: "There he [the Savior][14] preached to them the everlasting gospel, the doctrine of the resurrection and the redemption of mankind from the fall, and from individual sins on conditions of repentance" (D&C 138:19). Then follows this conclusive pronouncement of President Smith: "The dead who repent will be redeemed" (D&C 138:58). The Atonement was and is being taught to the dead, and furthermore, it is efficacious for those among them who choose to repent.

TOO LATE FOR REDEMPTION?

What then of those mortal men and earth-departed spirits who have fully heard the gospel and rejected it with finality? Does there come a time in man's sojourn when the cleansing power of the Atonement can no longer be applied? Is there a time when it is "too late," a time when the blessings of redemption will no longer be available? Samuel the Lamanite spoke of such a time when preaching to the wicked Nephites: "Your days of probation are past; ye have procrastinated the day of your salvation until it is everlastingly too late, and your destruction is made sure" (Helaman 13:38).

Amulek likewise envisioned and taught of such a day. He pleaded with his people not to "procrastinate the day of your repentance until the end; for after this day of life, which is given us to prepare for eternity, behold, if we do not improve our time while in this life, then cometh the night of darkness wherein there can be no labor performed" (Alma 34:33; see also 3 Nephi 27:33). Amulek then focused on that crucial moment in time when the glorious principle of repentance would no longer be available, when the last ray of hope will have vanished for the unrepentant, the final sliver of light will have faded, and night will have descended in all its blackness. Amulek continues:

"Ye cannot say, when ye are brought to that awful crisis, that I will repent, that I will return to my God. Nay, ye cannot say this. . . . For behold, if ye have procrastinated the day of your repentance even until death, behold, ye have become subjected to the spirit of the devil, and he doth seal you his; therefore, the Spirit of the Lord hath withdrawn from you, and hath no place in you, and the devil hath all power over you; and *this is the final state* of the wicked" (Alma 34:34–35; emphasis added).

Mormon "saw that the day of grace was passed . . . both temporally and spiritually" for his unrepentant people (Mormon 2:15). Hosea prophesied of that day when "repentance shall be hid from mine [God's] eyes" (Hosea 13:14). The Lord has given a generous period in which his healing powers are extended, but there finally comes a time when the spiritual balm is no longer available. Emily Dickinson spoke of such a moment:

> *Is Heaven a physician?*
> *They say that He can heal;*
> *But medicine posthumous*
> *Is unavailable.*[15]

At that point in time we will know, "The harvest is past, the summer is ended, and my soul is not saved!" (D&C 56:16; see also Jeremiah 8:20; D&C 45:2).

The Atonement does apply throughout "the endless expanses of eternity,"[16] retroactively and prospectively. That was the clear pronouncement of the Lord, for salvation will come "not only [to] those who believed after he came in the meridian of time, in the flesh, but [to] all those from the beginning, even as many as were before he came" (D&C 20:26). The effects of Christ's Atonement are eternal; the time for repentance is not. For those who do repent, however, the cleansing process is more than a temporary whitewash—it is a permanent healing for the sins of all such men, in all ages, in all stages of their existence. In addition, the resurrection lasts through time immemorial. Accordingly, the Atonement is infinite in time. Paul spoke of its timelessness when he taught that Christ "offered one sacrifice for sins *for ever*" (Hebrews 10:12; emphasis added). That was also the testimony of the Savior: "My salvation shall be *for ever*" (Isaiah 51:6, emphasis added; see also Isaiah 51:8). And so it is.

NOTES

1. Elder Bruce R. McConkie explains this scripture to mean that in every state of the Savior's existence (including but not limited to his premortal life) he was "the possessor and personification of every godly attribute and characteristic in its fulness and perfection" (*Promised Messiah*, 197).

2. Taylor, *Mediation and Atonement*, 97.

3. "Gospel of Philip," 132; emphasis added. The Gospel of Philip is one of the books of the Nag Hammadi library. These were Christian writings which were first discovered in December 1945 near the Egyptian town of Nag Hammadi.

4. Dickens, *A Christmas Carol*, 151.

5. Roberts, *Seventy's Course in Theology*, Fourth Year, 123, note c.

6. Smith, *Doctrines of Salvation*, 1:58–59.

7. Ibid., 59.

8. McConkie, *Mormon Doctrine*, 108–9.

9. Smith, *Religious Truths Defined*, 94.

10. Snow, "O My Father," in *Hymns*, no. 292.

11. Pratt, *The Seer*, 1 (no. 4): 54; emphasis added.

12. Matthews, "The Price of Redemption," 4.

13. Webster, *An American Dictionary of the English Language*, s.v. "Innocent."

14. In verses 29–32 of this same section, President Joseph F. Smith makes it clear that it was not the Savior who personally preached the gospel to the "wicked and disobedient" but that he "organized his forces" among the righteous and sent them forth to preach.

15. Dickinson, *"Life LVI,"* in *Emily Dickinson*, 42.

16. McConkie, *Mormon Doctrine*, 64.

CHAPTER 12

INFINITE IN COVERAGE

MAN, ANIMALS, PLANTS, AND THE EARTH

Are the mortals who walk this earth the only beneficiaries of the Atonement? What about other worlds and other forms of life? Who saves them from temporal, and where necessary, spiritual death?

The Atonement covers more than mankind. Elder Joseph Fielding Smith spoke directly to this point: "It is a very inconsistent notion which is held by some, that the resurrection will only come to human souls, that the animals and plants have no spirits and therefore are not redeemed by the sacrifice of the Son of God, and hence they are not entitled to the resurrection."[1] Joseph Smith taught: "I suppose John saw beings there [in heaven], that had been saved from ten thousand times ten thousand earths like this, strange beasts of which we have no conception all might be seen in heaven. John learned that God glorified himself by saving all that his hands had made whether beasts, fowl, fishes or man."[2] The Lord promised that "all old things shall pass away, and all things shall become new, . . . both men and beasts, the fowls of the air, and the fishes of the sea" (D&C 29:24). But how does the Atonement apply to these other forms of life? Are they resurrected and granted immortal bodies for eternity? Do they also need to overcome spiritual death? Elder McConkie addresses this issue by asking the following question as though it were a statement of response:

"Is it the doctrine of the gospel . . . that this temporal death passed upon all forms of life, upon man and animal and fish and fowl and plant life; *that Christ came to ransom man and all forms of life from the effects of the temporal death* brought into the world through the Fall, *and in the case of man from a spiritual death also; that this ransom includes a resurrection for man and for all forms of life?*"[3]

Jacob seems to confirm that redemption from spiritual death is limited to man, for he taught that Christ "suffereth the pains of all men, yea, the pains of every living creature, both men, women, and children, *who belong to the family of Adam*" (2 Nephi 9:21; emphasis added).

What of the earth itself? Does it have a need for redemption? It does. Like plants and animals it needs to be redeemed from physical death. President Brigham Young expressed such sentiments:

"Christ is the author of this Gospel, of this earth, of men and women, of all the posterity of Adam and Eve, and of every living creature that lives upon the face of the earth, that flies in the heavens, that swims in the waters, or dwells in the field. Christ is the author of salvation to all this creation; to all things pertaining to this terrestrial globe we occupy. . . . he has redeemed the earth; he has redeemed mankind and every living thing that moves upon it."[4]

Elder McConkie discusses certain heresies concerning the Fall, one being that Adam was the final product of the evolutionary process. In response he comments, "When those who espouse this view talk of a fall and an atonement, they falsely assume such applies only to man rather than to the earth and all forms of life, as the scriptures attest."[5] Elder Talmage shared similar feelings: "We learn from Scripture that Adam's transgression brought about a fallen condition, not of mankind alone, but likewise of the earth itself. In this and in numerous other epochal events, . . . nature is seen to be in intimate relation with man."[6]

How then, has the Savior redeemed the earth? Will it die? The scriptures clearly so state. Isaiah spoke of the time when "the earth shall wax old like a garment, and they that dwell therein shall die in like manner" (Isaiah 51:6; see also 2 Nephi 8:6). Latter-day revelation confirms this truth, for in speaking of this terrestrial sphere the Lord observed, "It shall be sanctified; yea, notwithstanding it shall die, it shall be quickened again, and shall abide the power by which it is quickened, and the righteous shall inherit it" (D&C 88:26). Joseph Fielding Smith likewise spoke of the death of the earth and its subsequent quickening or resurrection made possible only by the Atonement: *The earth, as a living body, will have to die and be resurrected, for it, too, has been redeemed by the blood of Jesus Christ.*[7]

Evidently the earth's resurrection will occur when it dies and is renewed and restored to its paradisiacal glory. Will any further redemption of the earth, other than its "resurrection" be necessary? The fall of Adam not only brought about physical death for man and the earth, but it also brought about spiritual death for man in the form of a fall from God's presence, known as the first spiritual death. Did the earth likewise undergo a fall from God's presence? The Prophet Joseph taught, "This earth will be rolled back into the presence of God, and crowned with celestial glory."[8] How could the earth be "rolled back into the presence of God" unless it were geographically located there in the first place? Lorenzo Snow, no doubt, learned this truth from the Prophet Joseph, for he spoke in similar terms of the earth's fall and return: "The earth shall be rolled back in pristine purity, into its primeval orbit, and the inhabitants thereof dwell upon it in perfect peace and righteousness."[9]

John Taylor taught that the earth "was first organized, near the planet Kolob."[10] This gives us some idea of the earth's proximity to God at the time of its creation, since Kolob is the planet nearest to God (Abraham 3:3, 16; facsimile No. 2, Figure 1).

Brigham Young taught that the earth "was banished from its more glorious state or orbit of revolution for man's sake."[11] Elsewhere he taught: "When man fell, the earth fell into space, and took up its abode in this planetary system. . . . This is the glory the earth came from, and when it is glorified it will return again unto the presence of the Father."[12] Such were the sentiments of Elder Bruce R. McConkie: "When Adam fell, the earth fell also and became a mortal sphere."[13]

Adam's transgression not only resulted in man's death and fall from God's presence, but also the earth's death and fall from the presence of God. The consequences affecting the earth following the Fall mirrored the consequences that came upon man. In fact, it is startling when we recognize the remarkable similarities between the earth and man. Both are subject to death, both will be resurrected, both fell from the presence of God, both need to be born of the water to be cleansed (i.e., the earth being baptized at the time of Noah), both need to be cleansed by fire (i.e., the earth being baptized by fire at the Second Coming and also prior to its final judgment), and both seek the day of their celestialization and return to God's presence. Through the powers of the Atonement, the earth will be "resurrected" and restored to the physical presence of the Holy One. Each of the negative consequences of the Fall, whether they affected man or this earthly globe, will be corrected by the Atonement. We can glimpse how sweeping the atoning powers must be, even for the earth, when we reflect upon the pained cry from the depths of the earth's bowels: "When shall I rest, and be cleansed from the filthiness which is gone forth out of me? When will my Creator sanctify me, that I may rest, and righteousness for a season abide upon my face?" (Moses 7:48).

Animals, fish, fowl, trees, and even the earth itself are heirs to the plan of redemption. So all-inclusive and so glorious are the Atonement's far-reaching powers that every form of life will "praise the name of the Lord" (Psalm 148:13; see also Revelation 5:7–9, 13), and "declare his name forever and ever!" (D&C 128:23; see also D&C 77:2–3).

The Atonement is universal, not selective in its coverage. All forms of life are freed from temporal death. In addition, man's ransom includes escape from all forms of spiritual death. Suffice it to say, the Atonement fully extends its redemptive powers to this earth and to all forms of life thereon to the extent necessary to save them from physical and, where necessary, spiritual death.

THE REDEEMER OF THE UNIVERSE

Does the Savior's Atonement extend beyond this world? Elder McConkie taught: "Our Lord's jurisdiction and power extend far beyond the limits of this one small earth on which we dwell. He is, under the Father, the Creator of worlds without number. (Moses 1:33.) And through the power of his atonement the inhabitants of these worlds, the revelation says, 'are begotten sons and daughters unto God' (D&C 76:24), *which means that the atonement of Christ, being literally and truly infinite, applies to an infinite number of earths.*"[14]

What a mind-expanding concept! Moses postulated that even if we could number millions of earths, "it would not be a beginning to the number of thy [God's] creations; and thy curtains are stretched out still" (Moses 7:30). Elder Marion G. Romney, who authored an article on Christ as the creator of worlds without number, wrote: "Jesus Christ, in the sense of being its Creator *and Redeemer, is the Lord of the whole universe.* Except for his mortal ministry accomplished on this earth, his service and relationship to other worlds and their inhabitants are the same as his service and relationship to this earth and its inhabitants."[15] Elder Romney discussed the Savior's role in the premortal existence as the chosen Redeemer and added, "In short, Jesus Christ, through whom God created the universe, was chosen [as the Redeemer in the pre-earthly councils] to put into operation throughout the universe Elohim's great plan 'to bring to pass the immortality and eternal life of man.'"[16] He concluded with his witness of the Savior's universality as the Atoning One:

"All who have a true concept of Jesus Christ and who have received a witness by the spirit of his divinity are ever stirred by the records of his life. They see in all that he said and did confirmation of his universal Lordship, both as Creator and Redeemer."[17]

Evidently the Prophet Joseph taught this doctrine in a poem attributed to him in which he lyricized a portion of Doctrine and Covenants 76:

> *And I heard a great voice, bearing record from heav'n,*
> *He's the Saviour, and only begotten of God—*
> *By him, of him, and through him, the worlds were all made,*
> *Even all that career in the heavens so broad,*
>
> *Whose inhabitants, too, from the first to the last,*
> *Are sav'd by the very same Saviour of ours;*
> *And, of course, are begotten God's daughters and sons,*
> *By the very same truths, and the very same pow'rs.*[18]

The headnote to Doctrine and Covenants 76 summarizes verses 18–24 in this manner: "*Inhabitants of many worlds* are begotten sons and daughters unto God through the atonement of Jesus Christ" (emphasis added). Lorenzo Snow alluded to this doctrine when speaking of the Father's trust in his Son. He observed: "Thousands of years before He [the Savior] came upon earth, the Father had watched His course and knew that He could depend upon Him when the salvation of *worlds* should be at stake; and He was not disappointed."[19]

In other words, the Savior is a multi-planet redeemer. This seems consistent with the fact he is also a multi-planet creator, as taught through Moses, "Worlds without number have I created; . . . and by the Son I created them, which is mine Only Begotten" (Moses 1:33). Paul taught the same: "God . . . hath in these last days spoken unto us by his Son, . . . by whom also he made the *worlds*" (Hebrews 1:1–2; emphasis added). Since the Son "made the worlds," a fair interpretation of Doctrine and Covenants 76:42—"that through him *all might be saved* whom the Father had put into his power and *made by him*" (emphasis added)— would suggest that the Savior saved all people from all worlds "made by him." The next verse seems to further substantiate this point: "Who [the Savior] glorifies the Father, and saves all the works of his hands" (D&C 76:43). Elder Russell M. Nelson confirmed these thoughts, "The mercy of the Atonement extends not only to an infinite number of people, but also to an infinite number of worlds created by Him."[20]

Hugh Nibley quotes the Gospel of Truth, which says, "All the other worlds look to the same God as to a common sun," and then adds his own observation, "The crucifixion is effective in worlds other than this one."[21] Brother Nibley cites other ancient writers who had insights into the Savior's universal lordship. Speaking of other worlds, the Twelfth Ode of Solomon records: "They know Him who made them because they are in concord. They have a common ruler, *a common lord,* so they are in concord with each other, and they communicate with Him and through Him with each other, for the mouth of the Most High has spoken to them."[22] Another writing of the ancient church (1 Clement) records: "God is the Father of all the worlds. . . . As the Father of greatness is in the glorious world, so his Son rules among those cosmoses as first chief lord of all the powers."[23] Finally, Robert J. Matthews put it about as simply as it can be stated: "The question often arises, Is Jesus the Savior of other worlds? The answer is yes."[24]

Doctrine and Covenants 88 speaks of "the earth and all the planets" (D&C 88:43). It then refers to these creations collectively as "kingdoms" (D&C 88:46). These kingdoms are likened unto a man with a field who sends his servants to dig and prepare the soil. The lord of the field visits each kingdom (i.e., planet) in its due time, one in the first hour, another in the second hour and finally the last in the twelfth hour, that each might behold the joy of his countenance. A portion of the parable reads as follows:

"And *thus they all received the light of the countenance of their lord,* every man in his hour, and in his time, and in his season—beginning at the first, and so on unto the last; every man in his own order, . . . that his lord might be glorified in him, and he in his lord, *that they all might be glorified. Therefore, unto this parable*

I will liken all these kingdoms [i.e. planets], and the inhabitants thereof" (D&C 88:58–61; emphasis added).

Who is this Lord who visits these planets and their inhabitants, that they might be glorified? Orson Pratt gives the answer. He speaks of the Savior's millennial reign and the pure in heart who will be made glad by his countenance for a thousand years. Then, Orson Pratt says:

"He withdraws. What for? To fulfill other purposes; for he has other worlds or creations and other sons and daughters, perhaps just as good as those dwelling on this planet, and they, as well as we, will be visited, and they will be made glad with the countenance of their Lord. Thus he will go, in the time and in the season thereof, from kingdom to kingdom or from world to world, causing the pure in heart, the Zion that is taken from these creations, to rejoice in his presence."[25]

Why should these other inhabitants be glorified in the presence of our Savior (D&C 88:60)? Because he was also their Savior. Since Christ also created them, he loved them and he redeemed them. He is the Savior of all the works of his hands. He is not only the Creator, but also the Redeemer and Lord of the entire universe.

WHY THIS EARTH AS THE REDEMPTIVE PLANET?

If the Atonement had such infinite consequences among infinite worlds, one might wonder, why was *this* earth selected from all the rest, "yea, millions of earths like this" (Moses 7:30)? Why this earth as the proving ground—the redemptive planet? Following are three possibilities.

The first possibility is that Christ may have come to this earth to counterbalance its great wickedness. After Enoch had built his "City of Holiness" and some mortal men knew perfect peace and happiness, Enoch saw in vision the time when the earth would be inundated with extreme wickedness. The Lord would tragically observe, "I can stretch forth mine hands and hold all the creations which I have made; and mine eye can pierce them also, *and among all the workmanship of mine hands there has not been so great wickedness as among thy brethren"* (Moses 7:36; emphasis added).

Evidently this earth knew greater depths of wickedness than could be found on any other of God's creations. What a tragic commentary! Millions, billions of worlds, even more than man can number, and this world stands out preeminent for its wickedness. As Elder Joseph Fielding Smith testified, "His presence was needed here because of the extreme wickedness of the inhabitants of this earth."[26] Hopefully the opposite is likewise true, that such depths of wickedness are countered by unparalleled heights of righteousness. It may be that the Savior's mortal life, and thus his Atonement, was reserved for this earth as a leveling influence, a counterbalancing measure to offset its great wickedness.

A second possible reason Christ came to our world may be that no other world was wicked enough to crucify their God. Enoch reminds us that the Savior would come "in the meridian of time, in the days of wickedness and vengeance" (Moses 7:46). So degenerate would be the spiritual condition of the people in this time period that Nephi commented, "and there is none other nation on earth that would crucify their God" (2 Nephi 10:3). How seemingly unfathomable! When we consider the myriad nations that have occupied this earth, the wars and crime and immorality fostered by their leaders, the widespread decadence among civilized and uncivilized countries alike, we must wonder how it can be that only one nation would crucify their God. Yet the scriptures declare it was so. Since only one nation on this earth would crucify their God, and since this world had greater wickedness than any other (Moses 7:36), then where amidst God's infinite creations would he find another nation that would crucify their Savior? Elder Joseph Fielding Smith contemplated this proposition: "Perhaps this is the reason Jesus Christ was sent here instead of to some other world, for in some other world they would not have crucified him."[27]

There exists at least a third possibility as to why Christ came to this particular earth. Perhaps here he would find a comprehensive cross-section of his children, from the best to the worst—representatives of whom would be witnesses of his Atonement.

So wicked was the earth in the days of Christ's ministry that President Joseph F. Smith observed: "Notwithstanding his mighty works, and miracles, and proclamation of the truth, in great power and authority, there were but few who hearkened to his voice" (D&C 138:26). This rejection was so pervasive that the Lord said, "I came unto my own, and my own received me not" (3 Nephi 9:16). Fortunately, amidst such widespread wickedness there could be found people of supreme righteousness. Peter, James, and John were among the best blood this earth had ever known. They were spiritual giants in a nation of spiritual infants. The law of opposites was in full force and effect: good and evil were at their extremes. Charles Dickens' observation of the times preceding the French Revolution seems apropos to the time of the mortal Christ: "It was the best of times, it was the worst of times"[28]; and to this might be added—these were the best of men, these were the worst of men. Noah Webster spoke of this cultural diversity: "The history of the Jews presents the true character of man in all its forms. All the traits of human character, good and bad; all the passions of the human heart; all the principles which guide and misguide men in society, are depicted in that short history, with an artless simplicity that has no parallel in modern writings."[29]

Such a climate of contrasts seemed ripe for the Savior's arrival. There would be mocking, taunting, disbelief, and finally crucifixion. On the other hand, there would be unrelenting devotion, faith, understanding, and appreciation among a humble few. The nation of Israel was simultaneously experiencing the depths of wickedness and heights of righteousness. The Savior's Atonement would be misunderstood, yet understood, unappreciated, yet appreciated, by the extremes in this spiritual divergence. The opposing consequences of moral agency were in full bloom. There would be some who would betray him, others who would pay "large money" (Matthew 28:12) to silence the lips of those who knew. There would be apathetic ones, some who were almost persuaded to be Christians, and others who were on the brink of perfection but could not quite consecrate their all. Amidst this backdrop of the masses who fell short, there were a few who held back nothing, not even their lives—who boldly, fearlessly, and fervently bore testimony of his divine mission.

Perhaps it was such opposing conditions of consummate goodness and unrestrained evil that made this earth "ripe" for Christ's mortal sojourn. The inhabitants of this earth ran the entire gamut of spirituality. This was the Lord's cross-section of humanity. This was a planet where the Atonement could be simultaneously witnessed, then rejected or embraced by a comprehensive sample of the universal race and so, perhaps for this reason, it became the chosen testing ground.

Whatever the reason may be, God certainly had a purpose in selecting this earth from his infinite creations. Lehi spoke the truth when he declared, "All things have been done in the wisdom of him who knoweth all things" (2 Nephi 2:24).

NOTES

1. Smith, *Answers to Gospel Questions,* 5:7.
2. Smith, *Words of Joseph Smith,* 185.
3. McConkie, "Seven Deadly Heresies," 7–8; emphasis added.
4. *Journal of Discourses,* 3:80–81.
5. McConkie, *New Witness,* 99.
6. Talmage, *Essential James E. Talmage,* 211.
7. Smith, *Doctrines of Salvation,* 1:74. On another occasion he wrote, "Through his death, through his ministry, the shedding of his blood, he has brought to pass redemption from death to *all men,* to *all creatures*— not alone to man, but to *every living thing,* and *even to this earth itself,* upon which we stand, for we are informed through the revelations that it too shall receive the resurrection" (Smith, *Doctrines of Salvation,* 1:138).
8. Smith, *Teachings of the Prophet Joseph Smith,* 181.
9. Snow, *Biography and Family Record of Lorenzo Snow,* 333.
10. Taylor, *The Mormon,* Aug. 29, 1857.
11. Smith, *Words of Joseph Smith,* 84, note 12.
12. *Journal of Discourses,* 17:143; see also *Journal of Discourses,* 9:317.
13. McConkie, *Mormon Doctrine,* 211; see also *Times and Seasons* 3: (1 Feb. 1842) 672.

14. McConkie, *Mormon Doctrine,* 65; emphasis added.

15. Romney, "Jesus Christ, Lord of the Universe," 46; emphasis added.

16. Ibid., 48.

17. Ibid., 48.

18. Holzapfel, "Eternity Sketch'd in a Vision," 145. While it is believed that Joseph Smith wrote or at least approved this poem, see ibid., 141–43, for a further discussion of the authorship of the poem.

19. Snow, *Teachings of Lorenzo Snow,* 93; emphasis added.

20. Nelson, "The Atonement," 35.

21. Nibley, *Old Testament and Related Studies,* 142.

22. Ibid., 142; emphasis added.

23. Ibid., 143.

24. Matthews, *A Bible!,* 210.

25. *Journal of Discourses,* 17:332.

26. Smith, *Signs of the Times,* 10.

27. Ibid., 10.

28. Dickens, *Tale of Two Cities,* 35.

29. Bennett, *Our Sacred Honor,* 397.

CHAPTER 13

INFINITE IN DEPTH

───∞───

HE DESCENDED BENEATH IT ALL

If the Atonement covers all of God's creations and all forms of life thereon, the next question is, "Does the Atonement cover all our sins and pains, or are there some who have sinned and suffered beyond Christ's redeeming grace?" In *A Winter's Tale,* Shakespeare wrote of Leontes, a man who seemed beyond redemption. He was consumed in jealousy. He unjustly imprisoned his wife, rejected the oracle of Delphos, and finally exiled his infant daughter. In a chain-like reaction, a series of calamitous events unfolded in response to his unseemly deeds. Unable to bear it any longer, Paulina, the wife of one of Leontes' lords, excoriated him as follows:

> *Do not repent these things, for they are heavier*
> *Than all thy woes can stir. Therefore betake thee*
> *To nothing but despair. A thousand knees*
> *Ten thousand years together, naked, fasting,*
> *Upon a barren mountain, and still winter*
> *In storm perpetual, could not move the gods*
> *To look that way thou wert.*[1]

This was a grim forecast, but fortunately Paulina underestimated God's mercy for the truly repentant. The Savior descended beneath all sins, all transgressions, all ailments, and all temptations known to the human family. He knew the sum total of the human plight, not just because he witnessed it, but because he embraced it. On one occasion the Lord spoke to Joseph Smith about trials he might yet face, saying, "If thou shouldst be cast into the pit, or into the hands of murderers, and the sentence of death passed upon thee; if thou be cast into the deep; if the billowing surge conspire against thee; if fierce winds become thine enemy; if the heavens gather blackness, and all the elements combine to hedge up the way; and above all, if the very jaws of hell shall gape open the mouth wide after thee, know thou, my son, that all these things shall give thee experience, and shall be for thy good" (D&C 122:7).

The scripture then adds this concluding, compelling thought: "The Son of Man hath descended below them all. Art thou greater than he?" (D&C 122:8). In other words, the Lord was saying, "Joseph, no matter what the world throws at you; no matter what you suffer, no matter what temptations you face—I faced it all and more."

The Savior's plunge into humanity was not a toe-dipping experience. It was a total immersion. He did not experience some pains and not others. His life was not a random sampling, a spot audit; it was a total confrontation with and internalization of every human experience, every human plight, every human trial. Somehow his sponge alone would absorb the entire ocean of human affliction, weakness, and suffering. For this descent he would fully bare his human breast. There would be no godly powers exercised that would shield him from one scintilla of human pain. Paul knew this: "For verily he [the Savior] took not on him the nature of angels; but he took on him the seed of Abraham. Wherefore in all things it behoved him to be made like unto his brethren" (Hebrews 2:16–17).

Christ's Atonement was a descent into the seemingly "bottomless pit" of human agony. He took upon himself the sins of the most wretched of all sinners; he descended beneath the cruelest tortures devised by man. His downward journey encompassed the transgressions of those who ignorantly sinned; it incorporated that quantum of suffering unrelated to spiritual error, but nonetheless viably acute in stinging proportions—the agony of loneliness, the pain of inadequacy, the suffering of infirmities and sickness. In the course of his divine descent he was assaulted with every temptation inflicted on the human race.

After our futile attempts to explain the awesome depths of this "terrible trip," we come back again to those simple but expressive words of the scriptures, "He descended below all things" (D&C 88:6). There need be no equivocation, no back-pedaling, no apologizing—the Atonement is infinite in its depth.

If the totality of human suffering and anxiety could be categorized, it might be broken down as follows: first, suffering caused by sin; second, suffering that flows from innocent transgression of the law; third, suffering related to infirmities, weaknesses, inadequacies, or trials that have nothing to do with sin or transgression; fourth, suffering incidental to our confrontation with the temptations of the world; and fifth, suffering or anxiety necessitated by the exercise of faith. The scriptures are replete with evidence that the Savior did not exempt himself from any of these, but rather faced each of them "square on."

SUFFERING CAUSED BY SIN

Peter explained that the Savior "suffered for sins, the just for the unjust, that he might bring us to God" (1 Peter 3:18). Such suffering was not limited to a few recreant sinners. The Savior himself declared that he "suffered these things for *all*" (D&C 19:16; emphasis added; see also D&C 18:11). John, in announcing the Savior, introduced him as "the Lamb of God, which taketh away the sin of the world" (John 1:29). When the Savior visited the Nephites he spoke of the bitter cup from which he drank "in taking upon me the sins of the world" (3 Nephi 11:11). There was no partial drinking of the cup, no selective discrimination in absorbing certain sins and not others; he would take upon him, as the scriptures said, "the sins of the whole world" (1 John 2:2). Nothing would be left on the table. That was the revelatory doctrine as taught by Joseph Smith, that Jesus was "crucified for the world, and to bear the sins of the world, and to sanctify the world, and to cleanse it from *all* unrighteousness" (D&C 76:41; emphasis added).

The Savior's suffering would include those who were "the very vilest of sinners" (Mosiah 28:4), he who was known as "a very wicked and an idolatrous man" (Mosiah 27:8), he who was "a blasphemer, and a persecutor" (1 Timothy 1:13), those who had "gone astray" and "were full of all manner of wickedness" (Alma 13:17), those who were "snatched" from their "awful, sinful, and polluted state" (Alma 26:17), those who were "in the darkest abyss" (Alma 26:3), and those who acknowledged they "were the most lost of all mankind" (Alma 24:11). It would even include the suffering of those who chose not to repent. In other words, the Savior suffered not only for those whom he knew would repent, but even for those who would choose never to embrace his sacrificial offering. Brigham Young made this clear: "He [the Savior] had paid the full debt, whether you receive the gift or not."[2] He would be "numbered," as Isaiah said, "with the transgressors" (Isaiah 53:12).

Are there some limits to the Atonement's seemingly infinite powers? Are there some depths to which even the Savior has not sunk? The scriptures give the answer: "He [the Savior] descended below all things" (D&C 88:6). In fact, "He suffered the pain of *all* men, that *all* men might repent and come unto him" (D&C 18:11; emphasis added).

But what of the unpardonable sin? The Prophet Joseph spoke of the predicament of those who so sinned: "After a man has sinned against the Holy Ghost, there is no repentance for him. . . . He has got to deny Jesus Christ when the heavens have been opened unto him, and to deny the plan of salvation with his eyes open to the truth of it."[3]

In essence, such people "crucify to themselves the Son of God afresh, and put him to an open shame" (Hebrews 6:6; see also D&C 76:35; 132:27). For these people, known as the sons of perdition, there is a resurrection and a return to God's presence for judgment purposes, but there is no escape from the second spiritual death. This is not because the Atonement lacks in any degree in its infinite nature, but rather because these souls rejected the gift of repentance that had been offered. It reminds one of the friend of Galileo who refused to look through his telescope "because he really did not want to see that which he had so firmly denied."[4] So, too, these sons of perdition have rejected that instrument (i.e., the Atonement) that provides the cleansing power to redeem their lives. The scriptures speak of the sorry state of all who will not repent: "For what doth it profit a man if a gift is bestowed upon him, and he receive not the gift? Behold, he rejoices not in that which is given unto him, neither rejoices in him who is the giver of the gift" (D&C 88:33).

The unpardonable sin is an informed, calculated, irreversible rejection of the Savior and his atoning sacrifice. To then claim that the Atonement is not infinite would be to argue that the son who rejected his father's bequest was robbed of his inheritance. Suffice it to say, to reject a gift is not to disprove its existence. The sons of perdition have chosen to spiritually disinherit themselves, to make of themselves spiritual orphans. The Lord spoke to Alma of those who "would not be redeemed" (Mosiah 26:26; see also D&C 88:33). How could anyone claim the Atonement not to be infinite when the sole reason for its nonapplication in his life is his rejection of the gift? Under such circumstances we have no claim on mercy. This is exactly what Mormon warned: "He that doeth this shall become like unto the son of perdition, for whom there was no mercy, according to the word of Christ!" (3 Nephi 29:7).

The scriptures declare that the Savior "saves *all* the works of his hands, except those sons of perdition who deny the Son after the Father has revealed him. Wherefore, he saves all except them" (D&C 76:43–44; emphasis added). In other words, the Savior saves everyone from outer darkness except the sons of perdition, for "they love darkness rather than light" (D&C 10:21; see also D&C 29:44). There is one reason and one reason only why he cannot save them—because they have chosen to reject him and his saving powers. Tragically, they, like Cain, "loved Satan more than God" (Moses 5:18). They have become subject to the condemnation spoken of by President Joseph F. Smith: "If any man object to Christ, the Son of God, being King of Israel, let him object, and go to hell just as quick as he please."[5]

The Atonement saves all of us in the sense that we are all resurrected and return to God's presence for judgment purposes without any effort on our part. It cannot, however, exalt us unless we repent. If a person does not achieve exaltation, the issue is not the infinite nature of the Atonement; the issue is the repentant spirit of the individual. He can have exaltation if he will but repent. Each of us has the key that unlocks the cleansing powers of the Atonement, but we must turn it. Simply put, the Atonement can open the door to godhood if we will but turn the key.

Just as true omnipotence is being able to do anything, anytime, anyplace within the confines of the inexorable laws of justice, so too the infinite nature of the Atonement redeems every person from every sin in every age throughout the universe, as far as is possible within the laws of justice. At some point the laws of justice require effort on our part, a softening of our hearts, and a refining of our souls before exaltation can be achieved.[6] Alma taught this principle: "Mercy cometh because of the atonement . . . and also mercy claimeth all which is her own; and thus, none but the truly penitent are saved" (Alma 42:23–24).

Recognizing the Savior's merciful outpouring, Truman Madsen spoke these consoling words: "Men have stood at pulpits and elsewhere—great men—and have testified that their knees have never buckled, that as one said of another, 'He had nothing to hide.' We have had monumental men who did not need redemption as much as they needed power, and who never fell very far from the communing light of which I have spoken. I cannot bear that kind of testimony. But if there are some of you who have been tricked into the conviction that you have gone too far, that you have been weighed down with doubts on which you alone have a monopoly, that you have had the poison of sin which makes it impossible ever again to be what you could have been—then hear me.

"I bear testimony that you cannot sink farther than the light and sweeping intelligence of Jesus Christ can reach. I bear testimony that as long as there is one spark of the will to repent and to reach, *he is there.* He did not just descend *to* your condition; he descended *below* it, 'that he might be in all and through all things, the light of truth' (D&C 88:6)."[7]

The Atonement of the Savior covers every repentable sin known to man.[8] This is both logical and reassuring. Certainly in the premortal council the Lord must have known of the depths to which mankind would sink. He was no novice at creating. He had been over the course time and time again. He had observed our spirits throughout the eons. He understood the inner workings of each man's heart. As he told the prophet Samuel, "The Lord seeth not as man seeth; for man looketh on the outward appearance, but the Lord looketh on the heart" (1 Samuel 16:7). He had witnessed the tragic war in heaven and seen one-third of his spirit brothers and sisters turn against him to choose the most notorious infidel of all time. Surely he understood there would be Sodoms and Gomorrahs and crimes of most heinous proportions. And surely he took this into account as he worked with the Father in planning a redemption that would encompass it all.

The Prophet Joseph confirms both the Lord's omniscient foresight and universal redemption: "The great Jehovah contemplated the whole of the events connected with the earth, pertaining to the plan of salvation. . . . *He knew of the fall of Adam, the iniquities of the antediluvians, of the depth of iniquity that would be connected with the human family,* their weakness and strength, their power and glory, apostasies, their crimes, their righteousness and iniquity; *He comprehended the fall of man, and his redemption;* He knew the plan of salvation and pointed it out; He was acquainted with the situation of all nations and with their destiny; He ordered all things according to the council of His own will; *He knows the situation of both the living and the dead, and has made ample provision for their redemption."* [9]

King Benjamin was not unmindful of these comprehensive premortal plans, for he taught that the Atonement "was prepared from the foundation of the world for all mankind, which ever were since the fall of Adam, or who are, or who ever shall be" (Mosiah 4:7).

In summary, the Savior's Atonement saves all men from the first spiritual death, because the laws of justice are not violated, and, in addition, exalts all men who repent, because the laws of mercy so allow. The Atonement cannot, however, exalt anyone who has rejected it or irreversibly closed the doors of repentance, for the laws of justice are not so permissive. That was the message of Amulek to Zeezrom: "Ye cannot be saved in your sins" (Alma 11:37; see also Matthew 1:21). Abinadi knew this, for when speaking of those who died in their sins, he observed, "The Lord hath redeemed none such; yea, neither can the Lord redeem such; for he cannot deny himself; for he cannot deny justice when it has its claim" (Mosiah 15:27; see also Alma 11:37). As long as we have the slightest spark of repentance within us, Christ and his Atonement are standing in the wings, anxiously waiting to be summoned. The question is not whether the Savior paid the purchase price for all sins—He did—but whether we are willing to avail ourselves of his sacrifice by repenting.

TRANSGRESSION OF LAWS

Not only did the Savior suffer for our conscious, deliberate sins, but he also suffered for our innocent transgressions and for those who died "in their ignorance, not having salvation declared unto them" (Mosiah 15:24). This was consistent with the Mosaic law. Moses taught, "If the whole congregation of Israel sin through ignorance, . . . the priest shall make an atonement for them, and it shall be forgiven them" (Leviticus 4:13, 20). King Benjamin joined in declaring the expansiveness of the Atonement's cleansing powers: "For behold, and also his blood atoneth for the sins of those who have fallen by the transgression of Adam, who have died not knowing the will of God concerning them, or who have ignorantly sinned" (Mosiah 3:11; see also Alma 34:8). Such Atonement, however, was not without its cost. Even when a law is innocently violated, a price must nevertheless be paid. One may innocently drink poison, but the physical consequences will be the same as for the person who drinks with suicidal motives. When a law is broken there must be a payment. This payment involves suffering, and whether it be for the innocent or repentant, that suffering is centered in the atoning sacrifice of the Savior.

Jacob observed that "where there is no law . . . the mercies of the Holy One of Israel have claim upon them, because of the atonement" (2 Nephi 9:25). He then added, "The atonement satisfieth the demands of his justice upon all those who have not the law given to them" (2 Nephi 9:26). Certainly this includes little children as well as those who have not yet heard the gospel message. Mormon addressed this same theme: "All little children are alive in Christ, and also all they that are without the law. For the power of redemption cometh on all them that have no law" (Moroni 8:22; see also D&C 137:7–10). The Savior explained why little children are saved: "Little children are whole. . . . Wherefore the curse of Adam is taken from them in me" (Moroni 8:8; see also Moroni 8:20). The Savior taught this same lesson to his disciples: "These little ones have no need of repentance, and I will save them" (JST, Matthew 18:11).

While King Benjamin clearly understood that little children and "innocent" sinners are protected by the Atonement, he also knew that the time would come when the "knowledge of a Savior shall spread throughout every nation, kindred, tongue, and people. . . . And . . . none shall be found blameless before God, except it be little children, only through repentance and faith on the name of the Lord God Omnipotent" (Mosiah 3:20–21). Isaiah likewise saw that day when "all flesh shall know that I the Lord am thy Saviour and thy Redeemer" (Isaiah 49:26; see also Jeremiah 31:34). So complete will be this flood of knowledge that

Habakkuk prophesied, "For the earth shall be filled with the knowledge of the glory of the Lord, as the waters cover the sea" (Habakkuk 2:14; see also 2 Nephi 30:15). These prophets foretold the time when the gospel would be preached worldwide. In that day none shall fall within the confines of the "ignorant sinner" for the gospel message will be worldwide. No doubt this condition will not exist until the millennial era (D&C 101:25–29).

The Atonement not only descends beneath the deeds of the willful sinner who repents, but also beneath the broken laws of those little children who "are not capable of committing sin" (Moroni 8:8) and, in addition, to those more mature souls who have not yet heard the truth and, therefore, have "ignorantly sinned" (Mosiah 3:11).

SUFFERING UNRELATED TO SIN OR TRANSGRESSION

Jacob placed no qualifiers when he said the Savior would suffer "the pains of every living creature, both men, women, and children, who belong to the family of Adam" (2 Nephi 9:21). These were pains both related and unrelated to sin or transgression. In other words, the Savior voluntarily took upon himself not only the cumulative burden of all sin and transgression, but also the cumulative burden of all depression, all loneliness, all sorrow, all mental, emotional, and physical hurt, and all weakness of every kind that afflicts mankind. He knows the depth of sorrow that stems from death; he knows the widow's anguish. He understands the agonizing parental pain when children go astray; he has felt the striking pain of cancer and every other debilitating ailment heaped upon man. Impossible as it may seem, he has somehow taken upon himself those feelings of inadequacy, sometimes even utter hopelessness, that accompany our rejections and weaknesses. There is no mortal condition, however gruesome or ugly or hopeless it may seem, that has escaped his grasp or his suffering. No one will be able to say, "But you don't understand my particular plight." The scriptures are emphatic on this point—"he comprehended all things" because "he descended below all things" (D&C 88:6; see also D&C 122:8). All of these, Elder

Neal A. Maxwell explains, "were somehow, too, a part of the awful arithmetic of the Atonement."[10]

President Ezra Taft Benson taught, "There is no human condition—be it suffering, incapacity, inadequacy, mental deficiency, or sin—which He cannot comprehend or for which His love will not reach out to the individual."[11] This is a staggering thought when we contemplate the Mount Everest of pain required to make it so. What weight is thrown on the scales of pain when calculating the hurt of innumerable patients in countless hospitals? Now, add to that the loneliness of the elderly who are forgotten in the rest homes of society, desperately yearning for a card, a visit, a call—just some recognition from the outside world. Keep on adding the hurt of hungry children, the suffering caused by famine, drought, and pestilence. Pile on the heartache of parents who tearfully plead on a daily basis for a wayward son or daughter to come back home. Factor in the trauma of every divorce and the tragedy of every abortion. Add the remorse that comes with each child lost in the dawn of life, each spouse taken in the prime of marriage. Compound that with the misery of overflowing prisons, bulging halfway houses and institutions for the mentally disadvantaged. Multiply all this by century after century of history, and creation after creation without end. Such is but an awful glimpse of the Savior's load. Who can bear such a burden or scale such a mountain as this? No one, absolutely no one, save Jesus Christ, the Redeemer of us all.

The prophets have long testified of the Savior's infinite, suffering nature. Years before his birth, Isaiah declared, "Surely he hath borne our griefs, and carried our sorrows" (Isaiah 53:4), and later, "In all their affliction he was afflicted" (Isaiah 63:9; see also D&C 133:53). Alma understood the extent of the Savior's descent when he observed, "He shall go forth, *suffering pains and afflictions and temptations of every kind;* and this that the word might be fulfilled which saith he will take upon him the pains and the sicknesses of his people" (Alma 7:11; emphasis added). So extensive would be this descent that King Benjamin observed, "He shall suffer temptations, and pain of body, hunger, thirst, and fatigue, even more than man can suffer" (Mosiah 3:7). No one in the limited experiences of mortality will scratch the surface of pain laid upon the Infinite One. He carried it all, even that aggregate of pain that has no origins in sin or transgression.

SUFFERING INCIDENT TO TEMPTATIONS

Part of the human experience is to confront temptation. No one escapes. It is omnipresent. It is both externally driven and internally prompted. It is like the enemy that attacks from all sides. It boldly assaults us in television shows, movies, billboards, and newspapers in the name of entertainment or free speech. It walks down our streets and sits in our offices in the name of fashion. It drives our roads in the name of style. It represents itself as political correctness or business necessity. It claims moral sanction under the guise of free choice. On occasion it roars like thunder; on others it whispers in subtle, soothing tones. With chameleon-like skill it camouflages its ever-present nature, but it is there—always there.

Every temptation proves a crossroad where we must choose between the high road and the low road. On some occasions it is a trial of agonizing frustration. On other occasions, it is a mere annoyance, a nuisance of minor proportions. But in each case there is some element of uneasiness, anxiety, and spiritual tugging—ultimately a choosing that forces us to take sides. Neutrality is a nonexistent condition in this life. We are always choosing, always taking sides. That is part of the human experience—facing temptations on a daily, almost moment-by-moment basis—facing them not only on the good days but on the days we are down, the days we are tired, rejected, discouraged, or sick. Every day of our lives we battle temptation—and so did the Savior. It is an integral part of the human experience, faced not only by us but also by him. He drank from the same cup.

We know little of the Savior's youthful years, but no sooner had his mission commenced than he "was left to be tempted of the devil" (JST, Matthew 4:2). The Savior was triumphant, but Satan would return. The scriptures record, "He [Satan] departed from him for a season" (Luke 4:13). The Pharisees would tempt him on multiple occasions; a lawyer would try to entrap Him—all to no avail. Even on the cross, Satan would spew forth his final poison dart: "If thou be the Son of God, come down from the cross" (Matthew 27:40).

The Savior's temptations were not limited to direct confrontations with the Evil One and his emissaries. Alma knew that he would suffer "temptations of every kind" (Alma 7:11). This would include temptations relating to "pain of body, hunger, thirst, and fatigue" (Mosiah 3:7). No doubt he would face temptations of greed, power, and fame. Every temptation of the flesh would face him. As Paul said, he "was in *all points* tempted like as we are" (Hebrews 4:15; emphasis added). Abinadi made it clear, however, that while he "suffereth temptation," he "yieldeth not to the temptation" (Mosiah 15:5). The Doctrine and Covenants confirms this same truth: "He suffered temptations but gave no heed unto them" (D&C 20:22). There were choices, confrontations, and encounters, but never internalization, rationalization, or indulgence. Stephen Robinson beautifully expresses this same principle:

"Do not misunderstand me. I am not suggesting here that Jesus in any way indulged in unclean thoughts, for that would be sin, and he indulged nothing sinful. I do not believe that he 'struggled' or 'wrestled' with temptations. My only point is that he was as vulnerable to suggestions and impulses coming into his mind from his mortal nature, a nature inherited from his mortal mother, as any of us. He simply paid no attention to those suggestions, and he immediately put them out of his mind. The ability of the flesh to suggest, to entice, was the same for him as it is for us, but unlike the rest of us, he *never* responded to it. He didn't ponder, deliberate, or entertain the sinful options even as theoretical possibilities—'he gave no heed unto them.'"[12]

President David O. McKay wrote poetic lines that echoed similar statements:

Though waves of temptation around me did roll,
They but tempered my manhood; untainted's my soul![13]

The question always lingers, Why did the Savior confront temptation? Why so condescend? And the answer is always the same: "In that he himself hath suffered being tempted, he is able to succour them that are tempted" (Hebrews 2:18). By doing so, he could now become our "advocate, who knoweth the weakness of man and how to succor them who are tempted" (D&C 62:1). Brigham Young spoke to this same point: "It must be that God knows something about temporal things, and has had a body and been on an earth, were it not so he would not know how to judge men righteously, according to the temptations and sin they have had to contend with."[14]

Some may contend that the Savior cannot empathize with those who succumb to temptation because he never yielded and, therefore, he could not understand the apparently unique circumstances of those who did. The fallacy of such an argument is exposed by C. S. Lewis: "No man knows how bad he is till he has tried very hard to be good. A silly idea is current that good people do not know what temptation means. This is an obvious lie. Only those who try to resist temptation know how strong it is. After all, you find out the strength of the German army by fighting it, not by giving in. You find out the strength of a wind by trying to walk against it, not by lying down. A man who gives in to temptation after five minutes simply does not know what it would have been like an hour later. That is why bad people, in one sense, know very little about badness. They have lived a sheltered life by always giving in. *We never find out the strength of the evil impulse inside us until we try to fight it: and Christ, because He was the only man who never yielded to temptation, is also the only man who knows to the full what temptation means—the only complete realist.*"[15]

EXERCISE OF FAITH

The scriptures suggest that the Savior endured all the sin, pain, and temptation experienced by the human race. But could there have been some human experience he never fully encountered because of his unique nature? Was he ever required to exercise faith, or did his unique spiritual knowledge and divine heritage exclude this possibility? Does not each of us confront those moments in life when faith and the reason of the world are seemingly incompatible and we must choose between the two? We find ourselves at a spiritual crossroad—one path paved with the knowledge and reason of man, the other paved with faith in God. It may come when there is a lack of funds to pay our tithing. It may knock when the Lord calls us to a position far beyond our natural abilities. It may be when we are called to serve at a moment of inconvenience. It may come with the loss of a job, the death of a loved one, or a sudden unexpected illness, but come it will. Do not all men, at some time in their lives, face that dilemma—the reason of the world versus faith in Jesus Christ?

Moses experienced it. He had just freed the children of Israel. He now led them on a seemingly suicidal course direct for the Red Sea. The Egyptian armies were in hot pursuit. The powers of reason no doubt cried out: "Veer to the left or to the right. To proceed straight ahead is a death trap—pinned against the wall of the Red Sea on the one side, the fast-approaching Egyptian army on the other." But Moses was steadfast in his course. March they would, directly toward the Red Sea. The Israelites, seeing their fate, fearfully cried out, "It had been better for us to serve the Egyptians, than that we should die in the wilderness" (Exodus 14:12). Moses was alone. The power of reason and the power of the people combined against him with a raging fury. But deep within his soul was a power that far exceeded the powers known to man, a power that drove him on against the world, against all seeming odds, against all that was rational and reasonable in life. It was the power of faith. It proved to be his—and his people's—temporal and spiritual salvation.

Peter faced such a moment. The Savior was preaching on the shores of Galilee. Nearby were two empty ships. Their fishermen were on the shore washing their nets. All night long they had toiled and caught nothing for their tireless vigil. The Savior spoke to Simon Peter and said, "Launch out into the deep, and let down your nets for a draught" (Luke 5:4). Peter, surprised, replied, "Master, we have toiled all the night, and have taken nothing" (Luke 5:5). How ridiculous the Savior's suggestion must have seemed to the rational minds of this world. Did he not know these were seasoned fishermen? This was their trade, their livelihood, their business, "their" lake. All night long they had cast out the net, retrieved it, and cast it again and again with unfailing repetition. They knew this lake, the currents, the winds, the fishing patterns. Why waste their efforts and try again? Here was but a carpenter. What did he know of fishing? Peter was now at a crossroad. He must choose between reason and faith. Then came Peter's stirring reply: "Nevertheless at thy word I will let down the net" (Luke 5:5). Then came the miracle. A great multitude of fish was caught—so many their nets could not hold them all. Another ship was beckoned to help with the bounty. The Lord did not send these faithful fishermen out to catch a fish or two, a basketful. No—there would be nothing penurious about his blessing nature. They had passed the test of faith and would be blessed abundantly.

Each of us faces the time when the powers of reason come in direct conflict with faith. All the logic, all the understanding of men may swell in unison, and there alone, in opposition, stands faith—unalterable, unassailable, unmovable—the anchor to our souls. The tides of trial can come, the ocean waves of worldly reason pound against our souls, the current and popular trends tug with all their mighty sway, but there unmoved, unfazed, unharmed is the soul that is anchored by faith. Philosopher George Santayana wrote of those who fail to choose this "better part":

> O world, thou choosest not the better part!
> It is not wisdom to be only wise,
> And on the inward vision close the eyes,
> But it is wisdom to believe the heart.
> Columbus found a world, and had no chart,
> Save one that faith deciphered in the skies;

To trust the soul's invincible surmise
Was all his science and his only art.
Our knowledge is a torch of smoky pine
That lights the pathway but one step ahead
Across a void of mystery and dread.
Bid, then, the tender light of faith to shine
By which alone the mortal heart is led
Unto the thinking of the thought divine.[16]

Job possessed such a faith. He had been stripped of family, wealth, health, and friends. Even his wife could see no reason in the trials. Finally she cried out, "Curse God, and die" (Job 2:9). Later, Job, a pillar of faith, would respond, "Though he slay me, yet will I trust in him" (Job 13:15). Nothing in all this world could extinguish his flame of faith.

That same flame burned brightly in the soul of Nephi as he headed back to Laban's home one more time: "I was led by the Spirit, not knowing beforehand the things which I should do" (1 Nephi 4:6). This was pure, absolute, unadulterated faith. All the powers of reason had been exhausted. Nephi and his brethren had requested the plates of Laban and been denied; they had offered the whole of their family wealth and had been rejected. It seemed that all the options had been played out. Nephi had no idea what solution would unfold. Who in a million years would have dreamed of the Lord's answer? But faith, that unseen power, drove him on.

Moses, Peter, Job, Nephi, and faithful saints of all ages have had to make that difficult choice on multiple occasions—faith or reason. But did the Savior, with his infinite faculties, both spiritually and intellectually, ever really face that dilemma? Was there ever a time he did not know the end from the beginning? Like all other mortals, did he ever have to choose faith in God over his own powers of reason? Was this, too, a part of his experience? If not, did he truly experience the totality of the human plight?

There are moments in the Savior's life that suggest he, too, was required to proceed on faith. Luke tells us that as a youth he "increased in wisdom" (Luke 2:52), implying that omniscience was not conferred at a singular moment of time. Evidently his knowledge and reasoning powers progressed step by step during his mortal sojourn. Such a progression suggests times when he was not all-knowing.

Even at the conclusion of his mortal life, when the knowledge of his mission was paramount and his reasoning powers supreme, it seems there were unresolved issues, even for him. The plea "O my Father, if it be possible, let this cup pass from me" (Matthew 26:39) was an honest request to seek another alternative, if there were any, to the atoning sacrifice. His probing mind sorted out all the options and all the possibilities but could find no alternative, so he turned in hope to that one being who knew and had experienced even more than he. The response was in the negative; there was no other way. He must place his trust in God and proceed on faith.

C. S. Lewis spoke of Christ's foreknowledge preceding his impending death. He also believed the Savior must experience all the conditions of mortality, including the anxieties that accompany the exercise of faith. He reconciled these seemingly conflicting positions as follows: "It is clear that this knowledge [of his death] must somehow have been withdrawn from Him before He prayed in Gethsemane. He could not, with whatever reservation about the Father's will, have prayed that the cup might pass and simultaneously known that it would not. That is both a logical and psychological impossibility. You see what this involves? Lest any trial incident to humanity should be lacking, the torments of hope—of suspense, anxiety—were at the last moment loosed upon Him—the supposed possibility that, after all, He might, He just conceivably might, be spared the supreme horror. There was precedent. Isaac had been spared: he too at the last moment, he also against all apparent probability. . . . But for this last (and erroneous) hope against hope, and the consequent tumult of the soul, the sweat of blood, perhaps He would not have been very Man. To live in a fully predictable world is not to be a man."[17]

To live a fully predictable life as suggested by C. S. Lewis, a life devoid of anxiety, suspense, and faith, is a pseudo-human life—it is no more than a facade. But this was not the case with the Savior. Never was more faith required of any man, at any hour, than when the Savior faced the terrifying aloneness of the hours surrounding the cross. This was the moment when the Father withdrew His spirit and left him comfortless.

The Savior's experience had some similarities to that of the Prophet Joseph's confinement in Liberty Jail. For months he had languished in that cramped and foul-smelling cell without any relief in sight. He was separated from wife, children, and friends. His petitions and appeals had fallen on what appeared to be deaf ears. In that desperate, seemingly hopeless state of affairs, Joseph cried out: "O God, where art thou? And where is the pavilion that covereth thy hiding place? How long shall thy hand be stayed . . . ?" (D&C 121:1–2). We can understand his frustration. He had been called to a high and holy calling. There was much work to do, and then in the midst of his mission he felt temporarily abandoned by the very One who called him. The heavens seemed unresponsive.

The Savior also had his time of abandonment. The climax of his mission was at hand. If there were any time he needed support and comfort, it was now. Only hours earlier he had declared, "I am not alone, because the Father is with me" (John 16:32). Surely he knew of the prophesied day of "aloneness"—but absent the actual experience perhaps he was unable to fully comprehend its terrible, even horrifying, magnitude. And so, in his moment of agony, he cried out, "My God, my God, why hast thou forsaken me?" (Matthew 27:46).

The Savior was facing his great trial with nothing to support him but his will and his faith. More faith was required of him than was ever exacted from any mortal. Mortals recognize their intellectual inferiority compared to God. In other words, they know they do not know all. They expect to have moments when faith is required. But here was a God whose knowledge reigned supreme, yet there was still a "why"—a gap between his cognitive powers and empirical senses. He had encountered a dark zone, an intellectual "out of bounds," even for him. Perhaps he did not expect this. Perhaps he did not contemplate a total abandonment. Perhaps he did not comprehend in advance the totality of the aloneness he must endure. Perhaps his infinite mind knew and understood all that is possible to know in advance, but even this fell short of the hard-core reality that comes from actual experience. In any event, it was a soul-wrenching moment. Would he continue to have faith in that God who had now withdrawn? David's Messianic psalm gives us further insight into the pathos of that moment when we reflect upon the Savior's soul-searching question, "Why art thou [the Father] so far from helping me, and from the words of my roaring?" (Psalm 22:1). This was a crisis hour of ultimate faith. Elder Erastus Snow spoke of that critical moment and the Savior's need for faith:

"At length the time came when the Father said, You must succumb, you must be made the offering. And at this dark hour the power of the Father withdrew itself measurably from him. . . . And when he was led to exclaim in his last agony upon the cross, My God, my God, why hast thou forsaken me? the Father did not deign to answer; the time had not yet come to explain it and tell him. But after a little, when he passed the ordeal, made the sacrifice, and by the power of God was raised from the dead, then all was clear, all was explained and comprehended fully."[18] It was as though the lost piece of the spiritual puzzle was not given to him until after the resurrection. Then the picture was complete.

In the meantime, the Savior was willing to proceed, knowing there was but one path through Gethsemane and Calvary, the unseen path of faith.

We have little in our mortal experience to which we can compare Christ's experience—the child jumping in darkness to a father she can hear but cannot see; the trapezist making the death-defying leap to his partner's arms without the safety net below; Moses, not knowing, but proceeding straight for the Red Sea; Job, not understanding, but trusting; Abraham wondering, but committed; Nephi, answerless, but going back one more time; Joseph Smith, asking why, and being told that no matter what happens, even if "the sentence of death [be] passed upon thee," even "if the very jaws of hell shall gape open the mouth wide after thee," that "the Son of Man hath descended below them all. Art thou greater than he?" (D&C 122:7–8).

The Savior had faith; he exercised faith; and by the power of that faith he forged ahead in uncharted waters to consummate the atoning sacrifice. As Lorenzo Snow confirmed, "It required all the power that He had and *all the faith that He could summon* for Him to accomplish that which the Father required of Him."[19]

The Atonement was accomplished by an infinite being of infinite power, but, of equal import, the effects of that Atonement were infinite in time, coverage, and depth. This event has no geographical limitations—no state, country, or galactic boundaries that it cannot or does not cross. It knows no time constraints. It descends beneath all transgressions, all pain, all temptations, and every demand for faith. Its influence and effect pervade all space, all worlds, and all forms of life. There is no crevice it has not filled, no abyss it has not plumbed. The Atonement is infinite in its depth.

NOTES

1. Shakespeare, *Winter's Tale*, 3.2.209–15.
2. Young, *Discourses of Brigham Young*, 156.
3. Smith, *Teachings of the Prophet Joseph Smith*, 358.
4. Maxwell, *A More Excellent Way*, 66.
5. Smith, *Gospel Doctrine*, 72.
6. Evidently the informed, deliberate murderer has so hardened his heart, perhaps irreversibly so, that in the scale of justice he has advanced his judgment day as to the issue of his exaltation and forever closed the door of eternal progress. The repentant Anti-Nephi-Lehies realized this tragic possibility. They had shed blood before their days of gospel enlightenment. Now they realized the dire consequences if they should take up the sword once more, "for perhaps, if we should stain our swords again they can no more be washed bright through the blood of the Son of our great God" (Alma 24:13).
7. Madsen, *Christ and the Inner Life*, 14; emphasis added.
8. As previously discussed, there is no repentance for the "unpardonable sin."
9. Smith, *Teachings of the Prophet Joseph Smith*, 220; emphasis added.
10. Maxwell, "Willing to Submit," 73.

11. Benson, "Jesus Christ," 6.

12. Robinson, *Believing Christ,* 115.

13. McKay, *Home Memories of President David O. McKay,* 33.

14. *Journal of Discourses,* 4:271.

15. Lewis, *Inspirational Writings of C. S. Lewis,* 337–38; emphasis added.

16. Santayana, "O World," in Untermeyer, *Treasury of Great Poems,* 1034.

17. Lewis, *Joyful Christian,* 171–72.

18. *Journal of Discourses,* 21:26.

19. Snow, *Teachings of Lorenzo Snow,* 98; emphasis added.

CHAPTER 14

INFINITE IN SUFFERING

———∞———

DID THE SAVIOR SUFFER AS WE DO?

The Atonement of Jesus Christ cost the blood and life and indescribable suffering of a God. Contrary to the thoughts of some, it was not mental suffering alone; it was intense, prolonged anguish, "*both* body and spirit" (D&C 19:18; emphasis added). It was physical, spiritual, intellectual, and emotional pain of the highest order, all wrapped into one. It was of such colossal magnitude that it caused "even God, the greatest of all, to tremble because of pain, and to bleed at every pore" (D&C 19:18).

As significant as the Savior's suffering seemed, was it tempered by the fact that he possessed godly attributes? Did he have superhuman powers of resistance that allowed him to more easily face and endure the human plight? In other words, did he have a shield when everyone else was fighting without one? True, he may have fasted forty days—but inwardly was he hungry, did his body crave food, his lips thirst for water, his muscles quiver, and his body ache? Or did superhuman powers give him an edge over his mortal counterparts? Some might contend that he went through the motions, but never internalized the hurt—that like Shadrach, Meshach, and Abednego, he walked through the furnace of life never feeling the heat of the flames. Paul contemplated the question and issued the response: "For verily he took not on him the nature of angels; but he took on him the seed of Abraham. Wherefore in all things it behoved him to be made like unto his brethren" (Hebrews 2:16–17). Later, Paul would confirm that the Savior was "touched with the feeling of our infirmities" (Hebrews 4:15).

Mortal life for Christ was not just an academic exercise; it was hard-core reality that pressed the "feeling" of a man into the being of a God. Paul observed that the Savior would "taste death for every man" (Hebrews 2:9). Those words, *feeling* and *taste,* are painfully descriptive. This was not just an intellectualization, but an internalization of the human plight. Alma taught this truth, that "the Son of God suffereth according to the flesh" (Alma 7:13). Jacob added his testimony that the Savior "suffereth himself to become subject unto man in the flesh" (2 Nephi 9:5; see also Philippians 2:7). Paul preached that Christ "was made in the likeness of men" (Philippians 2:7). And Isaiah prophesied he would be "a man of sorrows, and acquainted with grief" (Isaiah 53:3). Again and again the prophets testify that the Savior not only suffered what we suffer, but in like manner. Perhaps Robert Browning wrote more than of himself when he penned:

> I was ever a fighter, so—one fight more,
>   The best and the last!
> I would hate that death bandaged my eyes, and forbore,
>   And bade me creep past.
> No! let me taste the whole of it, fare like my peers
>   The heroes of old,
> Bear the brunt, in a minute pay glad life's arrears
>   Of pain, darkness and cold.[1]

The Savior both felt and tasted the whole of it. He fared like his mortal peers and so much more. Nephi understood: "The God of our fathers . . . yieldeth himself . . . as a man, into the hands of wicked men" (1 Nephi 19:10).

Elder Bruce R. McConkie quoted scholar Alfred Edersheim in his discussion of the Savior's humiliation and self-abasement.

Elder McConkie then elaborated: "When Edersheim speaks of Jesus' self-exinanition, he means that our Lord voluntarily abased himself, or, rather, emptied himself of all his divine power, or enfeebled himself by relying upon his humanity and not his Godhood, so as to be as other men and thus be tested to the full by all the trials and torments of the flesh."[2] C. S. Lewis wrote with feeling: "God could, had He pleased, have been incarnate in a man of iron nerves, the Stoic sort who lets no sigh escape him. Of His great humility He chose to be incarnate in a man of delicate sensibilities."[3]

The Savior voluntarily let his humanity take precedence over his divinity. Isaiah spoke prophetically of those days of Messianic submission: "I gave my back to the smiters . . . : I hid not my face from shame and spitting" (Isaiah 50:6). For those few moments in the eternal spectrum called mortality the Savior yielded to the mortal plight; he submitted to the inhumanity of man; his body longed for sleep; he hungered; he felt the pains of sickness. He was in all respects subjected to every mortal failing experienced by the human family. Not once did he raise the shield of godhood in order to soften the blows. Not once did he don the bulletproof vest of divinity. That he also had godly powers did not make his suffering any less excruciating, any less poignant, or any less real. To the contrary, it is for this very reason that his suffering was more, not less, than his mortal counterparts could experience. He took upon him infinite suffering, but chose to defend with only mortal faculties, with but one exception—his godhood was summoned to hold off unconsciousness and death (i.e., the twin relief mechanisms of man) that would otherwise overpower a mere mortal when he reached his threshold of pain. For the Savior, however, there would be no such relief. His divinity would be called upon, not to immunize him from pain, but to enlarge the receptacle that would hold it. He simply brought a larger cup to hold the bitter drink.

BLEEDING FROM EVERY PORE

Luke substantiates the reality of his suffering: "And being in an agony he prayed more earnestly" (Luke 22:44). Were not all his prayers earnest? Can we comprehend the intensity of suffering, the depth of pain that caused him now to pray even *more* earnestly? What overwhelming burden must he have been shouldering to have elicited from a God the admission that he was "exceedingly sorrowful" (Matthew 26:38)? What torment pressed upon him so deeply that he "fell on his face" in prayerful pleading (Matthew 26:39)? This was a crisis moment in the galaxy.

As his agony accelerated, and eventually raced towards its climax without restraint and without release, his physical body finally revolted, and he sweat great drops of blood. Some years ago I attended a Sunday School class in which the teacher suggested the Savior did not literally sweat blood, but rather sweat in such a manner that his perspiration fell to the ground *like* drops of blood. This teacher sought support from the words of Luke who wrote, "His sweat was *as it were* great drops of blood falling down to the ground" (Luke 22:44; emphasis added). King Benjamin, however, saw with prophetic eyes the true state of affairs: "Behold, blood cometh from every pore, so great shall be his anguish for the wickedness and the abominations of his people" (Mosiah 3:7; see also JST, Luke 22:44). Beyond this, we have the incontestable testimony of the one person who was present, the Savior himself, who declared, "Which suffering caused myself, even God . . . to bleed at every pore" (D&C 19:18). His body, in violent reaction to the superhuman pain thrust upon him, literally, not figuratively, shed forth blood from every pore.

WHY MUST BLOOD BE SHED?

Paul preached that "almost all things are by the law purged with blood; and without shedding of blood is no remission" (Hebrews 9:22; see also Hebrews 9:17–18). Such a truth was taught since ancient times. Moses declared, "It is the blood that maketh an atonement for the soul" (Leviticus 17:11). It is "the blood of Jesus Christ" that "cleanseth us from all sin" (1 John 1:7). The Savior's blood acts as the cleansing agent by which our "garments are made white" (1 Nephi 12:10). We even learn that the land of America was "redeemed" by "the shedding of blood" (D&C 101:80). Thus, somehow, blood acts as a cleansing, redeeming agent. How it is done we do not know. John Taylor taught: "Why it was necessary that his blood should be shed is an apparent mystery. . . . Without the shedding of blood there is no remission of sins; but why this? Why should such a law exist? It is left with us as a matter of faith."[4] Joseph Fielding Smith came to the same conclusion: "Just how the shedding of the Savior's blood atoned for a fall . . . is not completely explained by our Heavenly Father."[5]

Paul does give us a partial insight, however, into why blood must be shed. While speaking of animal sacrifices under the Mosaic law and the redeeming powers of blood, he adds: "It was therefore necessary that the patterns of things in the heavens should be purified with these; but the heavenly things themselves with better sacrifices than these" (Hebrews 9:23). It is as though he is saying that animal sacrifices are an earthly prototype or counterpart of heavenly sacrifices, but that Christ is the actual or "better" sacrifice that satisfies all heavenly requirements for purification. President Joseph F. Smith hints at this same truth: "Things upon the earth, so far as they have not been perverted by wickedness, are typical of things in heaven. Heaven was the prototype of this beautiful creation."[6] Until further light is shed on the issue, we can take comfort in the consequences that flow from the Savior's shedding his blood without fully comprehending the underlying rationale for its necessity.

While Joseph Fielding Smith does not attempt to answer how the blood of Christ cleanses us, he does discuss why such blood had to be shed: "Since it was by the creation of blood that mortality came, it is by the sacrifice of blood that the redemption from death was accomplished, and all creatures freed from Satan's grasp. In no other way could the sacrifice for redemption of the world from death be accomplished."[7]

Reference to his sacrificial act in the Garden was the focus of the Savior's plea on our behalf before the Father: "By the virtue of the blood which I have spilt, have I pleaded before the Father for them" (D&C 38:4). After reminding the Father of "the blood of thy Son which was shed . . . that thyself might be glorified," Christ then pleaded to the Father that he "spare these my brethren that believe on my name" (D&C 45:4–5). As our advocate, he knew there was something in that act of such spiritual poignancy that it should form the crux of his plea for mercy. With unhesitating conviction he could declare that he had "wrought out this perfect atonement through the shedding of his own blood" (D&C 76:69).

THE SHEDDING OF BLOOD IS SYMBOLIC

Among other things, the shedding of blood is symbolic. The shedding of a man's blood brings about physical death. On the other hand, the shedding of Christ's blood brings about spiritual life. Again and again in the scriptures the same symbol can have dual, even opposite, meanings. In the Garden of Eden it was the serpent that represented the devil, the father of death and darkness. Later, however, it was the brazen serpent that represented the Savior, the source of life and light. The waters of Noah's day destroyed all but eight souls, yet the waters of baptism symbolically cleanse and save every soul who seeks eternal life. Fire is the token of punishment for the anguished in hell, but Isaiah spoke of the righteous who shall dwell in "everlasting burnings" (Isaiah 33:14; see also Revelation 15:2). At the Second Coming it is fire that will destroy the wicked, but in the interim it is the fire of the Holy Ghost that purges and preserves the spiritually repentant. In similar dualistic fashion, it is the shedding of man's blood that symbolizes death, but it is the shedding of Christ's blood that symbolizes life eternal.

It seems appropriate that the place for this shedding of blood should be a garden called Gethsemane. As Truman Madsen explains: "*Geth* or *gat* in Hebrew means 'press,' *Shemen* means 'oil.' This was the Garden of the olive press." Brother Madsen then explains how the olive press worked: "To produce olive oil, the refined olives had to be crushed in a press. The mellowed and seasoned olives were placed in strong bags and flattened on a furrowed stone. Then a huge crushing circular rock was rolled around on top, paced by a mule or an ox and a stinging whip. Another method used heavy wooden levers or screws twisting beams downward like a winch upon the stone with the same effect: *pressure, pressure, pressure—until the oil flowed*."[8]

And so there was the "pressure, pressure, pressure" of infinite sins until the blood flowed from every pore. "Indeed," as Brother Madsen observed, "the symbolism of the place is inescapable."[9]

AN ANGEL STRENGTHENS HIM

What was the Savior's state of mind, physical body, and spirit at this crisis hour in the garden that an angel from heaven should need to come "strengthening him" (Luke 22:43), a God? Do we presume that he, a God, was so weakened by this ordeal that he now needed strengthening? What divine messenger offered such aid? Was it Adam? Noah? Abraham? Certainly at such a critical moment in the destiny of man, this angel must have been a being of towering stature. Elder Bruce R. McConkie suggests it was "mighty Michael [Adam]."[10] While we do not know with certainty the identity of this heaven-sent comforter, there are at least four reasons why it may indeed have been Adam.[11] First, Adam, who was a joint creator of this earth and father of mortal man, would have had a supreme interest in man's ultimate destiny. Certainly he had a vested interest to see that this earth and all its dominions were not created in vain. Second, it seems appropriate that he who triggered in part the need for the Atonement should now be the agent for mankind to assist Him who pled for its redemption. Third, as taught by Joseph Smith, Adam has a presiding role in the hierarchy of divine beings, since all "angels are under the direction of Michael or Adam,"[12] and thus it seems no messenger would be more suited to strengthen and bless than he who was the presiding archangel. Fourth, Adam enjoyed a unique relationship with the Savior. Not only did he join with him in the creation process, but likewise as he led the heavenly forces in battle (Revelation 12:7). Now, once again, Adam might momentarily stand by him as the Savior participated in the most crucial battle of all. Adam could not take the Savior's place (for the Savior must bear this alone), but what he could do, he no doubt wanted to do. Perhaps he was there to console him, to comfort him, to support him, maybe even to bless him.

The scriptures are silent as to the nature of the exchange between Christ and his angelic visitor. No doubt this was one of those moments so sacred it was not to be recorded in the annals of man.[13] Evidently certain thoughts of the spirit are so lofty, so poignant, that they cannot be reduced to the oral language or written word of man. They simply defy mortal expression. Surely this was one of those moments.

Whatever the details of that divine encounter, surely the angelic guest must have extended to Christ the fullest blessing heaven could offer. Certainly this was a moment of transcendent pathos. Perhaps each wept and transmitted an intensity of love known only by the gods and angels. Perhaps the angel offered words of comfort and reassurance. Or perhaps the strength of his silent presence was sufficient. Whatever the divine exchange may have been, the Savior found sufficient strength, in the midst of unfathomable pain, to press on. Truman Madsen reminds us that the angel came "strengthening—not delivering."[14]

The time had now come. History's most crucial moment was here. The words of the lyricist were never more applicable than now: "The hopes and fears of all the years are met in thee tonight."[15] All other events, as significant as they may have seemed, paled in comparison to this. Without this moment all history was for naught.

THE DEPTHS OF HIS SUFFERING

Christ had fasted for forty days, confronted Satan face to face, weathered mocking, taunting, and abuse; he had endured the stinging pangs of rejection, even the brutal blow of betrayal. To what new depths must he now have sunk to cry out, "O my Father, if it be possible, let this cup pass from me" (Matthew 26:39)? *But it was not possible!*

Perhaps those closest to the Lord can best understand his suffering, a suffering that surpassed the finite understanding of man. President John Taylor gave us this insight: "There came upon Him the weight and agony of ages. . . . Hence His profound grief, His indescribable anguish, His overpowering torture, all experienced in the submission to the eternal fiat of Jehovah and the requirements of an inexorable law. . . . Groaning beneath this concentrated load, this intense, incomprehensible pressure, this terrible exaction of Divine justice, from which feeble humanity shrank, and through the agony thus experienced sweating great drops of blood, He was led to exclaim, 'Father, if it be possible, let this cup pass from me.'"[16]

President Taylor focuses our attention on the vision of Enoch, who "beheld the Son of Man lifted up on the cross, . . . and the heavens were veiled; and all the creations of God mourned; and the earth groaned; and the rocks were rent" (Moses 7:55–56). He then comments: "Thus, such was the torturing pressure of this intense, this indescribable agony, that it burst forth abroad beyond the confines of His body, convulsed all nature and spread throughout all space."[17] Just as man trembles at pain and suffering, so too does nature seem to respond in like fashion.

One might wonder if nature's response in the New World to the Savior's atoning sacrifice was indicative of what occurred on other worlds. Whatever the environmental response in the Old World, corresponding manifestations of greater magnitude appeared in the New World. There seems to be a divine law of compensation—those nations and worlds that were not privileged with the Savior's mortal ministry received greater physical witnesses as a compensating testimony. The Old World had its heavenly star to introduce the Savior's mortal entrance. In the New World, there were "many signs and wonders in heaven" (Helaman 14:6)—but the most conclusive witness of all was a day, a night, and a day of light. So powerful and convincing was this witness that "all the people . . . were so exceedingly astonished that they fell to the earth" (3 Nephi 1:17). The Old World had its quakings and its three hours of darkness, but such events pale when placed beside the cataclysmic events of the New World.

Those lands where the Savior's physical presence was absent no doubt responded with more powerful elemental reactions as a compensating witness. The New World suffered exceeding sharp lightnings, terrible thunderings, tempests, whirlwinds, and an earthquake of such monumental consequence "that it did shake the whole earth as if it was about to divide asunder" (3 Nephi 8:6). But there was more. Darkness, thick, vaporous, total darkness enveloped the land for three days. This was not a shadowy darkness, a dim-lit darkness, a darkness to which the eyes eventually adjust; no, this was impenetrable blackness, "so that there could not be any light at all" (3 Nephi 8:21). This was cold, unyielding, oppressive darkness, symbolizing evil and tragedy in their fullest measure. This was darkness similar to that which was cast over Egypt in Moses' day, "even darkness which may be felt. . . . And there was a thick darkness in all the land of Egypt three days" (Exodus 10:21–22).

Nature and all her components were joined in horrifying harmony. Even the kings of the isles of the sea exclaimed, "The God of nature suffers" (1 Nephi 19:12). The elements wrenched and writhed in all their fury as undeniable proof of a suffering that was no doubt galactic—that affected every man, every animal, every fish, every plant, and every element in that expanse of space called the universe. The Savior's suffering was like a prodigious boulder thrown into the midst of a glassy pond—the ripples emanating from Gethsemane and Calvary would, as President John Taylor said, "spread throughout all space"[18] and for the moment "all eternity is pained" (D&C 38:12).[19] John Taylor understood that the Savior's suffering affected universal nature:

> World upon world, *eternal things,*
> *Hang on thy anguish, King of kings.*[20]

As inadequate as words may be to describe this infinite ordeal, perhaps Frederik Farrar has best articulated, with an eloquence of words and a precision of thought, what others have attempted:

"Jesus knew that the awful hour of His deepest humiliation had arrived—that from this moment till the utterance of that great cry with which He expired, nothing remained for Him on earth but the torture of physical pain and the poignancy of mental anguish. All that the human frame can tolerate of suffering was to be heaped upon His shrinking body; every misery that cruel and crushing insult can inflict was to weigh heavy on His soul; and in this torment of body and agony of soul even the high and radiant serenity of His divine spirit was to suffer a short but terrible eclipse. Pain in its acutest sting, shame in its most overwhelming brutality, all the burden of the sin and mystery of man's existence in its apostasy and fall—this was what He must now face in all its most inexplicable accumulation."[21]

As if this were not enough, Farrar continues:

"It is as natural to die as to be born. The Christian hardly needs to be told that it was no such vulgar fear which forced from his Saviour that sweat of blood. No, it was something infinitely more than this: infinitely more than the highest stretch of our imagination can realize. It was something far deadlier than death. It was the burden and the mystery of the world's sin which lay heavy on His heart; it was the tasting, in the divine humanity of a sinless life, the bitter cup which sin had poisoned. . . . It was the endurance, by the perfectly guiltless, of the worst malice which human hatred could devise; it was to experience in the bosom of perfect innocence and perfect love, all that was detestable in human ingratitude, all that was pestilent in human hypocrisy, all that was cruel in human rage. It was to brave the last triumph of Satanic spite and fury, uniting against His lonely head all the flaming arrows of Jewish falsity and heathen corruption—the concentrated wrath of the rich and respectable, the yelling fury of the blind and brutal mob. It was to feel that His own, to whom he came, loved darkness rather than light—that the race of the chosen people could be wholly absorbed in one insane repulsion against infinite goodness and purity and love.

"Through all this He passed in that hour which, with a recoil of sinless horror beyond our capacity to conceive, foretasted a worse bitterness than the worst bitterness of death."[22]

Even the best of minds, the most fluent of speech cannot adequately describe the Savior's ordeal. Farrar reminds us that it "transcended all that, even in our purest moments, we can pretend to understand."[23] It is beyond any experience known or conceived by man. John Taylor simply stated, "In a manner to us incomprehensible and inexplicable, he bore the weight of the sins of the whole world."[24] Elder Orson F. Whitney shared in this feeling: "Our little finite afflictions are but as a drop in the ocean, compared with the infinite and unspeakable agony borne by him for our sakes because we were not able to bear it for ourselves."[25] In an inspired effort to define his suffering, Elder Neal A. Maxwell called it "*enormity* multiplied by *infinity.*"[26] However hard we try, the Lord reminds us of our inability to fully empathize, for while speaking to the Prophet Joseph he describes his own sufferings: "How sore *you know not,* how exquisite *you know not,* yea, how hard to bear *you know not*" (D&C 19:15; emphasis added). The suffering endured by the Savior cannot be translated into some quantifiable mass or reduced to some mathematical equation. The simple truth is, we have no tools to measure it or sufficient language to explain it. Part of the sacredness of this event lies in the fact that we feel much more than we can tell. The words of the hymn so observe:

> *We may not know, we cannot tell,*
> *What pains he had to bear,*
> *But we believe it was for us*
> *He hung and suffered there.*[27]

If suffering is proportionate to one's physical, intellectual, spiritual, and emotional sensitivities, then the Savior suffered more than mortal man, because he knew more, felt more, and cared more than any other mortal had ever done. Joseph Fielding Smith testifies of his unique suffering:

"A mortal man could not have stood it—that is, a man such as we are. I do not care what his fortitude, what his power, there was *no man ever born into this world that could have stood under the weight of the load that was upon the Son of God, when he was carrying my sins and yours. . . .* [It] was beyond the power of mortal man either to accomplish or endure."[28]

The Savior's sacrifice required inexhaustible stamina in order to bear the consequences of our sins and weather the temptations of the Evil One. But his suffering must have been more than a resigned submissiveness or a fist-clenching "taking of the stripes." It must have been more than a defensive "holding of the fort" or raising of the shield to ward off the fiery darts of the Evil One. Part of the Savior's atoning quest must have included an element of conquering, an offensive struggle of sorts. There was a need for the Savior to voluntarily lay down his life so he could "[break] the bands of death" (Mosiah 15:8) and to "destroy him that had the power of death" (Hebrews 2:14; see also 1 Corinthians 15:26). There was a need to rescue and deliver souls from "the chains of hell" (Alma 12:11). This part of the battle may have necessitated an invasion of Satan's turf, perhaps even an intrepid trespass into the dark abyss of the Devil's domain. Orson F. Whitney alludes to these moments of classic conflict:

> For flaming falchion, sword of light,
> Swift-flashing from its sheath,
> It cleft the realms of darkness and
> Dissolved the bands of death.
> Hell's dungeons burst! Wide open swung
> The everlasting bars,
> Whereby the ransomed soul shall win
> Those heights beyond the stars.[29]

The Savior's redemption was a one-man rescue mission to deliver the prisoners of all ages from death and hell, of which Satan was the ever-so-vigilant guard. Tennyson's description of

"The Light Brigade" may bear some similarities to the Savior's battle in Gethsemane:

> *Cannon to right of them,*
> *Cannon to left of them,*
> *Cannon in front of them*
> *Volley'd and thunder'd;*
> *Storm'd at with shot and shell,*
> *Boldly they rode and well,*
> *Into the jaws of Death,*
> *Into the mouth of hell.*[30]

The Savior's charge, however, would be alone; alone he would ride into the jaws of death and hell. This was all-out war. This was a "wrestle . . . against principalities, against powers, against the rulers of the darkness of this world, against spiritual wickedness in high places" (Ephesians 6:12). This was a fight to the finish— a fight to the death of all deaths. We have seen men fight against incredible odds to save self, men fight with reckless abandon to preserve country and freedom, and men fight with almost super-human strength to protect both wife and child, but now the cause was grander than all these. Elder James E. Talmage addresses the fierceness of this battle at the atoning "hour": "The frightful struggle incident to the temptations immediately following the Lord's baptism was surpassed and overshadowed by this supreme contest with the powers of evil."[31]

With merciless fury Satan's forces must have attacked the Savior on all fronts—frantically, diabolically, seeking a vulnerable spot, a weakness, an Achilles' heel through which they might inflict a "mortal" wound, all in hopes they could halt the impend-ing charge, but it was not to be. The Savior pressed forward in bold assault until every prisoner was freed from the tenacious ten-tacles of the Evil One. This was a rescue mission of infinite impli-cations. Every muscle of the Savior, every virtue, every spiritual reservoir that could be called upon would be summoned in the struggle. No doubt there was an exhaustion of all energies, a straining of all faculties, an exercise of all powers. Only then, when seemingly all had been spent, would the forces of evil abandon their posts and retreat in horrible defeat. Only then did Christ deliver "his saints from that awful monster the devil, and death, and hell" (2 Nephi 9:19). David saw this terrifying, yet glorious moment of triumph when he sang, "Thou hast delivered my soul from the lowest hell" (Psalm 86:13). Nephi also rejoiced: "He hath redeemed my soul from hell" (2 Nephi 33:6). Eventually, the saints of all ages will acknowledge "the Son of God as their Redeemer and Deliverer from death and the chains of hell" (D&C 138:23; see also Revelation 20:13). The Great Deliverer has rescued us—saved the day, saved eternity. But, oh, what a battle! What wounds! What love! What cost!

Perhaps mortals will never fully comprehend Gethsemane, for death would have come to other men as a welcome relief long before the intensity and duration of this infinite ordeal had reached its zenith. There was no such early release, however, for the Savior, because he would "suffer temptations, and pain of body, hunger, thirst, and fatigue, *even more than man can suffer*" (Mosiah 3:7; emphasis added). The Prophet Joseph so testified: "[The Savior] suffered greater sufferings and was exposed to more powerful contradictions than any man can be."[32]

Pain, agony, mocking, and insult would culminate in all their horrible fury to wrest from the Redeemer every last ounce of anguish that justice would demand and the Evil One could exact. Like mortals, his escape valve was death. He alone possessed the power to "lay down [His] life" (John 10:17), but he would not let go and free himself from pain one moment too soon. For him there would be no unconsciousness, no sedatives, no pain killers. Rather, there would be an acute awareness and stinging consciousness of all that was being thrust upon him. He would drink the overflowing cup. As he said to the Nephites, "I have drunk out of that bitter cup which the Father hath given me . . . in taking upon me the sins of the world" (3 Nephi 11:11). Edna St. Vincent Millay tells of a mortal who was momentarily endowed with omniscience, for which he "paid [the] toll / In infinite remorse of soul." The following lines, symbolic of the Savior's sacrifice, capture the anguish of his atoning hour:

> *All sin was of my sinning, all*
> *Atoning mine, and mine the gall*
> *Of all regret. Mine was the weight*
> *Of every brooded wrong, the hate*
> *That stood behind each envious thrust,*
> *Mine every greed, mine every lust.*
> *And all the while for every grief,*
> *Each suffering, I craved relief*
> *With individual desire,—*
> *Craved all in vain! And felt fierce fire. . . .*
> *All suffering mine, and mine its rod;*
> *Mine, pity like the pity of God.*
> *Ah, awful weight! Infinity*
> *Pressed down upon the finite Me! . . .*
> *And so beneath the weight lay I*
> *And suffered death, but could not die.*[33]

The last few words are telling: "but could not die." For the Savior it might better read, "but *would* not die." The full price would be paid. Every sin of Sodom, Gomorrah, Babylon, your sins and mine, would be accounted for, suffered for, and paid for before the Savior would choose to let death in.

It is a sobering thought to realize that *our* sins contributed to the immense suffering of our Savior! Elder James E. Faust so contemplated: "One cannot help wondering how many of those drops of precious blood each of us may be responsible for."[34]

THE SUFFERING CONTINUES ON THE CROSS

Elder McConkie expressed his belief that "these infinite agonies [in the Garden of Gethsemane]—this suffering beyond compare—continued for some three or four hours."[35] As intense and terrible as was the Savior's suffering, it was not to terminate in the Garden—he had yet to endure the cross. But why the cross? Why not stoning or some other form of death? The cross was considered the most terrible form of death man could inflict upon man. It was said by President J. Reuben Clark Jr. "to have been the most painful [death] that the ancients could devise."[36] It held the victim for hours at the brink of life, never quite releasing him, yet all the while inflicting upon the nerves and senses all he could painfully and consciously endure. It took man to his threshold of pain, but not beyond. Throbbing, pulsating pain was felt by a victim who would welcome death, but could find no such early relief. The Savior would nobly endure the cross, all that man could endure, and much, much more. Yet amidst it all, there was no revenge, no bitterness, no venom in his soul. Elder Maxwell observed, "Jesus partook of history's bitterest cup without becoming bitter!"[37] Eliza R. Snow put it poetically:

> *Although in agony he hung,*
> *No murm'ring word escaped his tongue.*[38]

Those who have belittled the Savior's sacrifice as no superhuman feat, because others have been so crucified and died so "nobly," have forgotten the moments in the Garden. The physical pain of the cross alone, when compared to the accumulated pain of the Garden and the cross, was as a penlight to the sun. Perhaps the cross was chosen because the Savior wanted us to know he had endured man's greatest form of inhumanity to man; but even then, such anguish was relatively insignificant when compared to the spiritual agony in the Garden, which was extended on the cross. Elder Joseph Fielding Smith attests to this truth: "A great many people have an idea that when he was on the cross, and nails were driven into his hands and feet, that was his great suffering. His great suffering was before he ever was placed upon the cross. It was in the Garden of Gethsemane."[39]

Elder McConkie makes this comparison between the Garden and the cross: "As he came out of the Garden, delivering himself voluntarily into the hands of wicked men, the victory had been won. There remained yet the shame and the pain of his arrest, his trials, and his cross. But all these were overshadowed by the agonies and sufferings in Gethsemane."[40]

Elder Marion G. Romney shared similar feelings: "Jesus then went into the Garden of Gethsemane. There he suffered most. He suffered greatly on the cross, of course, but other men had died by crucifixion; in fact, a man hung on either side of him as he died on the cross. But no man, nor set of men, *nor all men put together, ever suffered what the Redeemer suffered in the garden.*"[41]

What a doctrine! The composite suffering of all men of all ages, of all worlds does not surpass the Savior's suffering in the Garden. How can we begin to comprehend the cumulative suffering of all mankind, or as taught by Elder Orson F. Whitney, "the piled up agony of the human race"?[42] What is thrown on the scale of remorse, as observed by Truman Madsen, when we aggregate "the cumulative impact of our vicious thoughts, motives, and acts"?[43] What, as Elder Vaughn J. Featherstone inquired, is the "weight and immensity of the penalties of all broken laws crying from the dust and from the future—an incomprehensible tidal wave of guilt"?[44] How many searing consciences has this world produced and to what depths of depravity has this earthly sphere sunk? Can anyone possibly fathom the horrendous consequences of such sin? Not only did the Savior fathom it—he felt it, and he suffered it.

Many writers contrast the infinite pain suffered by the Savior while in the Garden with the finite pain of physical death while on the cross. This comparison is appropriate, since the Garden is the place where the Savior commenced his suffering for sins and where he bled from every pore in response to such suffering. Accordingly, the Garden is often referred to as the place or symbol of his spiritual suffering, while the cross is referred to as the place or symbol of his physical suffering. I do not believe, however, that all such authors mean to imply that the Savior's suffering for sins was *solely* confined to the Garden. Such scholars as Elder Talmage and Elder McConkie help us understand that there is no such sharp line of demarcation between the Garden and the cross. Rather, they suggest, the sufferings of Gethsemane continued to afflict the Savior on the cross. "It seems," Elder Talmage opines, "that in addition to the fearful suffering incident to crucifixion, the agony of Gethsemane had recurred, intensified beyond human power to endure. In that bitterest hour the dying Christ was alone, alone in most terrible reality."[45] Elder McConkie felt similarly: "Again, on Calvary, during the last three hours of his mortal passion, the sufferings of Gethsemane returned, and he drank to the full the cup which his Heavenly Father had given him."[46] On another occasion he echoed like sentiments: "To this we add, if we interpret the holy word aright, that all of the anguish, all of the sorrow, and all of the suffering of Gethsemane recurred during the final three hours on the cross, the hours when darkness covered the land."[47] Commenting on the darkness surrounding the crucifixion, Elder McConkie queried, "Could it be that this was the period of his greatest trial, or that during it the agonies of Gethsemane recurred and *even intensified?*"[48]

Elder McConkie and Elder Talmage believed that the pain that commenced in Gethsemane, but concluded on Calvary, far outweighed the physical pain associated solely with the cross. Those who diminish the Savior's sacrifice because two thieves on either side suffered similarly have completely missed the point. Of course the physical suffering on the cross was tremendous; of course the two thieves felt the same physical pangs of crucifixion as the Savior felt. But the anguish of the nails was far overshadowed by the spiritual, emotional, and physical suffering absorbed by the Savior as he took upon himself the sins and infirmities of the world—an offering that evidently continued on the cross. This doctrine is consistent with Peter's observation that the Savior "*bare our sins* in his own body *on the tree*" (1 Peter 2:24; emphasis added). Other scriptures, while not necessarily definitive, suggest that the Savior's role on the cross included his confrontation with sin. Paul spoke of the Savior's reconciliation through "the blood of his cross" (Colossians 1:20). Nephi recorded that he saw the Savior "lifted up upon the cross and slain for the sins of the world" (1 Nephi 11:33). Later, the Prophet Joseph Smith added his testimony "that Jesus was crucified by sinful men for the sins of the world" (D&C 21:9).

The concluding events in the Savior's life, as discussed below, suggest that the trials of Gethsemane did in fact recur and even intensify on the cross.

First, following the harrowing Garden experience the Savior underwent a night of scourging, mocking, and taunting that left him exhausted and abandoned. In the Garden he could draw upon his full physical, emotional, and mental faculties to face the torrential barrage of pain thrust upon him. When he entered the Garden, he was at his "best." An angel came to his side with the express mission of "strengthening him" (Luke 22:43). But now, while stretched out upon the cross, his physical and emotional reservoirs were rapidly dissipating. His life-giving substance had already ebbed from every pore. He had been scourged, spat upon, and smitten. The sleepless hours were taking their toll on his temporal frame. One of the Twelve had betrayed him. Another had denied him. The increasing onslaught of pain would find him devoid of mortal or divine comfort. Every temporal and heavenly resource was being methodically stripped and withdrawn from him until nothing was left but selfless love and the commitment to atone.

Perhaps some who only days before hailed him as their king and shouted "Hosanna to the Son of David" (Matthew 21:9) now tragically joined in that damning chant, "Crucify him, crucify him" (Luke 23:21). Is it any wonder he should in a future day lament, "These wounds are the wounds with which I was wounded in the house of my friends" (D&C 45:52; see also Zechariah 13:6). The Savior had become "disowned by his people" (Mosiah 15:5). As he tragically observed, "I came unto my own, and my own received me not" (3 Nephi 9:16). If there were a moment of particular susceptibility to temptation for the Savior, it seemed to be now. In such a wearied and rejected condition he would face the cross. One wonders how he could have any resistance left, any will to fight back, any reservoir of strength to overcome, any more love to give. He was walking the fine line that separates death from life, consciousness from unconsciousness. From Satan's perspective, the time of vulnerability was here.

No wonder Satan came at such a propitious moment, spewing

forth his insidious temptation through the lips of his mortal pawns: "If thou be the Son of God, come down from the cross" (Matthew 27:40). The Savior's body writhed in pain; his pure, spotless spirit revolted in violent reaction to sin and its consequences. The heavens seemed as brass. Oh, how tempting this suggestion from the Evil One may have seemed, even to a God—to step down from the cross and obtain relief, even if only momentarily, from such exquisite pain. Farrar spoke of an analogous moment when Satan confronted the Savior in his weakened condition following his forty-day fast:

"This was the tempter's moment. The whole period had been one of moral and spiritual tension. During such high hours of excitement men will sustain, without succumbing, an almost incredible amount of labor, and soldiers will fight through a long day's battle unconscious or oblivious of their wounds. But when the enthusiasm is spent, when the exultation dies away, when the fire burns low, when Nature, weary and overstrained, reasserts her rights—in a word, when a mighty reaction has begun, which leaves the man suffering, spiritless, exhausted—then is the hour of extreme danger, and that has been, in many a fatal instance, the moment in which a man has fallen a victim to insidious allurement or bold assault. It was at such a moment that the great battle of our Lord against the powers of evil was fought and won."[49]

That Satan came at such a moment on the cross is indicative that the Savior was reaching the threshold of his pain, the climax of his mission. This was Satan's last chance, his final desperate hope to frustrate the redemptive plan. It was now or never. There was no angel to strengthen the Holy One, no sustaining influence of the Father. Surely Satan liked the odds. Milton wrote of similar odds as he envisioned the Savior's commission to face the rebellious forces in the premortal war. Jehovah, in prelude to confronting the evil forces, noted that he would go forth against them,

That they [the rebellious forces] may have
their wish, to try with me
In battle which the stronger proves, they all,
Or I alone against them.[50]

This was the showdown: Satan, accompanied perhaps by his legions of nefarious forces, against the Savior in all his compelling loneliness—the Savior in his weakened, almost lifeless condition battling a universal accumulation of suffering. Satan's timing was impeccable. The Father's healing light was being withdrawn; the torturous forces of man's most heinous form of death were peaking; and nature was about to revolt in seismic language. Meanwhile, Satan lurked in the wings, waiting to confront his adversary at the exact moment when the Savior was most vulnerable and the consequences of sin were most acute. This was the crisis moment in time when Satan was at his "strongest," the Savior at his "weakest." This was the crisis moment on the cross, the moment the Savior's pain was most intense and his vulnerability most acute; but Milton was right: "Heavenly love shall outdo hellish hate."[51]

A second factor evidencing the intensification of the suffering on the cross is the withdrawal of God's Spirit. The scriptures repeatedly affirm that the Savior had "trodden the wine-press alone" (D&C 76:107; D&C 88:106; D&C 133:50). However, he seems not to have been completely alone in the Garden, for it was here the angel came to offer divine comfort. If "aloneness" were part of his descent, part of his infinite suffering, part of the climax of his agony, then that requirement seems not to have been fully consummated in the Garden, but on the cross where the angel was absent, the Father was withdrawn, and the cry of abject loneliness was heard in all its stark reality—"My God, my God, why hast thou forsaken me?" (Matthew 27:46; Mark 15:34). Certainly the physical consequences of the cross did not dictate such a withdrawal of God's Spirit; rather it may have been a natural response to the avalanche of evil heaped upon the Innocent One. When the Savior reached the climax of his ordeal—when the infinite sins of infinite worlds pressed upon Him—God's

138

Spirit retreated from the consequences of such universal evil. Isaiah taught this truth when he declared, "Our iniquities, like the wind, have taken us away," and furthermore, God hid his "face from us . . . because of our iniquities" (Isaiah 64:6, 7). If God withdrew his Spirit due to the worlds' iniquities being assumed by Jesus, then the sufferings of Gethsemane were indeed recurring on the cross.

Third, Elder Talmage believed the Savior literally died on the cross of a broken heart, suggesting this event was the culmination and conclusion of his mission. Perhaps this was the physical sequel to his bleeding from every pore. Not unmindful of the Savior's control over life and death, Elder Talmage gave this perspective: "While, as stated in the text, the yielding up of life was voluntary on the part of Jesus Christ, for He had life in Himself and no man could take His life except as He willed to allow it to be taken, (John 1:4; 5:26; 10:15–18) there was of necessity a direct physical cause of dissolution. . . . The strong, loud utterance, immediately following which He bowed His head and 'gave up the ghost,' when considered in connection with other recorded details, *points to a physical rupture of the heart as the direct cause of death.* . . . Great mental stress, poignant emotion either of grief or joy, and intense spiritual struggle are among the recognized causes of heart rupture."[52]

Talmage then added, "The present writer believes that the Lord Jesus died of a broken heart."[53] Perhaps the inspired psalmist saw literally and figuratively the cause of the Savior's demise when he sang, "Reproach hath broken my heart" (Psalm 69:20). If the Savior's broken heart was the last straw, the final blow symbolizing the quintessence of suffering in all of its terrible reality, then such a rupture might likewise symbolize that moment of climax when his mortal and spiritual frame could neither endure any more, nor need do so. He had given his all. His heart had broken in the giving process. There was nothing left to give nor any further price to pay.

It is appropriately symbolic that we must likewise have a "broken heart" to enjoy the blessings of the atoning sacrifice. Lehi taught that "he [Christ] offereth himself a sacrifice for sin . . . unto all those who have a broken heart and a contrite spirit" (2 Nephi 2:7). The Savior taught the Nephites that they, too, must sacrifice in like manner, for he commanded, "Ye shall offer for a sacrifice unto me a broken heart and a contrite spirit" (3 Nephi 9:20; see also D&C 59:8). Like the Savior, we must also consecrate our all, both temporally and spiritually, to be eligible for the crowning blessings of Christ's infinite sacrifice. Rudyard Kipling recognized this age-old spiritual remedy:

> The tumult and the shouting dies;
> The captains and the kings depart:
> Still stands Thine ancient sacrifice,
> An humble and a contrite heart.[54]

At first thought we might conclude that the Savior's greatest suffering was in the Garden when he bled at every pore. There the intensity of his offering manifested itself in a physical phenomenon that resulted in blood oozing from every pore. This external release seemed to be a physical response to the superhuman pain being thrust upon him. But this raises the question, "If the Savior suffered in equal or greater measure on the cross, why was there not a similar physical reaction on that cruel timber—a bleeding from every pore or some other form of extreme physical response?" Perhaps such a physical response came in the form of his broken heart. If indeed his heart ruptured or broke in response to infinite suffering, then the fact that it happened on the cross, not in the Garden, would suggest that the cross may indeed have been the climax of his universal suffering.

A PERSONAL ATONEMENT

At some point the multitudinous sins of countless ages were heaped upon the Savior, but his submissiveness was much more than a cold response to the demands of justice. This was not a nameless, passionless atonement performed by some detached, stoic being. Rather, it was an offering driven by infinite love. This was a personalized, not a mass atonement. Somehow, it may be that the sins of every soul were *individually* (as well as cumulatively) accounted for, suffered for, and redeemed for, all with a love unknown to man. Christ tasted "death for *every* man" (Hebrews 2:9; emphasis added), perhaps meaning for each individual person. One reading of Isaiah suggests that Christ may have envisioned each of us as the atoning sacrifice took its toll— "when thou shalt make his soul an offering for sin, he shall *see* his seed" (Isaiah 53:10; emphasis added; see also Mosiah 15:10–11). Just as the Savior blessed the "little children, one by one" (3 Nephi 17:21); just as the Nephites felt his wounds "one by one" (3 Nephi 11:15); just as he listens to our prayers one by one; so, perhaps, he suffered for us, one by one.

President Heber J. Grant spoke of this individual focus: "Not only did Jesus come as a universal gift, He came as an individual offering with a personal message to each one of us. For each one of us He died on Calvary and His blood will conditionally save us. Not as nations, communities or groups, but as individuals."[55] Similar feelings were shared by C. S. Lewis: "He [Christ] has infinite attention to spare for each one of us. He does not have to deal with us in the mass. You are as much alone with Him as if you were the only being He had ever created. When Christ died, He died for you individually just as much as if you had been the only man in the world."[56] Elder Merrill J. Bateman spoke not only of the Atonement's infinite nature, but also of its intimate reach: "The Savior's atonement in the garden and on the cross is intimate as well as infinite. Infinite in that it spans the eternities. Intimate in that the Savior felt each person's pains, sufferings, and sicknesses."[57] Since the Savior, as a God, has the capacity to simultaneously entertain multiple thoughts, perhaps it was not impossible for the mortal Jesus to contemplate each of our names and transgressions in concomitant fashion as the Atonement progressed, without ever sacrificing personal attention for any of us. His suffering need never lose its personal nature. While such suffering had both macro and micro dimensions, the Atonement was ultimately offered for each one of us.

Moses' vision of the world may offer some insights on how the pains and infirmities of countless individuals could be perceived in a relatively short time, perhaps even concurrently. Moses saw the numerous inhabitants of the earth, but the scriptures make it clear this was not merely some mass panoramic vision, a microsecond panning of the hosts of mankind, like some epic film being run at the speed of light. To the contrary, the sacred record reads, "There was *not a soul which he beheld not;* and he discerned them by the Spirit of God" (Moses 1:28; emphasis added; see also Ether 3:25). What an awesome, yet comforting thought. No one, "not a soul," was forgotten or slighted or neglected in the redeeming process. It was personal, focused, intimate, one-on-one sacrificing and caring for you and me.

WHY DID GOD WITHDRAW HIS SPIRIT?

Unlike the Garden experience, an angelic minister was not to be found at the cross. Instead, the Father's healing light appears to have been withdrawn in full measure, at which moment of extremity the Savior, a God in his own right, uttered that never-to-be forgotten cry, "My God, my God, why has thou forsaken me?" (Matthew 27:46; Mark 15:34). Brigham Young taught that at this moment of crisis, "The Father withdrew Himself, withdrew His Spirit, and cast a vail [sic] over him." At this heartrending moment, the Son pled with the Father not to forsake him, to which the Father replied, "'No, . . . you must have your trials, as well as others.'"[58] The Savior now knew in the fullest measure what it was like to be cut off from the presence of God. His suffering for sins was no academic experience. It was bitter reality.

This raises the underlying question, "Why was it necessary for God to withdraw his Spirit?" Perhaps this can best be answered by addressing another question: "What happens with God's Spirit when we sin?" Of necessity, the Spirit withdraws. When we sin, our spirit is estranged or separated from God and his divine

Spirit. King Benjamin taught, "If ye should transgress . . . ye do withdraw yourselves from the Spirit of the Lord, that it may have no place in you" (Mosiah 2:36; see also D&C 97:17). As the Savior assumed the infinite sins of infinite worlds and all their attendant consequences, it appears that God's Spirit naturally withdrew. It was but a fulfillment of the law that "the Lord is far from the wicked" (Proverbs 15:29). The Savior, of course, was not wicked, but he certainly bore the sins of the wicked. If this withdrawal had not taken place, the Savior would not have fully known the consequences of sin as experienced by those for whom he suffered. If this were the case, men might say, "He never fully understood the total ramifications of sin. True, he suffered, he agonized, but he never felt the loneliness, the rejection, the estrangement that accompanies the withdrawal of God's light." But such was not the case.

Finally the Savior's ordeal had reached its climax. The storm of guilt, remorse, embarrassment, shame, and hopelessness that accompanies sin pressed with its full weight and fury upon him. His pure and sensitive soul, which had no blemish, no spot, which had never known sin in any degree, at any time, at any place was now facing evil of cataclysmic proportions. The price for evil in infinite measure was accounted for and paid for. All the senses a man has—intellectual, emotional, spiritual, and psychological (so much more attuned in the Savior's sensitive soul)—were monopolized by the effects that follow evil. The last trace of God's healing light withdrew, to let the unrestrained effects of evil run their full course. No longer could the Father's Spirit remain in the presence of infinite evil, now being assumed by the very one who embodied infinite goodness. At that point, the Son of Man, acutely alone in the fullest sense of that term, cried out in a moment of ultimate pathos, "My God, my God, why hast thou forsaken me?" (Matthew 27:46; Mark 15:34). No one could claim he was spared any consequence of sin. There was no softening of the blow. He descended beneath it all.

Such a withdrawal of the Spirit was felt in small measure by the Prophet Joseph Smith when the 116 pages of the Book of

Mormon manuscript were lost. On that occasion the Lord said: "I command you again to repent, lest I humble you with my almighty power; and that you confess your sins, lest you suffer these punishments of which I have spoken, of which in the smallest, yea, *even in the least degree you have tasted at the time I withdrew my Spirit*" (D&C 19:20; emphasis added).

So overwhelming was the cloud of this moment that Joseph's mother, Lucy Mack Smith, would later comment: "I well remember that day of darkness, both within and without. To us, at least, the heavens seemed clothed with blackness, and the earth shrouded with gloom. I have often said within myself, that if a continual punishment, as severe as that which we experienced on that occasion, were to be inflicted upon the most wicked characters who ever stood upon the footstool of the Almighty—if even their punishment were no greater than that, I should feel to pity their condition."[59]

How can we extrapolate from such an experience to that of the Savior, who felt not in the "least degree," but rather, in infinite degree, the Father's withdrawal? The truth is, we cannot.

HE BORE IT ALONE

Elder James E. Talmage suggested another compelling reason for the Father's withdrawal of his Spirit: "That the supreme sacrifice of the Son might be consummated in all its fulness, the Father seems to have withdrawn the support of His immediate Presence, leaving to the Savior of men the glory of complete victory over the forces of sin and death."[60] There was something in the comprehensiveness of his sacrifice, in the depth of it, that required him to sever all mortal and heavenly ties, and to stand alone, absolutely alone.

Thus, in the final moments of darkness when God the Father withdrew his Spirit and even nature itself cried out, the Savior of mankind suffered the combined burden of the cross and the burden of the Garden and bore them *alone!* Of this truth, he himself bore fervent testimony: "I have trodden the winepress alone; and of the people there was none with me. . . . And I looked, and there was none to help" (Isaiah 63:3, 5; see also D&C 76:107; 88:106; 133:50).

Were there none with him, none to help? What of his three chief apostles in the Garden? Did they not comfort and sustain him in his hour of need? Mark records those moments in the Garden—and tells us of the apostles' sore amazement. Evidently they could not reconcile in their hearts that the promised Messiah would succumb to death. It seems that messiahship and martyrdom were to them irreconcilable theologies. The moment of truth was here and it was temporarily more than they could bear. Mark so records:

"They came to a place which was named Gethsemane, which was a garden; and the disciples began to be sore amazed, and to be very heavy, *and to complain in their hearts, wondering if this be the Messiah.* And Jesus knowing their hearts, said to his disciples, Sit ye here, while I shall pray. And he taketh with him, Peter, and James, and John, and *rebuked them,* and said unto them, My soul is exceeding sorrowful, even unto death; tarry ye here and watch" (JST, Mark 14:36–38; emphasis added).

As good as these men were, they momentarily questioned Jesus' messiahship. In his hour of supreme need, when his spirit yearned for mortal support, those whom he had trusted most, the three chief apostles who would later lead the church, would only doubt, and then sleep on. Three times the request came for them to watch with him and three times sleep conquered them. How stinging those words of chastisement must have been to Peter, "What, could ye not watch with me one hour?" (Matthew 26:40). David's Messianic psalm was tragically unfolding: "Reproach hath broken my heart; and I am full of heaviness: and *I looked for some to take pity, but there was none; and for comforters, but I found none*" (Psalm 69:20; emphasis added).

The twilight of Gethsemane faded into the darkest of all nights. The chief priests and elders were led by Judas to the Savior's holy retreat. Now, at that moment, when conspiracy and betrayal were crimson red with their sinister stain, the scriptures reveal, "Then all the disciples forsook him, and fled" (Matthew 26:56). This came as no surprise to the Savior: "Behold, the hour cometh, yea, is now come, that ye shall be scattered, every man to his own, and shall leave me alone" (John 16:32; see also Mark 14:27). Samuel Taylor Coleridge's description of the ancient mariner is reminiscent of the Savior's plight:

> *Alone, alone, all, all alone,*
> *Alone on a wide, wide sea!*
> *And never a saint took pity on*
> *My soul in agony.* [61]

Moroni tasted, in part, this unenviable condition of stark solitude. He recorded: "I am alone. My father hath been slain in battle, and all my kinsfolk, and I have not friends nor whither to go" (Mormon 8:5). Moses had Aaron and Hur to hold him up in his hour of need—but for the Savior none would be found. There was no loneliness like his—no comforting words,[62] no arm upon his shoulder, no angel to strengthen him on the cross, and, ultimately, no remnant of his Father's Spirit. He stood acutely alone against sin, death, and all the vile assaults of the evil one until he could say with triumphant glory, "It is finished" (John 19:30).

The Savior then lay down his life. His sacrifice of infinite dimensions was completed, but his mission was not yet finished. He had yet to overcome death through the power of the resurrection. Elder Joseph F. Smith helps put these concluding events of the Savior's life in their proper perspective: "It is believed by many in the Christian world, that our Savior finished his mission when he expired upon the cross, and his last words on the cross, as given by the Apostle John—'*it is finished,*' are frequently quoted as evidence of the fact; but this is an error. Christ did not complete his mission upon the earth until after his body was raised from the dead. . . . Further, the mission of Jesus will be unfinished until he redeems the whole human family, except the sons of perdition, and also this earth from the curse that is upon it, and both the earth and its inhabitants can be presented to the Father redeemed, sanctified and glorious."[63]

CAN INFINITE SUFFERING BE COMPRESSED INTO FINITE TIME?

How could the Savior in the "limited" moments of Gethsemane and Calvary suffer in such a manner that he could succor those who had suffered over extended periods? Is there any way that one can equate the suffering in Gethsemane and upon the cross to the pain and agony of one who battled cancer for twenty years, to the loneliness of the widow whose husband died in the flower of his youth? The scriptures unequivocally state, "The Son of Man hath descended below them all" (D&C 122:8). The real question is not whether he so suffered, but how did he do it? How did he compress into a "brief" moment suffering of such magnitude that he could claim to have experienced everything that mortals have suffered and more? The following thoughts are not given as doctrinal certainties, but only as possible considerations.

First, in the context of the Atonement perhaps time is immaterial or at least of diminished consequence. With our finite minds we translate all action into time, but Alma taught, "Time only is measured unto men" (Alma 40:8). For God there seems to be no past, present, or future; instead, "All things are present before [God's] eyes" (D&C 38:2; see also D&C 130:7). He does not live moment by moment or day by day. He does not wear a watch or turn a calendar, rather "all is as one day with God" (Alma 40:8). Since God knows all things, the future is as real as the present. There is no dividing line between now and then. Joseph Smith observed that "the past, the present, and the future were and are, with Him, one eternal 'now.'"[64] C. S. Lewis shared similar feelings:

"God, I believe, does not live in a time series at all. His life is not dribbled out moment by moment like ours. . . . All the days are 'Now' for Him. He does not remember you doing things yesterday; He simply sees you doing them, because, though you have lost yesterday, He has not. He does not 'foresee' you doing things tomorrow; He simply sees you doing them; because, though tomorrow is not yet there for you, it is for Him."[65]

Moroni had a small taste of timelessness as he looked into the distant future and noted, "Behold, I speak unto you as if ye were present, and yet ye are not" (Mormon 8:35). Perhaps the Savior experienced a similar sense of timelessness as he took upon himself our sins. In such a setting the words "brief" or "extended" would be meaningless. Accordingly, it may be that the quantum of pain borne by the Savior simply cannot be measured by man's time constraints.

Second, it is common knowledge that the area of a rectangle is equal to its length multiplied by its width. No matter how small the width is made, the area may be held constant by proportionately increasing the length. Could that also be true with suffering? Perhaps the totality of suffering is expressed by a similar formula: Suffering = Intensity of Pain x Time. If this is so, could one decrease the time and inversely increase the pain so a lifetime of suffering could be compressed into one day, one hour, even one second, and yet the total suffering remains constant?

Man's concept of pain is shortsighted at best. When we reach our threshold of pain, a release valve "kicks in." We either lapse into unconsciousness or we die. Accordingly, we cannot know nor can we relate to an intensity of pain that transcends death or unconsciousness.

In the case of the Savior, however, there was no such escape mechanism. The pain would continue to escalate far beyond that ever experienced or envisioned by any mortal man. Elder Erastus Snow suggested that at this crisis moment, when the "end was nigh at hand, all the infirmities of the flesh, as it were, crowded upon him."[66] King Benjamin reminds us that the Savior suffered "even more than man can suffer" (Mosiah 3:7). If there were no death or unconsciousness, and pain could escalate without limit, then it seems not unreasonable to suppose that suffering could remain constant—even if the time factor were drastically decreased.

Third, perhaps the suffering of the Savior was not limited to the Garden and the cross. Perhaps a portion of his suffering was found not only in the triggering event that brought the pain, but also in the anticipation of the act. Joseph Smith taught, "There is no pain so awful as that of suspense."[67] Such pain gnaws at the defendant while he breathlessly waits for the jury to render its verdict. Such pain causes anxious mothers to sleeplessly wrestle away the night wondering if sons are safe in distant battlefields. Such pain is more than psychological. It too is real. It too is suffering.

If anticipation be pain, then in one sense the Savior's suffering did not commence with manhood, but eons before—in the premortal existence when he proclaimed these words, "Here am I, send me" (Abraham 3:27). The anticipation of his Atonement since premortal times did not replace the staggering reality of Gethsemane and the cross (which was beyond even his telescopic expectations), but certainly it must have added to the magnitude of pain he bore. In this sense, his suffering extended far beyond the confines of the Garden and the cross.

Fourth, in another way the suffering of the Savior is not "brief," but endless. It involves more than the Garden and the cross, more than his mortal sojourn, more than the pain of suspense. If God suffers as mortal parents do when one of their children suffers, then as long as God procreates, he will suffer. As long as his creations experience sin, loneliness, disease, rejection, or any of the travails that constitute the human plight, God will suffer and weep. On one occasion Abigail Adams expressed to a friend her deep devotion for her presidential husband: "When he is wounded, I bleed."[68] In like manner the Savior continues to "bleed" with each of our wounds and hurts. When Satan was cast from God's presence, "the heavens wept over him" (D&C 76:26). When Enoch saw in vision the inhabitants of the earth, he marveled that "the God of heaven looked upon the residue of the people, and he wept" (Moses 7:28). After the Savior learned of Lazarus' death and the accompanying sorrow of Mary and

Martha, the scriptures read, "Jesus wept" (John 11:35). It was this same Jesus who experienced a "fulness of joy" when he visited the Nephites, yet prophesied to them that "it sorroweth me because of the fourth generation" from that time (3 Nephi 27:31–32).[69] God has felt and will yet feel our infirmities because he loves us, rejoices with us, suffers with us, and weeps with us. His suffering is a never-ending process of which the Atonement was an integral part. In this sense the Savior's suffering continues, worlds without end. B. H. Roberts was in full accord with this concept: "The suffering of Jesus Christ was not a single episode,—one short hour, one short three years: the suffering of Jesus Christ was the revelation of the eternal fact that God is from eternity the Life-giver, and that giving life costs God something as it costs us something."[70]

As much as we weigh and sift and analyze, we must admit that we do not know with certainty how the Savior encompassed man's entire gamut of woes. Perhaps future revelation will tell; perhaps our minds must acquire more infinite-like qualities before we can fully comprehend. At present we can only surmise. Such a "predicament" may remind one of John Keats's reflections concerning an ancient Greek urn, spoken of in his poem, "Ode on a Grecian Urn":

> *Thou, silent form, dost tease us out of thought*
> *As doth eternity.*

Then this consolation:

> *"Beauty is truth, truth beauty,"—that is all*
> *Ye know on earth, and all ye need to know.*[71]

The Savior "descended below all things" (D&C 88:6). That is the important doctrinal conclusion. We know the consequence—someday we will know the means. In the interim, that is all we need to know.

DID THE SAVIOR KNOW IN ADVANCE
OF HIS INTENSE SUFFERING?

Was the Savior forewarned of Gethsemane and Calvary? Could he have exercised his full agency if he were led into it blindly or if he were inadequately informed? Can credit or blame exist in all its glory or infamy when one acts having only partial information? The answer to these questions should be self-evident. No principle in the celestial realm is more sacred than the right to agency. It is the keystone upon which heaven and earth are governed. Without informed decisions agency would be but a mockery. The Savior was informed and knowledgeable of his impending ordeal.

But how did he know? Perhaps his far superior mind knew all things past, present, and future, even those things that had never been experienced before. Or perhaps the Father revealed to him all he needed to know—teaching, instructing, and preparing him for the divine ordeal.[72] Whatever method was employed to prepare the Savior for his moments in Gethsemane and on the cross, one point seems clear—his submission was founded on knowledge, not lack of it. "As he went into Gethsemane," Elder McConkie declared, "it was with a *total awareness* of what lay ahead."[73] Elder Vaughn J. Featherstone expressed similar feelings: "Our Lord summoned all the powers of His Godhood and His mortal, physical strength with an absolute, uncluttered comprehension of what was yet to come in those few brief moments. He was prepared for that night."[74] No doubt the Savior knew intellectually all that one could know in advance of the event; nothing was hidden or unknown. During the last supper he made it clear he knew of his impending fate: "I have desired to eat this passover with you *before* I suffer" (Luke 22:15; emphasis added). Another version reads, "Jesus *knew* that his hour was come" (John 13:1; emphasis added). John further observed that "Jesus . . . [knew] all things that should come upon him" (John 18:4). He came to the altar of sacrifice with a total intellectual understanding of what lay ahead. It was this knowledge that permitted him to proceed with full agency. Yet one wonders if there were not, even for him, some gap between what he knew intellectually and what he would soon know experientially. Elder Neal A. Maxwell taught that there was: "Jesus knew cognitively what He must do, but not experientially. He had never personally known the exquisite and exacting process of an atonement before. Thus, when the agony came in its fulness, it was so much, much worse than even He with his unique intellect had ever imagined!"[75]

The Lord's soul-cry, "My God, my God, why hast thou forsaken me?" (Mark 15:34) was not a rhetorical question. It was the earnest pleading of a divine being, who, under intense pain, sought answers and comfort in his hour of need. There comes a time in each man's life, regardless of his intellectual acumen, when he must rely on faith and faith alone. Abraham experienced it as he drew his knife from the sheath on Mt. Moriah; Moses felt it as he marched toward the Red Sea. In each case there was no apparent solution at hand other than to simply obey; all the options of mortal reasoning had been exhausted. There was only faith to cling to, faith in its purest form.

Now the Savior had come to such a moment, with the Father withdrawn, alone on the cross. Why should he be forsaken? Was he not the Chosen Lamb? The Savior knew in advance of this telling moment, that he would stand alone, for the prophets had so spoken (Psalm 22:1; 69:20; Isaiah 63:3)—but when the moment of truth actually came, perhaps it was so much more acute in reality than in contemplation that even his mind could not fully fathom the horrendous physical, emotional, and spiritual trauma to be thrust upon him. This experience simply could not be intellectualized. So it is with love. However exhaustively we may read of the subject, it will always fall short of the actual experience. And so it may have been with the Savior in his atoning hour. At this crisis moment it was faith, not omniscience, that sustained him.

Once again the Savior proved to be the Great Exemplar. Not only did he know the totality of mortal temptation, not only did he know the pain and infirmities of man, not only did he know the consequences of all sin, but now he knew what it was like to have every vestige of reason stripped away, so that faith and faith alone is all that remains to carry one forward. All that he had intellectually was an unanswered *why*, but what he had spiritually was faith, and with that faith he pressed forward and descended beneath it all.

When the Savior asked to have the cup removed, he demonstrated his comprehension of the situation. He knew intellectually what the cup contained or he would not have asked to have it taken from him. Both the option and the power to retreat, to withdraw, or to abandon the ordeal at any stage were readily available. Satan's final taunt, "If thou be the Son of God, come down from the cross" (Matthew 27:40), was not an idle suggestion, but a powerful reminder that he could!

In every sense of the term, his was a conscious, deliberate decision. He knew all that could be known (or that his Father desired him to know) in advance of the infinite suffering that would soon be his and his alone. His eyes were wide open when he tendered the most loving offer of all time: "Here am I, send me" (Abraham 3:27).

There is no question: the Savior's suffering was infinite. He bore it all—knowingly, willingly, and lovingly.

NOTES

1. Browning, "Prospice," in Untermeyer, *Treasury of Great Poems,* 876; emphasis added
2. McConkie, *Mortal Messiah,* 3:88, footnote 1.
3. Lewis, *Inspirational Writings of C. S. Lewis,* 501.
4. *Journal of Discourses,* 10:114.
5. Smith, *Religious Truths Defined,* 121.
6. Smith, *Gospel Doctrine,* 21.
7. Smith, *Answers to Gospel Questions,* 3:103.
8. Madsen, "Olive Press," 58; emphasis added.
9. Ibid., 60.
10. McConkie, "Purifying Power," 9.
11. While this conclusion seems logical, it is not a scriptural certainty. Elder Maxwell wrote of this heavenly messenger, "An angel, whose identity *we*

do not know came to strengthen Him" ("Enduring Well," 10; emphasis added).

12. Smith, *Teachings of the Prophet Joseph Smith*, 168.

13. Nephi spoke of a similarly tender moment. The Savior knelt upon the earth and prayed to his Father for the Nephites who had survived the destruction. It was an outpouring that pierced and filled every heart. One must reread the account to sense the overwhelming emotion and joy that was felt by all who were present. Nephi observed: "The things which he [the Savior] prayed cannot be written . . . neither hath the ear heard, before, so great and marvelous things as we saw and heard Jesus speak unto the Father; and no tongue can speak, neither can there be written by any man, neither can the hearts of men conceive so great and marvelous things as we both saw and heard Jesus speak" (3 Nephi 17:15–17).

14. Madsen, "Olive Press," 61.

15. Phillips Brooks, "O Little Town of Bethlehem," in *Hymns*, no. 208.

16. Taylor, *Mediation and Atonement*, 149–50.

17. Ibid., 152.

18. Ibid., 152.

19. While the context of this scripture refers to the "last days," it was inserted here because the truth it teaches seems to have dual applicability to the Atonement.

20. Taylor, *Mediation and Atonement*, 151; emphasis added.

21. Farrar, *Life of Christ*, 575.

22. Ibid., 579.

23. Ibid., 577.

24. Taylor, *Mediation and Atonement*, 148–49.

25. Whitney, *Baptism*, 4.

26. Maxwell, "Willing to Submit," 73.

27. Cecil Frances Alexander, "There Is a Green Hill Far Away," in *Hymns*, no. 194.

28. Smith, *Doctrines of Salvation*, 1:130–31.

29. Whitney, *Saturday Night Thoughts*, 149.

30. Tennyson, "The Charge of the Light Brigade," in *Harvard Classics*, 42:1006.

31. Talmage, *Jesus the Christ*, 613.

32. Smith, *Lectures on Faith*, 59.

33. Millay, "Renascence," in Cook, *Famous Poems*, 175–76.

34. Faust, "Supernal Gift," 13.

35. McConkie, "Purifying Power," 9.

36. Clark, Conference Report, Oct. 1955, 24.

37. Maxwell, "Enduring Well," 10.

38. Snow, "Behold the Great Redeemer Die," in *Hymns*, no. 191.

39. Smith, *Doctrines of Salvation,* 1:130.

40. McConkie, *Mortal Messiah,* 4:127–28.

41. Conference Report, Oct. 1953, 35; emphasis added.

42. Whitney, *Saturday Night Thoughts,* 152.

43. Madsen, *Christ and the Inner Life,* 4.

44. Featherstone, *Disciple of Christ,* 4.

45. Talmage, *Jesus the Christ,* 661.

46. McConkie, "Seven Christs," 33.

47. McConkie, *Mortal Messiah,* 4:232, note 22.

48. Ibid., 225; emphasis added.

49. Farrar, *Life of Christ,* 115.

50. Milton, *Paradise Lost,* 192.

51. Ibid., 100.

52. Talmage, *Jesus the Christ,* 668–69, note 8; emphasis added.

53. Ibid., 669, note 8.

54. Kipling, "Recessional," in Untermeyer, *Treasury of Great Poems,* 1047.

55. Grant, "Marvelous Growth," 697.

56. Lewis, *Quotable Lewis,* 248.

57. Bateman, "Power to Heal," 14.

58. *Journal of Discourses,* 3:206.

59. Smith, *History of Joseph Smith,* 132.

60. Talmage, *Jesus the Christ,* 661.

61. Coleridge, "The Rime of the Ancient Mariner," in Untermeyer, *Treasury of Great Poems,* 673.

62. This must be tempered by the degree to which the three Marys and John the Beloved may have provided comfort by their mere presence as they "stood by the cross" (John 19:25), as well as by the blessing provided by the "many women [who] were there beholding afar off, which followed Jesus from Galilee, ministering unto him" (Matthew 27:55).

63. *Journal of Discourses,* 23:173, 175.

64. Smith, *Teachings of the Prophet Joseph Smith,* 220.

65. Lewis, *Inspirational Writings of C. S. Lewis,* 475–77.

66. *Journal of Discourses,* 7:357.

67. Smith, *Teachings of the Prophet Joseph Smith,* 288.

68. Bennett, *Our Sacred Honor,* 137.

69. Perhaps in this respect, the Savior is like the Three Nephites, who did "not suffer pain nor sorrow save it were for the sins of the world" (3 Nephi 28:38; see also 4 Nephi 1:44).

70. Roberts, *The Seventy's Course in Theology,* 158–59.

71. In Cook, *Famous Poems,* 151.

72. The Apostle John addressed this latter possibility: "For the Father loveth the Son, and *sheweth* him all things that himself doeth" (John 5:20;

emphasis added). Elder McConkie quoted this scripture, and then paraphrased the words of Jesus as follows, "I have seen in vision all the works of the Father; I have seen what he did in ages past; what he does even now; and he has manifest to me his future works, even 'all things that himself doeth'" (*Mortal Messiah,* 2:71). Joseph Fielding Smith shares a similar opinion, "The statement of our Lord that he could do nothing but what he had seen the Father do, means simply that *it had been revealed to him what his Father had done*" (*Doctrines of Salvation,* 1:32–33; emphasis added). In such a manner the Savior may have learned the nature of the sacrifice he was contemplating.

73. McConkie, *Mortal Messiah,* 4:126; emphasis added.

74. Featherstone, *Disciple of Christ,* 3.

75. Maxwell, "Willing to Submit," 72–73.

CHAPTER 15

INFINITE IN LOVE

———— ⬡ ————

SACRIFICE—THE HIGHEST FORM OF LOVE

If sacrifice for others is the highest manifestation of love, then the Atonement of Jesus Christ is the grandest demonstration of love this world has ever known. The compelling, driving force behind his sacrifice was love, not duty or glory or honor or any other temporal reward. It was love in its purest, deepest, most enduring sense.

President Joseph F. Smith's vision of the spirit world was preceded and prompted by his reflection upon "the great and wonderful love made manifest by the Father and the Son in the coming of the Redeemer into the world" (D&C 138:3). With similar feelings, Ammon spoke of "the matchless bounty of [the Savior's] love" (Alma 26:15).

It was this love that prompted the Savior's gift of the Atonement. Emerson helps put in perspective the value of this gift: "The only gift is a portion of thyself."[1] In this spirit, the Savior's sacrifice was the noblest gift of all because he who possessed all gave all. His spiritual, emotional, psychological, and life-giving powers were all laid on the altar of sacrifice without restraint. He gave until there was nothing left to give, nothing left to do—until he had fully drawn from that vast reservoir of virtues he possessed in order to work out an infinite sacrifice. Brigham Young noted: "There is not one thing that the Lord could do for the salvation of the human family that He has neglected to do; . . . all that can be accomplished for their salvation, independent of them, has been accomplished in and by the Savior."[2]

Of all the acts of love, the atoning sacrifice far exceeds and transcends them all. No one has ever given so much to so many so willingly. The words of the hymn are a poignant reminder:

> *He shed a thousand drops for you,*
> *A thousand drops of precious blood.*
> *Here's love and grief beyond degree.*[3]

THE LOVE OF THE SON

From the premortal council until he breathed his last breath on Calvary, the Savior was impelled by unfeigned love, for "in his love, and in his pity, he redeemed them" (D&C 133:53). Nephi was given an understanding of the abuse that would be heaped upon the Savior by an insensitive and ungrateful world: "They scourge him, and he suffereth it; and they smite him, and he suffereth it. Yea, they spit upon him, and he suffereth it" (1 Nephi 19:9). Why such submission? Nephi gives the simple but profound answer: "Because of his loving kindness and his long-suffering towards the children of men" (1 Nephi 19:9). There were no ulterior motives or hidden agendas in the Savior's ministry—only love, unrestrained and freely given.

John the Beloved, who walked side by side with the Savior, who shared with him the experience on the Mount of Transfiguration, who stood as close and saw as clearly as any mortal the atoning sacrifice, spoke of the Holy One in reverential tones as "him that loved us, and washed us from our sins in his own blood" (Revelation 1:5). Paul rightfully observed that "scarcely for a righteous man will one die. . . . But God commendeth his love toward us, in that, while we were yet sinners, Christ died for us" (Romans 5:7–8).

The Savior's love was not a love for the righteous only; it was not an abstract love; nor was it demonstrated by one dramatic sacrificial act and nothing more. To the contrary, it was a day-by-day, hour-by-hour, even moment-by-moment love! It was love that stretched from premortality into eternity. It was a love that thoughtfully prepared a little fire of coals with fish and bread for hungry and tired disciples as they emerged from an exhausting night of fishing on the Sea of Galilee. It was a love that blessed little children, healed the sick, and offered hope to the hopeless. It was a love that reached out to every individual as he or she was and lifted them to higher ground. Love was exhibited in every conscious, waking moment of his mortal life. Love flowed from every pore, every thought, every act. As naturally and regularly as we seek air, he sought to bless. Again and again in those moments of physical exhaustion and pressing "agendas" he was there for the one—to listen, to love, and to bless. His entire life was an accumulation of acts of love, capped by the most significant of all—his atoning sacrifice. Peter summed up his life in this simple but expressive phrase: "[He] went about doing good" (Acts 10:38).

Contemplate for a moment the love of a mother for her newborn child. Suppose now that the child were taken from her mother's arms. Though that mother should live to be a hundred years old, it is doubtful she would ever forget that heaven-sent child she held so tightly in her loving grasp. Some memories can never be erased, some relationships never severed, some feelings never forgotten; such things outlast both time and death. Knowing all this, the Lord asked, "Can a woman forget her sucking child, that she should not have compassion on the son of her womb?" (1 Nephi 21:15). Then the Lord makes his point: "Yea, they [mothers] may forget, *yet will I not forget thee,* O house of Israel" (1 Nephi 21:15; emphasis added). If there be any question about the Lord's commitment and love for the house of Israel, he has dispelled it. The magnitude of his caring has been put in perspective. It far surpasses anything man has to offer, even a mother's love for her child. Then he gives an awesome reminder to us all: "Behold, I have graven thee upon the palms of my hands" (1 Nephi 21:16). The wounds in his hands are his witness, his tangible and undeniable proof, of his sacrifice and his love.

Suppose we could turn back the pages of history to the meridian of time. Suppose we could have been there that night when the Savior declared from his celestial home, "Behold . . . on the morrow come I into the world" (3 Nephi 1:13). Suppose we had the power to see that quaint little town of Bethlehem, standing in such stark contrast to the Savior's divine abode. Who among us could fathom the depths of love that caused him that night to exchange his godhood for manhood? Thus the Savior, the omnipotent one, the creator of worlds without number, made his entrance into this world as a helpless babe.

But why—why all this for us? Why yield his power and honor for taunting, mocking, condemnation, and eventually crucifixion? Paul taught that Christ became "like unto his brethren, that he might be a merciful and faithful high priest" (Hebrews 2:17). And Alma wrote that the Lord took upon himself man's infirmities "that his bowels may be filled with mercy" (Alma 7:12). But the Savior answered the inquiry best: "Greater love hath no man than this, that a man lay down his life for his friends" (John 15:13). It was true—he "so loved the world that he gave his own life" (D&C 34:3; see also 1 John 3:16; Ether 12:33). President Ezra Taft Benson spoke of this unquenchable love: "We may never understand nor comprehend in mortality how He accomplished what He did, but we must not fail to understand why He did what He did. All that He did was prompted by His unselfish, infinite love for us."[4] This was the humble recognition of Nephi, who in response to the angel's query concerning the condescension of God replied, "I know that he loveth his children; nevertheless, I do not know the meaning of all things" (1 Nephi 11:17).

THE LOVE OF THE FATHER

Does not the Son's suffering and love, as significant as they are, only magnify the Father's even more? What loving Father, given the chance, would not eagerly, even desperately attempt to exchange places with his suffering son? King David, for example, when he learned of the death of a rebellious son, cried out, "O my son Absalom, my son, my son Absalom! *would God I had died for thee*" (2 Samuel 18:33; emphasis added; see also Alma 53:15). David knew firsthand that there can be a sacrifice greater than suffering for oneself. And what greater sacrifice than to witness a son's incomparable suffering while possessing the power to alleviate it?

Suppose at your command you could release your son from the exquisite pain that has caused him to cry, "Father, if thou be willing, remove this cup from me" (Luke 22:42). Which of us could resist such a request from a son who had never erred, never complained, never asked anything for himself—who all his life had honored and obeyed and served us, whose only thoughts were for others, and now in this moment of supreme agony pled for help, just this once, for himself? Would not our hearts have been bursting with compassion? Would not that cry of pathos, "My God, my God, why has thou forsaken me," offered by the purest of all beings, the most obedient of all sons, so overpower us as to break our hearts and weaken our resolve? How much could this most loving of all fathers stand? But the words of the Messianic psalm would pierce even deeper into the tender heart of the most loving of all fathers: "Why art thou so far from helping me, and from the words of my roaring?" (Psalm 22:1). Would the overwhelming emotion of the moment have so flooded our powers of reason, so diluted our vision that we would have yielded and released him? Would we in our wisdom have sent the legion of angels to heal the bleeding pores and remove the nails from his torn flesh? Fortunately, even with his incomparable love for his Son, our Father in Heaven did not relent.

Paul paid tribute to our Father, who chose not to exercise his saving power on behalf of his Only Begotten Son, so that we also might be saved: "He . . . spared not his own Son, but delivered him up for us all" (Romans 8:32). Truly, "God so loved the world, that he gave his only begotten Son" (John 3:16), or as John later observed, "In this was manifested the love of God toward us, because that God sent his only begotten Son into the world, that we might live through him" (1 John 4:9). Why did God not release his Son? Because he knew there was no other way to save the rest of his children. Christ was our only hope, our only means to salvation.

Elder Melvin J. Ballard, with a tender insight that seemed to penetrate the veil, commented on the Father's choice not to rescue his son:

"God heard the cry of his Son in that moment of great grief and agony, in the garden when, it is said, the pores of his body opened and drops of blood stood upon him, and he cried out: 'Father, if thou be willing, remove this cup from me.'

"I ask you, what father and mother could stand by and listen to the cry of their children in distress, in this world, and not render aid and assistance? . . .

"We cannot stand by and listen to those cries without its touching our hearts. The Lord has not given us the power to save our own. He has given us faith, and we submit to the inevitable, but he had the power to save, and he loved his Son, and he could have saved him. . . . He saw that Son finally upon Calvary; he saw his body stretched out upon the wooden cross; he saw the cruel nails driven through hands and feet, and the blows that broke the skin, tore the flesh, and let out the life's blood of his Son. He looked upon that.

"In the case of our Father, the knife was not stayed, but it fell, and the life's blood of his Beloved Son went out. His Father looked on with great grief and agony over his Beloved Son, until there seems to have come a moment when even our Savior cried out in despair: 'My God, my God, why hast thou forsaken me?'

"In that hour I think I can see our dear Father behind the veil looking upon these dying struggles until even he could not endure it any longer; and, like the mother who bids farewell to her dying child, has to be taken out of the room, so as not to look upon the last struggles, so he bowed his head, and hid in some part of his universe, his great heart almost breaking for the love that he had for his Son. Oh, in that moment when he might have saved his Son, I thank him and praise him that he did not fail us, for he had not only the love of his Son in mind, but he also had love for us."[5]

The words of Eliza R. Snow confirm this eternal truth:

> *How great the wisdom and the love*
> *That filled the courts on high*
> *And sent the Savior from above*
> *To suffer, bleed, and die!*[6]

A JOINT ACT OF LOVE

How does a God communicate a love such as this to mortals? Perhaps in our temporal state he cannot, but in the story of Abraham and Isaac we have our closest parallel. Jacob speaks of Isaac's sacrifice as "a similitude of God and his Only Begotten Son" (Jacob 4:5). Abraham had reached the century mark before a son was born who would bear the birthright. This son was all that he ever hoped a son could be. Then came the fateful day when the divine voice decreed, "Take now thy son, thine only son Isaac, whom thou lovest . . . and offer him . . . for a burnt offering upon one of the mountains which I will tell thee of" (Genesis 22:2). How could it be? This son was to bear the birthright, become a father of many nations. This was the promised son. Abraham would willingly give his land, his herds, his money, all the wealth the world had given him—"But please," he must have thought, "not my son." To Abraham's everlasting credit he did not resist, rather he humbly submitted to God's will.[7]

Early the next morning Abraham rose and began his journey with Isaac to the appointed place. As they ascended the mountain Abraham "took the wood of the burnt offering, and laid it upon Isaac his son" (Genesis 22:6), perhaps symbolic of the cross to be laid upon the Savior's back. Isaac then asked in innocence, "Where is the lamb for a burnt offering?" (Genesis 22:7). Abraham could only reply, "God will provide himself a lamb for a burnt offering" (Genesis 22:8). Genesis is silent as to the conversation that transpired between father and son on top of that holy mount. No doubt it was one of those sacred moments when silence thunders.

The Book of Jasher reports Isaac's first response to the news: "I will do all that the Lord spoke to thee with joy and cheerfulness of heart."[8] While the authenticity of this book is questioned, the principle taught seems correct. Abraham wanted to confirm that his son's feelings did not belie his words. Accordingly, he asked Isaac if he had any reservations. Isaac responded as recorded by Jasher: "There is nothing in my heart to cause me to *deviate* either to the right or to the left from the word that he has spoken to thee. . . . But I am of joyful and cheerful heart in this matter, *and* I say, Blessed is the Lord who has this day chosen me to be a burnt offering before Him."[9] Josephus noted the same obedient spirit: "Now Isaac was of such a generous disposition, as became the son of such a father, . . . and said, 'That he was not worthy to be born at first, if he should reject the determination of God and of his father. . . .' So he went immediately to the altar to be sacrificed."[10]

How like the Savior Isaac was. His sacrifice would not be given grudgingly, nor would it stem from duty. There would be no force, no coercion, not even gentle persuasion. Every element would be voluntary. Any painting, any story, any inference that suggests Abraham took Isaac by force would so undermine the parallel with the Savior's sacrifice as to destroy the heart and substance of any meaningful similitude. The underlying and overriding principle of the Atonement was the Savior's voluntary response, "Here am I, send me" (Abraham 3:27). And so it must have been with Isaac—a prototype of the Savior.

The Book of Jasher captures the tenderness of this "final exchange" between father and son: "Abraham heard the words of Isaac, and he lifted up his voice and wept when Isaac spake these words; and Abraham's tears gushed down upon Isaac his son."[11] Abraham then bound Isaac upon the altar, perhaps at Isaac's request, so he would not involuntarily obstruct the sacrificial act.

Abraham then stretched forth the knife to draw the lifeblood from this beloved son, when the angel of mercy cried out, "Lay not thine hand upon the lad, neither do thou any thing unto him: for now I know that thou fearest God, seeing thou hast not withheld thy son, thine only son from me" (Genesis 22:12). Abraham then found a ram caught in the thicket and offered him for a burnt offering in the place of his son—but for our Father in Heaven there was no angel to stay the hand of death, nor any ram to be found in the thicket. Every element of his sacrifice would be complete. There were no substitutes, no alternative ways, no easier paths to tread. This was the only possible way to save mankind.

Abraham now understood, more keenly than ever before, the meaning of the atoning sacrifice. As his heart was about to burst in that brief moment when he raised the knife, he felt a pain akin to the Father's pain and a love akin to the Father's love.

NOTES

1. Emerson, "Gifts," 5:220.
2. *Journal of Discourses,* 13:59.
3. Isaac Watts, "He Died! The Great Redeemer Died," in *Hymns,* no. 192.
4. Benson, *Teachings of Ezra Taft Benson,* 15.
5. Hinckley, *Sermons and Missionary Services of Melvin J. Ballard,* 153–54.
6. Snow, "How Great the Wisdom and the Love," in *Hymns,* no. 195.
7. The scriptures suggest that Abraham did not expect an angel of mercy to relieve him of the command he had received. Rather, he apparently believed that Isaac's life would be taken as directed, while thinking "that God was able to raise him up, even from the dead" (Hebrews 11:19). Perhaps Abraham believed that Isaac would be raised so that he might yet bear his seed in fulfillment of the divine promise.
8. *Book of Jasher,* 61.
9. Ibid., 62.
10. Josephus, *Complete Works,* 37.
11. *Book of Jasher,* 62.

CHAPTER 16

THE BLESSING OF THE RESURRECTION

⊸⊷⊶

A DEMONSTRATION OF MIGHTY POWER

The Atonement is infinite in its blessing powers. It results in "a multiplicity of blessings . . . forever and ever" (D&C 97:28; see also D&C 104:2). One such blessing is the resurrection. Some have wondered if the resurrection was part of the Atonement, or if instead the Atonement was completed on the cross, and the resurrection was a separate, unrelated act. In a restricted sense, the Atonement involves Christ's suffering in the Garden and on the cross in order to "atone" for our sins. In the more expanded and complete sense, it also encompasses the power exercised by the Savior to reconcile *all* the consequences of the Fall, including physical death. Accordingly, the Atonement was not only Christ's suffering in the Garden and on the cross, but likewise his exercise of the power necessary to resurrect us.

The LDS Bible Dictionary speaks of its comprehensive nature: "By . . . his sinless life, the shedding of his blood in the garden of Gethsemane, his death on the cross *and subsequent bodily resurrection from the grave, he made a perfect atonement for all mankind.*"[1] This is what Jacob understood, for he taught that without an "infinite atonement . . . this flesh must . . . rise no more" (2 Nephi 9:7), meaning that the resurrection was that necessary component of the Atonement that overcame physical death. Alma taught similarly: "The atonement bringeth to pass the resurrection of the dead" (Alma 42:23).

Jacob pointed out that absent some offsetting power, "This flesh must have laid down to rot and to crumble to its mother earth" (2 Nephi 9:7). This is a manifestation of entropy, which is the process of going from a more organized state to a less organized state. Hugh Nibley observes, "Without the resurrection, entropy—the good old Second Law of Thermodynamics—must take over."[2] It is no surprise that Jacob, who observed that "death hath passed upon all men," also observed that "there must needs be a *power* of resurrection" (2 Nephi 9:6; emphasis added). There had to be some reversing power to thwart the inexorable march of decay, decomposition, and ultimate disorder. Decay and death are constant forces, or powers, wreaking havoc upon God's creations. David called it "the power of the grave" (Psalm 49:15). Paul made reference to "him that had the power of death, that is, the devil" (Hebrews 2:14). It should be no wonder that in the scriptures he is sometimes called "the destroyer" (1 Corinthians 10:10). With poetic insight, Goethe called the evil one the "son of chaos."[3]

Isaiah saw the day when the Lord would finally "punish leviathan" (Isaiah 27:1), referred to in the footnotes of the LDS edition of the Bible as "a legendary seamonster representing the forces of chaos that opposed the Creator." As powerful as is this sinister force that promotes death, chaos, and destruction upon all living things, there is a countervailing, counteracting power that emanates from the Atonement. It is the power of the resurrection.

The Savior had power to lay down his own life and the "power to take it again" (John 10:18). He is "the resurrection, and the life" (John 11:25). The scriptures make it clear that he "will also raise up us by his own power" (1 Corinthians 6:14) and that while the body "is sown in weakness; it is raised in power" (1 Corinthians 15:43). The resurrection is an act of mighty power. Jacob referred to it as "the power of the resurrection which is in Christ" (Jacob 4:11; see also 2 Nephi 10:25). Alma spoke of "the resurrection of the dead . . . which was to be brought to pass through the power . . . of Christ" (Mosiah 18:2). Alma the Younger spoke of "the resurrection of the dead, according to the will and power and deliverance of Jesus Christ" (Alma 4:14). And Moroni spoke of death as that sleep from which "all men shall be awakened by the power of God" (Mormon 9:13).

Again and again the scriptures reveal the remedy for death. It is power—not manpower, not atomic power, but the divine power of resurrection. The effect of this divine power is far more than Lazarus being raised from the dead—multiplied many times over. It does not just restore the dead to mortal life. It does not just put the process of entropy in remission. This is infinite power, only found in an infinite being, bringing both a permanent cure and an eternal enhancement. This power somehow changes our bodies to a state free from the entropic process. An immortal, terrestrial body, like Adam's in the Garden, is exempt from decay. But a resurrected, exalted body is the direct antithesis of entropy. It has the powers of godhood, the power of endless seed, the power to create and people other worlds (see D&C 132:19–20).[4] As an exalted body exercises its creative powers, its offspring become divine agents to bring order and harmony to an otherwise increasingly chaotic universe. Such is but a glimpse of the awesome power of the resurrection.

How is such a power unleashed? By the Atonement of Jesus Christ. Jesus Christ broke the bands of death for all men and by so doing overcame physical death for all. Abinadi confirmed this truth: "The grave hath no victory, and the sting of death is swallowed up in Christ" (Mosiah 16:8).

What, then, is this resurrection? As death is the separation of body and spirit, so resurrection is the reverse. It is a permanent reuniting of body and spirit into an immortal being (see Alma 11:45). As to the exact process by which it occurs, we do not know—but we can rest assured, as did Alma, that it will happen: "The soul shall be restored to the body, and the body to the soul;

yea, and every limb and joint shall be restored to its body; yea, even a hair of the head shall not be lost; but all things shall be restored to their proper and perfect frame" (Alma 40:23).

THE PHYSICAL NATURE OF A RESURRECTED BODY

A resurrected body is not subject to pain or disease or exhaustion. There is no bullet that can harm it, poison that can pollute it, or cancer that can invade it. There is no resurrected being who suffers loss of limb, speech impediment, or failing sight. A resurrected personage has a glorified, immortal body, free from the destructive elements of this temporal world. The Savior personally testified to his disciples of the physical nature of his resurrected body: "Behold my hands and my feet, that it is I myself: handle me, and see; for a spirit hath not flesh and bones, as ye see me have" (Luke 24:39). Later he ate broiled fish and honeycomb in their presence, as further evidence of his corporeal nature. Certain witnesses testified that they also "did eat and drink with him after he rose from the dead" (Acts 10:41).

Despite such overwhelming evidence, many deny the physical resurrection of the Savior. Some believe his physical postmortal appearances were merely temporary manifestations to appeal to mortal man, but that his real nature was not "restricted" by a tangible body. Such a belief, however, is in direct opposition to the teachings of Paul. This learned apostle taught that the resurrected Lord "dieth no more" (Romans 6:9). This did not refer to the spirit body, because it does not die at all, let alone "no more." This had reference to physical death, since Christ had already died one physical death but would die "no more." Since the scriptures define death as "the body without the spirit" (James 2:26), Paul's statement must mean that the Savior's resurrected physical body can *never* be separated from his spirit; otherwise, he would again suffer physical death, the very event Paul declared could not recur. Amulek taught that the eternal union of Christ's body and spirit, following his resurrection, was a prototype that applies to all resurrected beings. Referring to the resurrection of all men, he spoke of "their spirits uniting with their bodies, never to be divided" (Alma 11:45).

All who die shall, like Christ, have bodies that will be restored to their "proper and perfect frame" (Alma 40:23). Joseph Fielding Smith made it clear that the prints of the nails in Christ's hands and feet are but temporary, acting as "a special manifestation"[5] to selected groups. When he appears to the Jews in their hour of distress, they will look upon him and he will say: "These wounds are the wounds with which I was wounded in the house of my friends. I am he who was lifted up. I am Jesus that was crucified" (D&C 45:52; see also Zechariah 12:10). When all are judged it seems the reason for his wounds will cease.

A resurrected body is composed of flesh and bone and spirit, not blood. The prophets have testified that blood, the mortal element that eventually brings death, will one day be replaced by a spiritual substance flowing through our veins. John Taylor wrote: "When the resurrection and exaltation of man shall be consummated, although more pure, refined and glorious, yet will he still be in the same image, and have the same likeness, without variation or change in any of his parts or faculties, except the substitution of spirit for blood."[6]

So spoke the Prophet Joseph: "When our flesh is quickened by the Spirit, there will be no blood in this tabernacle."[7] At that moment "our vile body" shall "be fashioned like unto his [God's] glorious body" (Philippians 3:21). In such a resurrected state one's countenance, one's outer glow and beauty will be but a manifestation of one's inner spirituality—thus, the inner and outer beings will be, in essence, mirrors of each other. Celestial bodies will radiate celestial glory; terrestrial bodies, terrestrial glory; and telestial bodies, telestial glory.

WHO WILL BE RESURRECTED?

What is the answer to Job's age-old question, "If a man die, shall he live again?" (Job 14:14). The answer, of course, is yes. Everyone who has had a mortal body will be resurrected—the righteous, the wicked, even the lukewarm—for the resurrection is universal. It is a free gift to all men regardless of their righteousness. But why? Why the disobedient, the scoundrel, the atheist? Is that fair? It is. Adam brought physical death into the world through his transgression and thus transmitted his mortal nature, the seeds of death, to all living creatures without any action on their part. They did nothing to merit death in their earthly sojourn, and so in return, the Savior restored immortal life without any redemptive action on the part of man. The plan is fair and just and merciful. With remarkable brevity, Paul crystallized this doctrine: "For as in Adam *all* die, even so in Christ shall *all* be made alive" (1 Corinthians 15:22; emphasis added). The solution proved to be as broad as the curse. This part of Christ's Atonement overcame physical death for all men. It was universal. In this sense all men will be saved.

Further, Elder McConkie observed that not just the inhabitants of this earth would be resurrected: "Just as the creative and redemptive powers of Christ extend to the earth and all things thereon, *as also to the infinite expanse of worlds in immensity,* so the power of the resurrection is universal in scope. Man, the earth, and all life thereon will come forth in the resurrection. *And the resurrection applies to and is going on in other worlds and other galaxies.*"[8]

CHRIST IS THE FIRSTFRUITS

The resurrection of Jesus Christ was foretold years in advance of the actual event. Centuries before that glorious day Nephi prophesied, "Behold, they will crucify him and after he is laid in a sepulchre for the space of three days he shall rise from the dead, with healing in his wings" (2 Nephi 25:13). Matthew records, "They shall kill him, and the third day he shall be raised again" (Matthew 17:23; see also Matthew 16:21). The third day did come. He was resurrected and became "the firstfruits of them that slept" (1 Corinthians 15:20), "the firstborn from the dead"

(Colossians 1:18), or as John declared, "the first begotten of the dead" (Revelation 1:5).

Elder Joseph Fielding Smith suggests that the Savior did not acquire the keys of the resurrection for all men until after he was crucified and overcame death. He said, "On the third day after the crucifixion he took up his body and gained the *keys of the resurrection,* and thus has *power to open the graves for all men,* but this he could not do until he had first passed through death himself and conquered."[9] Thus, the Savior could not have unlocked the graves of any of the dead until he first acquired the necessary keys through his own resurrection (see also Mosiah 16:7; Alma 11:42). With those keys Christ immediately opened the floodgates of the resurrection, for the scriptures tell us that both in Jerusalem and Book of Mormon lands the "graves were opened" (Matthew 27:52) and "many saints did arise and appear unto many" (3 Nephi 23:11). Perhaps these same keys simultaneously opened the graves of more distant spheres.

DEATH IS DESTROYED

What a devastating blow to death when Christ first unlocked the doors to the masses of imprisoned spirits who had so awaited the day of his triumphant resurrection! He arose from the grave "with healing in his wings" (2 Nephi 25:13) for all men. He opened the door that had been shut for thousands of years on billions of graves. He was the first to walk through that door, and then, in a display of unequaled mercy, he left it open for others to exit in a divinely determined sequence. John Donne captured that moment in these telling lines:

> *Death, be not proud, though some have called thee*
> *Mighty and dreadful, for thou are not so; . . .*
> *One short sleep past, we wake eternally,*
> *And Death shall be no more: Death, thou shalt die.*[10]

With the resurrection of Christ, the long-awaited words of Hosea had come to pass: "I will ransom them from the power of the grave; I will redeem them from death: O death, I will be thy plagues; O grave, I will be thy destruction" (Hosea 13:14). Is it any wonder that Ammon and his brethren, who had a burning, unflinching conviction of the future resurrection of Jesus, could face death again and again with no fear? The scriptures record, "They never did look upon death with any degree of terror, for their hope and views of Christ and the resurrection; therefore, death was swallowed up to them by the victory of Christ over it" (Alma 27:28). Such were the feelings of the righteous of past ages: "All these had departed the mortal life, firm in the hope of a glorious resurrection" (D&C 138:14).

WITNESSES OF HIS RESURRECTION

Christ's resurrection "was not done in a corner" (Acts 26:26). The witnesses to this event were both legion and varied. There were the women at the tomb (Luke 24:1–10), Mary Magdalene in the garden (John 20:11–18), the ten apostles (Luke 24:36–43), Thomas (John 20:24–29), the two disciples on the road to Emmaus (Luke 24:13–34), "above five hundred brethren at once" (1 Corinthians 15:6), and Paul on the road to Damascus (Acts 9:3–9). To his apostles Christ would say, "Ye are witnesses of these things" (Luke 24:48). Of all these firsthand accounts, none was more profound than the resurrected Savior's first appearance to the Nephites, as recorded in the Book of Mormon. A multitude of two thousand five hundred people—one by one—"went forth, and thrust their hands into his side, and did feel the prints of the nails in his hands and in his feet . . . until they had all gone forth, and did see with their eyes and did feel with their hands, and did know of a surety and did bear record, that it was he, of whom it was written by the prophets, that should come" (3 Nephi 11:15).

The resurrected Lord appeared to individuals, to groups, to multitudes. Men, women, and children constituted the spiritual witnesses of his resurrection. Some of these heard testimony from the Father of us all, some from angels, and others from the resurrected Lord. Some saw with their eyes, others felt with their hands, some heard with their ears, and yet others had their hearts burn within them. So widespread was the knowledge of Christ's resurrection to the spiritually enlightened that Peter testified, "God . . . shewed him *openly;* not to all the people, but unto witnesses chosen before of God" (Acts 10:40–41; emphasis added).

The resurrected Lord appeared in the quiet of the garden, on the dusty road to Emmaus, in the closed room where the apostles gathered, and at the temple site of Bountiful. As time marches on, the witnesses continue to mount—Joseph Smith, Oliver Cowdery, Sidney Rigdon, Lorenzo Snow, and, no doubt, a corps of the spiritually humble whose testimonies have been recorded in the heavenly journals, one day to be revealed to men in the flesh, as powerful reminders "that he lives!" (D&C 76:22).

Eventually, in the appointed hour, the resurrected Savior will visit all kingdoms over which he is the creator (D&C 88:58–61). Honest and credible witnesses of all ages will add their testimonies to that of the angelic messenger who proclaimed, "He is risen" (Matthew 28:6). And likewise, one day, those historic words will be spoken by each of us.

NOTES

1. LDS Bible Dictionary, 617.
2. Nibley, *Approaching Zion,* 555.
3. Goethe, *Faust,* 163.
4. For further discussion on these doctrines, see chapter 21.
5. Smith, *Doctrines of Salvation,* 2:291.
6. Taylor, *Mediation and Atonement,* 166.
7. Smith, *Teachings of the Prophet Joseph Smith,* 367.
8. McConkie, *Mormon Doctrine,* 642; emphasis added.
9. Smith, *Doctrines of Salvation,* 1:128.
10. Donne, "Death, Be Not Proud," in Untermeyer, *Treasury of Great Poems,* 368.

CHAPTER 17

THE BLESSING
OF REPENTANCE

—⊗⊗⊗—

ANOTHER DEMONSTRATION OF MIGHTY POWER

One of the significant blessings of the Atonement emerges
from Christ's power to redeem the spiritually dead. Spiritual
death is a form of spiritual alienation or dissolution of the divine
relationship. But it is more than a geographic banishment from
God's presence. Just as the physical body weakens with the
onslaught of disease, it seems that in the same way we weaken
spiritually as we embrace each new sin. Perhaps we lose our capacity or will to absorb light and truth. Perhaps, like an injured
muscle, we lose strength and resiliency to confront each new
temptation. Whatever the mechanics, spiritual death seems to
result in a form of spiritual degeneration or entropy. As with
physical death, there needs to be some power to reverse the decay-
ing process, to heal our spiritual wounds, to strengthen our spiritual fiber. Again, the Atonement is the source of that reversing
power, that fount to which men "may look for a remission of their
sins" (2 Nephi 25:26).

The psalmist sang of the Savior's healing balm, "He restoreth
my soul" (Psalm 23:3). Helaman testified, "He hath power given

unto him from the Father to redeem them from their sins" (Helaman 5:11). The Savior queried, "Is my hand shortened at all, that it cannot redeem? or have I no power to deliver?" (Isaiah 50:2; see also Alma 7:13). He later answered his own question: "The Son of man hath power on earth to forgive sins" (Matthew 9:6). With that power "he quickened" those "who were dead in trespasses and sins" (Ephesians 2:1). Such quickening was a healing of our spiritual being. In the Savior's own words, he said, "Return unto me, and repent of your sins, and be converted, that I may heal you" (3 Nephi 9:13). Through this healing process he "delivered us from the power of darkness" (Colossians 1:13). Truly, Satan was overcome by the "blood of the Lamb" (Revelation 12:11).

Again and again, the scriptures reveal that the Atonement is the ultimate source of redeeming power. Jacob so concluded. He taught of redemption "from everlasting death by the power of the atonement" (2 Nephi 10:25). So all-encompassing is this power to save the otherwise spiritually lost that, while speaking of those who shall take part in the first resurrection, John conclusively pronounced, "on such the second death hath no power" (Revelation 20:6).

CLEANSING CONDITIONED ON REPENTANCE

There is no question but that the Atonement generated sufficient power to restore and cleanse the errant soul. But how is it done, and who is eligible for the benefits of such a blessed power? How could any person who has sinned be cleansed sufficiently to return to God's presence and enjoy sociality with him once again? Unlike the resurrection, this part of the Atonement was not universal; it was individual, meaning that God's suffering, which made the cleansing process possible, became efficacious only for those who repent. While "the Lord cannot look upon sin with the least degree of allowance," he has nonetheless promised, "he that repents and does the commandments of the Lord shall be forgiven" (D&C 1:31–32).

This conditional nature of a spiritual cleansing was revealed to the Prophet Joseph: "The Lord your Redeemer . . . suffered the pain of all men . . . that he might bring all men unto him, on conditions of repentance" (D&C 18:11–12). Samuel the Lamanite also taught that the Atonement brought "to pass the condition of repentance" (Helaman 14:18). In other words, if there were no Atonement, there would be no opportunity to repent. Men might feel sorrow; they might change their behavior within certain parameters; but no divine rehabilitation process would be in operation. Simply stated, without the Atonement, there would be no cleansing of the sinner's soul regardless of any actions on his part.

With the Atonement, that cleansing can come—but only if we repent. King Benjamin so taught: "For salvation cometh to none such except it be through repentance" (Mosiah 3:12). Elder Marion G. Romney emphasized the conditional nature of this phase of the Atonement: "He paid the debt for your personal sins and for the personal sins of every living soul that ever dwelt upon the earth or that ever will dwell in mortality upon the earth. But this he did conditionally. The benefits of this suffering for our individual transgressions will not come to us unconditionally in the same sense that the resurrection will come regardless of what we do. If we partake of the blessings of the atonement as far as our individual transgressions are concerned, we must obey the law."[1]

President David O. McKay declared: "Every principle and ordinance of the gospel of Jesus Christ is significant and important . . . , but there is none more essential to the salvation of the human family than the divine and eternally operative principle, repentance. Without it, no one can be saved. Without it, no one can even progress."[2] Why? Because it is the key that unlocks the cleansing power of the Atonement. That is exactly what Helaman taught: "He [Christ] hath power given unto him from the Father to redeem them from their sins *because* of repentance" (Helaman 5:11; emphasis added).

Repentance is not a negative principle, but rather a positive, most glorious one. It did not come from an angry, overbearing parent, but from the most loving Father of all. It is not for the wicked alone, but for every good and great person who wants to be better. It is for every individual who has not yet reached perfection. It is the only road to peace of mind, forgiveness of sin, and ultimately godhood itself.

WHAT IS REPENTANCE?

What, then, is true repentance and how does it relate to the Atonement? It is not just a five-step or seven-step process through which we mechanically advance. It is not merely the cessation of wrongdoing, the passage of time, or the expression of sorrow. None of these alone is true repentance. Alma the Younger described true repentance when he spoke to the people of Zarahemla. He recounted the life of his father, Alma the Elder, who had been one of the wicked priests of Noah. One day the prophet Abinadi entered the scene. Something about Abinadi's message penetrated the heart and soul of Alma's father. Alma the Younger observed, "According to his faith there was a mighty change wrought in his heart." Alma then added, "[My father] preached the word unto your fathers, and a mighty change was also wrought in their hearts." Then his sermon reached its climax: "And now behold, I ask of you, my brethren of the church, . . . Have ye experienced this mighty change in your hearts?" (Alma 5:12–14).

That is true repentance. It is a melting, softening, refining process that brings about a mighty change of heart. It is manifest by those who come forth with broken hearts and contrite spirits. It is a burning resolve to make amends with God at any cost. Such a change means "we have no more disposition to do evil, but to do good continually" (Mosiah 5:2). Lamoni and his servants experienced such a change. As they awoke from their spiritual slumber "they did all declare unto the people the self-same thing—that their hearts had been changed; that they had no more desire to do evil" (Alma 19:33).

What about those who do not experience this change but nonetheless obtain a temple recommend? What of those with dire sins who escape reprimand or disciplinary action where another in similar circumstances has borne his cross? President Harold B. Lee spoke directly to this point: "There are no successful sinners."[3]

Years ago a father shared with me some concerns he had about his teenage daughter. She had shared with him her plans. She wanted to "live it up" for a while, sowing her oats, and then three months before it was time to get married she would "clean up her act" and obtain a temple recommend. He was severely disappointed, and rightly so. One might appropriately ask, "Is that a broken heart and contrite spirit—a resolve to make amends with God at any cost?" Did she really believe that a bishop or stake president would sign a recommend for someone with an attitude such as that? Even if they did, it would fail to be a blessing in her life. Her attitude reflected the mentality of the Pharisees and Sadducees who looked upon the Jewish law as a long list of mechanical rules—so many steps to walk—so much time to pass. It had become a matter of form over substance. Ezekiel gave the key to the truth: "Cast away from you all your transgressions, . . . make you a new heart and a new spirit" (Ezekiel 18:31). Sanctification finally came to the Nephites "because of their yielding their hearts unto God" (Helaman 3:35). Repeatedly throughout the scriptures repentance is associated with the heart. It is a new heart, a broken heart, a changed heart, a contrite heart.

Elder Spencer W. Kimball told of Holman Hunt, the artist, who one day showed a friend his painting of Christ knocking at the door. Suddenly the friend exclaimed, "'There is one thing wrong about your picture.'"

"'What is it?' inquired the artist.

"'The door on which Jesus knocks has no handle,' replied his friend.

"'Ah,' responded Mr. Hunt, 'that is not a mistake. You see, this is the door to the human heart. It can be opened only from the inside.'" Elder Kimball then continued: "And thus it is. Jesus may stand and knock, but each of us decides whether to open."[4] Priesthood leaders may warn, counsel, discipline, and lovingly encourage, but all this will be in vain unless there is sometime, somewhere, an inward change of heart.

REPENTANCE OR RATIONALIZATION?

How does this change of heart occur? First, there must be an honest, unqualified recognition, not a rationalization, of our sins. Alma gave this wonderful counsel to his son Corianton: "Do not endeavor to excuse yourself in the least point because of your sins" (Alma 42:30). What a contrast to Korihor's philosophy that "whatsoever a man did was no crime" (Alma 30:17), or to the belief of the Lamanites "that whatsoever they did was right" (Alma 18:5). One must ultimately choose between these conflicting doctrines. There cannot simultaneously be repentance and rationalization. Rationalization is the world's answer to sin; repentance is the Lord's. They are two different roads with opposite destinations. Robert Frost tells of encountering a fork in the road he was traveling. He debated the road he should take, and then writes of his choice as follows:

> *I shall be telling this with a sigh*
> *Somewhere ages and ages hence:*
> *Two roads diverged in a wood, and I—*
> *I took the one less traveled by,*
> *And that has made all the difference.*[5]

Every time we sin we find ourselves at a spiritual crossroad. We may rationalize the sin away or repent it away. The road "less traveled by" will make "all the difference."

In Book of Mormon times the moral laws closely paralleled the civil laws. That is not true today. The civil law does not punish many serious moral crimes, such as adultery and abortion. We hear excuses for such sins under the labels of "free agency" or "everyone does it" or "no one will know." But there is no defense, no adequate excuse, no alibi for breaking the laws of God. That is what the Lord told Joseph Smith: "Thou art not excusable in thy transgressions" (D&C 24:2). When we honestly recognize that, we are on the road to repentance.

The principal barrier to repentance is always self. Thomas Carlyle put it this way: "The greatest of faults is to be conscious of none."[6] It was this warning that Alma was trying to give to his wayward son, Corianton: "Acknowledge your faults and that wrong which ye have done" (Alma 39:13). Those who choose instead to live a life of denial, to defend themselves against God's law, will discover the bitter truth: "Your sins have come up unto me, and are not pardoned, because you seek to counsel [rationalize] in your own ways" (D&C 56:14).

Rationalization is the intellectual drug that anesthetizes the sting of conscience. Mormon witnessed this deadly overdose at the time his people were "without principle, and past feeling" (Moroni 9:20). Nephi saw the danger signals in the lives of Laman and Lemuel when he noted, "[God] hath spoken unto you in a still small voice, but ye were past feeling" (1 Nephi 17:45). Contrast that with Nephi's lamentation: "O wretched man that I am! . . . My heart groaneth because of my sins; nevertheless, I know in whom I have trusted" (2 Nephi 4:17, 19). It is hard to imagine those words from a prophet of God. Nephi's life was one of devotion and obedience, yet he was ever more conscious of the distance still to be traveled for perfection. The more spiritual an individual becomes, the more sensitive he becomes to his imperfections. The better he becomes, the worse he realizes he was.

Since all of us, like Nephi, have sinned, the issue is not just whether we have done wrong, but whether having done wrong we are now willing to repent. John Donne spoke of the efficacy of repenting:

> Teach me how to repent; for that's as good
> As if thou'hadst seal'd my pardon, with thy [Christ's] blood.[7]

The purpose of this earth life is to serve as a probationary estate, to see if we will repent and follow Christ. The Lord appointed "unto man the days of his probation" (D&C 29:43). In fact, the Lord provided that Adam's seed "should not die as to the temporal death, until I, the Lord God, should send forth angels to declare unto them repentance and redemption" (D&C 29:42). That is what Lehi clearly taught: "The days of the children of men were prolonged . . . that they might repent while in the flesh" (2 Nephi 2:21). Alma likewise taught that if there had been no "space for repentance . . . the word of God would have been void, and the great plan of salvation would have been frustrated" (Alma 42:5).

Wickedness alone seldom, if ever, has been the cause of man's destruction; the greater tragedy is wickedness coupled with an unwillingness to repent. The predicted destruction of the wicked people of Nineveh was waived because they were willing to turn to God. The people of Melchizedek "waxed strong in iniquity" (Alma 13:17) but were spared because "they did repent" (Alma 13:18). Alma the Elder "did many things which were abominable in the sight of the Lord" (Mosiah 23:9), and the sons of Mosiah were called the "vilest of sinners" (Mosiah 28:4), yet each found the impetus to reverse his course. In each of these, the embers of repentance still glowed. For those who have let the embers die the Lord pronounced the consequence, "He that repents not, from him shall be taken even the light which he has received; for my Spirit shall not always strive with man" (D&C 1:33). It was the same message the Lord sent to the wicked people of Ammonihah: "If ye persist in your wickedness" and "repent not" then "your days shall not be prolonged in the land" (Alma 9:18). It was simple logic. The reason for this earth life was to provide a probationary period to repent; if a man refused to do so after every reasonable opportunity was offered, he forfeited his right to remain. At that point he was, as the scriptures term, "ripe for destruction" (Helaman 13:14).

At one point Oliver Cowdery had disassociated himself from the Church. Joseph was anxious that he repent and return. He instructed his clerk, "I wish you would write to Oliver Cowdery and ask him if he hasn't eaten husks long enough."[8]

Rationalization and procrastination bring the husks of life—repentance, the kernels.

GODLY SORROW

Those who experience a change of heart will manifest sorrow, not just any sorrow, but godly sorrow. Worldly sorrow and godly sorrow are a chasm apart. Paul distinguishes between the two: "I rejoice, not that ye were made sorry, but that ye sorrowed to repentance: for ye were made sorry after a godly manner. . . . For godly sorrow worketh repentance to salvation" (2 Corinthians 7:9–10). Not all sorrows are twins. There is wordly sorrow, which is an intellectual recognition of our error. It is the sorrow of the criminal that he is caught. It is the sorrow of the immoral youth that she became pregnant. It is the sorrow of the wrongdoer that his evil designs did not come to fruition. The prophet Mormon was a witness of this sorrow. He was the leader of the Nephite armies. Due to their wickedness, many had been slaughtered in battle. His heart momentarily rejoiced when he saw their lamentation and mourning before the Lord. But the scriptures then add, "But behold this my joy was vain, for their sorrowing was not unto repentance, . . . but it was rather the sorrowing of the damned, because the Lord would not always suffer them to take happiness in sin" (Mormon 2:13). To the contrary, Alma pled with his son, "Let your sins trouble you, with that trouble which shall bring you down unto repentance" (Alma 42:29).

Godly sorrow is of an infinitely transcending quality. There is no need for outside pressure. The transformation will come from within. The stream of tears may flow. There will be soul-wrenching, sometimes even exquisite pain. It may take us "down to the dust in humility" (Alma 42:30). Even the righteous, on occasion, may cry out, "O wretched man that I am!" (2 Nephi 4:17). The sons of Mosiah knew the process: "They suffered much anguish of soul . . . , suffering much and fearing that they should be cast off forever" (Mosiah 28:4). Alma acknowledged that his past history of misdeeds "caused me sore repentance"

(Mosiah 23:9). There will be newfound reservoirs of compassion for those who may have been hurt, perhaps sore embarrassment, and finally and always a willingness to submit to whatever is necessary—be it apology, confession, disciplinary action, or any other divine requirement—in order to make amends with God. There will be an absence of excuses, alibis, and blaming of others. There will be a complete acceptance of responsibility for our attitudes and actions, and an unyielding commitment to be right with God. In essence, repentance brings us to a moment of total intellectual, emotional, and spiritual integrity—when we can say we have mastered the counsel of Polonius, "To thine own self be true."[9]

The Savior taught that if we do not repent, we must suffer even as he suffered. This does not mean, however, that there is no suffering if we do repent. In fact, President Kimball taught that personal suffering "is a very important part of repentance. One has not begun to repent until he has suffered intensely for his sins."[10] President Kimball then added: "If a person hasn't suffered, he hasn't repented. . . . He has got to go through a change in his system whereby he suffers and then forgiveness is a possibility."[11] This suffering, intense as it may be, is nevertheless substantially less for the repentant soul than the unrepentant. The Savior "picks up" part of the burden for those who do repent. This principle is illustrated by a story B. H. Roberts loved to share:

"It is related of Lord Byron that when he was a lad attending school, a companion of his fell under the displeasure of a cruel, overbearing bully, who unmercifully beat him. Byron happened to be present, but knowing the uselessness of undertaking a fight with the bully, he stepped up to him and asked him how much longer he intended to beat his friend. 'What's that to you?' gruffly demanded the bully. 'Because,' replied young Byron, the tears standing in his eyes, 'I will take the rest of the beating if you will let him go.'"[12]

The Savior takes "the rest of the beating" for those who submit their will to his. Isaiah prophesied that he would be "bruised for our iniquities" and then promised that "with his stripes we are healed" (Isaiah 53:5; see also 1 Peter 2:24). Such a healing sprang from the medicinal roots of Gethsemane.

Elder Vaughn J. Featherstone tells of a young man who came to him for a mission interview. Elder Featherstone inquired as to the young man's transgressions. In a haughty manner the young man replied, "There isn't *anything* I haven't done." Elder Featherstone inquired as to specifics—morals, drugs, and so on. Again he replied, "I told you I have done *everything*." Elder Featherstone asked, "What makes you think you're going on a mission?" "Because I have repented," came the reply. "I haven't done any of these things for a year." Elder Featherstone then looked at the young man across the table—twenty-one years of age—sarcastic, haughty, with an attitude far removed from sincere repentance. "My dear young friend," he said, "I'm sorry to tell you this, but you are *not* going on a mission. . . . You shouldn't have been ordained an elder and you really should have been tried for your membership in the Church. What you have committed is a series of monumental transgressions. You haven't repented; you've just stopped doing something. Someday, after you have been to Gethsemane and back, you will understand what true repentance is." At this, the young man started to cry. It lasted for about five minutes. There was no exchange of words, only silence. Then he left Elder Featherstone's office.

About six months later Elder Featherstone was speaking to an institute group in Arizona. Following the meeting he saw this same young man walking up the aisle towards him, and the details of their interview flashed through his mind. Elder Featherstone reached down from the podium to shake his hand. As the young man looked up, Elder Featherstone could see that something wonderful had taken place in his life. Tears streamed down the young man's cheeks and an almost holy glow came from his countenance. "You've been there, haven't you?" asked Elder Featherstone. Through the tears he said, "Yes, Bishop Featherstone, I've been to Gethsemane and back." "I know," Elder Featherstone replied. "It shows in your face. I believe now that the Lord has forgiven you."[13]

A godly sorrow involves joining with the Savior in the sorrow of Gethsemane. It is a sorrow that fosters a new heart and a new spirit.

AN ABSOLUTE FORSAKING

But repentance requires more than sorrow. True repentance requires an absolute forsaking. Dante speaks of a soul who feigned repentance, who was long on promises but short on deeds. Believing that vows alone would save him, he argued for a celestial crown. Just before his hoped-for ascension, however, a "black cherubim" appeared on the scene. Dante's tragic figure, now in hell, recalled the encounter and the damning words of the infernal intruder:

> *"You shall not take him: cheat me not!*
> *For down among my minions he must come, . . .*
> *He who repents not, cannot be absolved:*
> *No more can he repent and act at once,*
> *Because the contradiction won't permit it!"*
> *Alas for me! How violently I shuddered*
> *When he laid hold on me and said: "Perhaps*
> *You did not think that I was a logician!"*[14]

Even the minions of the underworld knew there could be no forgiveness without forsaking.

Elder Matthew Cowley gives us the comforting assurance that the forsaking of any sin is possible: "There is not one of us here upon the earth that is not greater than his sins, is not greater than his weaknesses and his faults."[15] That is true. "But for how long must I forsake?" comes the oft-repeated inquiry. "How long before my membership can be reinstated or I can be rebaptized?" The answer is always the same—when there is a mighty change of heart and a new mind to make the Lord's will supreme in our lives, regardless of our own passionate desires—when there is an unequivocal resolve to put behind us our former ways. There is a measuring rod, but it is one primarily of attitude, not time.

Bjorn Borg, considered to be the finest tennis player of his era, was, as *Time* magazine reported, "unflappable on the court, a mannerly competitor who rarely disputed a linesman's calls, unleashed grimaces, tossed racquets, or bashed balls. 'Iceborg' they called him." The article continues: "He rules his emotions so completely that so much as an on-court frown leaves fans and fellow players awe-struck." But it was not always so. *Time* reveals a darker side before a remarkable change took place:

"At eleven young Bjorn cursed like a navvy, hurled his racquet, hectored officials and bellyached over every close call. 'I was crazy, a madman on the court. It was awful. Then the club I belonged to suspended me for five months, and my mother, she took my racquet and locked it in the closet. For five months, she locked up my racquet. After that I never opened my mouth again on the tennis court. Since the day I came back from that suspension, no matter what happened, I have behaved on the court.'"[16]

When we have the resolve to refrain from a certain course of conduct, no matter what happens, then repentance is in the works. We have forsaken when we have mastered the habit under any set of circumstances that may be thrown at us. It is not the passage of time, but a change of heart that is the key.

RESTITUTION

Repentance requires a full restitution in the spirit of Zacchaeus, who said, "If I have taken any thing from any man . . . , I restore him fourfold" (Luke 19:8; see also Leviticus 6:4). Such a spirit exuded from Elder Spencer W. Kimball when he was called to the apostleship. What about people he might have offended? Would they resent him? He visited each man with whom he did business to explain the situation. "'I've been called to a high position in my Church. I cannot serve in good conscience unless I know my life has been honorable. . . . If there was any injustice I want to make it right, and I've brought my checkbook.' Most shook hands and refused to hear any more. A couple of men[, however,] fancied that in fairness they should have got a few hundred dollars more on certain sales. [Elder Kimball] wrote the checks."[17]

Restitution comes in many forms. It may involve a return of funds, an apology, prayers offered on behalf of the injured party, making up for years of lost service by redoubling our efforts, or making up for negativism with positive deeds and words. The spirit of repentance demands a restoration of all that is possible, within our power.

The people of Anti-Nephi-Lehi understood this principle. Before they heard the gospel, in their unenlightened state, they had committed numerous murders and transgressions against the Nephites. In an honest attempt at restitution, the repentant king of the Lamanites made this offer to Ammon: "We will be [the Nephites'] slaves until we repair unto them the many murders and sins which we have committed against them" (Alma 27:8; see also Helaman 5:17). This humble king knew that his people could not restore to life those Nephites whom they had killed, but there burned within his heart a desire to do all he could do to make repairs. He and his people would serve those whom they had wronged and, if necessary, even be their slaves. This was the spirit of restitution. This was the spirit that burned in the hearts of the repentant sons of Mosiah, for they went about "zealously striving to repair all the injuries which they had done to the church" (Mosiah 27:35).

CONFESSION

True repentance, however, is a hard taskmaster. It requires yet more than the foregoing. Moses taught, "When he shall be guilty in one of these things, . . . he shall confess that he hath sinned in that thing" (Leviticus 5:5; see also Numbers 5:6–7; Nehemiah 9:3). David promised, "I will declare mine iniquity" (Psalm 38:18). Those who sought John in baptism came "confessing their sins" (Matthew 3:6). To the Prophet Joseph the Lord declared, "I command you again to repent . . . and . . . confess your sins" (D&C 19:20). Later he advised, "By this ye may know if a man repenteth of his sins—behold, he will confess them and forsake them" (D&C 58:43). Samuel Taylor Coleridge, speaking through the ancient mariner, well knew the pangs of nondisclosure:

> *Forthwith this frame of mind was wrench'd*
> *With a woeful agony,*
> *Which forced me to begin my tale;*
> *And then it left me free.*
>
> *Since then, at an uncertain hour,*
> *That agony returns:*
> *And till my ghastly tale is told,*
> This heart within me burns.[18]

Fortunately the truly repentant, unlike the ancient mariner, need not confess his sins over and over again once an honest confession has been made to the appropriate priesthood leader—but until such a confession occurs, oh, how the heart can burn. The Lord made it abundantly clear that "he that covereth his sins shall not prosper: but whoso confesseth and forsaketh them shall have mercy" (Proverbs 28:13). When Alma inquired of the Lord about how he should treat certain transgressors in the Church, the Lord responded, "If he confess his sins before thee and me, and repenteth in the sincerity of his heart, him shall ye forgive, and I will forgive him also" (Mosiah 26:29; see also D&C 64:7). But if they did not confess, "their names were blotted out" (Mosiah 26:36), meaning they were excommunicated from the Church.

When should we confess? When the sin is of such serious magnitude that it may trigger a disciplinary proceeding or continues to linger in our mind so that we cannot have peace. David understood this latter condition, as evidenced by his admission, "My sin is ever before me" (Psalm 51:3). If we then fail to confess, our spiritual horizons become limited. It is like being surrounded by a circular, impenetrable wall. In such a circumstance, we have some limited room in which to move, but we are trapped. We will look in vain for a slit through which we can squeeze, an opening through which we can pass, an end around which we can travel. There are no end runs, no secret openings, no hidden passages. Years of service do not obviate confession; years of abstinence do not erase its need; one-on-one pleading with the Lord is not a substitute. Somewhere, sometime, somehow we must face the wall square up and climb it. That is confession. When we do this, our spiritual horizons are broadened.

Oscar Wilde knew this truth as he unfolded the story of Dorian Gray. One day Dorian exchanged his soul for the promise of eternal youth. Wilde traces Dorian's downward plunge from an innocent young man to a passionless killer—until there was nothing left of him but the sordid visage of a wrecked wretch. Even in this state of seemingly moral hopelessness, Dorian's conscience flickered with one last hope: "Yet it was his duty to confess, to suffer public shame, and to make public atonement. There was a God who called upon men to tell their sins to earth as well as to heaven. *Nothing that he could do would cleanse him till he had told his own sin.*"[19]

And likewise, when necessary, there is nothing that can bring us to the desired cleansing except an honest confession to the Lord's appointed on earth.

In what spirit do we render such a confession? The Lord gave the key: "For I, the Lord, forgive sins, and am merciful unto those who confess their sins with humble hearts" (D&C 61:2). That is the spirit. There is no room for pretense or deceit, no coloring of the facts, not a divulgence of 99 percent and a withholding of one percent. It is a disclosure of the *whole* truth and nothing but the truth. The father of Lamoni had the proper spirit: "I will give away *all* my sins to know thee" (Alma 22:18; emphasis added). Confession and repentance involve an unqualified baring of the soul, an unconditional surrender of self. The outpouring comes voluntarily; it is not compelled by outside circumstance. One of Dante's damned souls discovered the hard way that deathbed confession would never invoke the cleansing process:

> *When I perceived that I had reached the age*
> *When every man of prudence takes in sail*
> *And gathers in his tackle for the storm,*
> *What I once revelled in now caused me shame:*

In penance I confessed, surrendering all.
Ah, hapless me—for still I was not saved! [20]

Resistance to confession comes, even from good saints. They may be ashamed or embarrassed. Perhaps they believe their priesthood leaders will think less of them once the sin is aired. We need to remember that bishops and other priesthood leaders are friends who desperately want to help and lift burdens. They are humans who have made mistakes but who want to be better. They are fathers to their flocks. I can honestly say that as a priesthood leader, I never thought less of a man or a woman who voluntarily, humbly confessed. To the contrary, I rejoiced that they were trying to put their lives in order. In each case I believe the bonds of brotherhood were strengthened, not weakened.

When Mahatma Gandhi was fifteen he stole from his brother. His brother carried a chunk of solid gold on his arm. Gandhi found it easy to clip off a little portion for himself. He said he felt the pangs of guilt so severely that he resolved never again to steal. Having cleared the debt with his brother, he said he also made up his mind to confess to his father—but he was afraid, not that his father would beat him, but for the pain it might cause him. Finally, he said, "I felt that the risk should be taken; that there could not be a cleansing without a clean confession." Gandhi resolved to write out his confession. He did so, confessing his guilt, pledging never to steal again, and asking for adequate punishment. He then closed by asking his father not to punish himself for what Gandhi had done. At the time, Gandhi's father was ill and confined to a bed that consisted of nothing more than a wood plank. Gandhi, trembling, handed the confession to his father, then sat opposite his father and anxiously waited for a response. In his own words he tells of the encounter:

"He read it through, and pearl-drops trickled down his cheeks, wetting the paper. For a moment he closed his eyes in thought and then tore up the note. . . . I could see my father's agony. If I were a painter I could draw a picture of the whole scene today. It is still so vivid in my mind.

"Those pearl-drops of love cleansed my heart, and washed my sin away. Only he who has experienced such love can know what it is. . . . It transforms everything it touches. There is no limit to its power.

"This sort of sublime forgiveness was not natural to my father. I had thought that he would be angry, say hard things, and strike his forehead. But he was so wonderfully peaceful, and I believe this was due to my clean confession. A clean confession, combined with a promise never to commit the sin again, when offered before one who has the right to receive it, is the purest type of repentance. *I know that my confession made my father feel absolutely safe about me, and increased his affection for me.*"[21]

What a beautiful observation. Honest confession increases, not decreases, a priesthood leader's affection for the repentant soul.

Elder Marion G. Romney observed, "My brothers and sisters, there are many among us whose distress and suffering are unnecessarily prolonged because they do not complete their repentance by confessing their sins."[22] Naaman the leper went to the prophet Elisha seeking to be healed. Elisha told Naaman to go wash himself seven times in the River Jordan. We might wonder what would have happened if Naaman the Syrian had dipped himself three times in the River Jordan and then abandoned the cause. Would he be three-sevenths clean? Or what if he had dipped himself six times and given up—would he be six-sevenths clean? We know the answer. The cleansing came only after the seventh dipping, after total submission to the word of God. And then what a cleansing followed! The scriptures record: "His flesh came again like unto the flesh of a little child" (2 Kings 5:14). So it is with the sinner, the spiritual leper. There must be a total submissiveness to the will of the Lord, a broken heart and a contrite spirit, even confession if necessary, to complete the seventh dipping, and then the spirit is made clean "like unto the spirit of a little child."

Why does the Lord require confession? It is so very hard. Perhaps because that one act more than any other drives us to our knees in the depths of humility. Speaking of the repentance process Alma declared, "Let it bring you down to the dust in humility" (Alma 42:30). But, oh, the promise to those who do: "If we confess our sins, he is faithful and just to forgive us our sins, and to cleanse us from all unrighteousness" (1 John 1:9). On the other hand, the Lord has warned, "He that covereth his sins shall not prosper" (Proverbs 28:13). What a man really is will always surface. Any disguise, any charade, any subterfuge may last for days, weeks, months, perhaps even years, but eventually a man's true character will be expressed by his words, betrayed by his actions, and manifested in his countenance. How much better to voluntarily disclose one's true character than to be involuntarily discovered. Confession is a means of bridging that gap.

A CLEANSING POWER

The fruits of repentance make us clean. Isaiah declared, "Though your sins be as scarlet, they shall be as white as snow" (Isaiah 1:18). In ancient Israel the Day of Atonement was symbolic of the consequences that would flow from the real day of atonement. The scriptures read: "For on that day shall the priest make an atonement for you, to cleanse you, that ye may be clean from all your sins before the Lord" (Leviticus 16:30; see also Leviticus 23:27–28). Such was possible only because of the Savior's future day of redemption. Through that Atonement, the Lord has promised that the righteous will have their "garments [made] white through the blood of the Lamb" (Ether 13:10; see also Alma 13:11).[23]

David pled with the Lord, "Wash me throughly from mine iniquity, and cleanse me from my sin." Then he described the miracle: "Purge me . . . and I shall be clean: wash me, and I shall be whiter than snow" (Psalm 51:2, 7). There is no such thing as a spotted, cream-colored repenter. There is no black mark that emerges from the waters of baptism, no stain that survives the rigors of repentance. The repentant soul becomes as white as the driven snow. For such a saint, it is as though the act were never even committed.[24] That is the miracle of repentance. As Elder Matthew Cowley said, "I believe when we repent there is some erasing going on up there so that when we get there we will be judged as we are for what we are and maybe not for what we have been." He also commented, "That's what I like about it—the erasing."[25] But for the unrepentant there is no such erasing. The Lord warned, "Behold, my blood shall not cleanse them if they hear me not" (D&C 29:17).

The Lord loves and longs to forgive each of his children. If we will but repent, "He will abundantly pardon" (Isaiah 55:7). Peter explained that the Lord was "not willing that any should perish, but that all should come to repentance" (2 Peter 3:9). Even Ahab, the reprobate king of Israel, had a transitory moment of repentance that was rewarded by the Lord: "Because he humbleth himself before me, I will not bring the evil in his days" (1 Kings 21:29). It is as though the Lord wants to bless every attempt, however small or feeble it may be, to put our life in his hands. To those who sincerely repent the Lord has promised, "Behold, he who has repented of his sins, the same is forgiven, and I, the Lord, remember them no more" (D&C 58:42). Ezekiel reassured us of this same great truth: "None of his sins that he hath committed shall be mentioned unto him" (Ezekiel 33:16; see also Ezekiel 18:22). It is a glorious thought—the Lord will judge us by what we have become, not by what we were. If we repent he will judge the new man, not the old man. This was David's plea: "Remember not the sins of my youth, nor my transgressions: according to thy mercy remember thou me for thy goodness' sake" (Psalm 25:7).

The Lord's forgiveness is total and unconditional once we have repented. Samuel the Lamanite told the Nephites that the Savior, through his Atonement, made possible "the condition of repentance" (Helaman 14:18). The Lord declared to the Prophet Joseph his feelings concerning this divine principle: "For behold, I, God, have suffered these things for all, that they might not suffer if they would repent; but if they would not repent they must suffer even as I" (D&C 19:16–17). Elder Neal A. Maxwell summarized it well: "We will end up either choosing Christ's manner of living or His manner of suffering!"[26] As we choose his manner of living we overcome spiritual death through the miraculous cleansing powers of the Atonement.

NOTES

1. Conference Report, Oct. 1953, 35.
2. McKay, *Gospel Ideals,* 13.
3. Lee, *Stand Ye in Holy Places,* 221.
4. Kimball, *Miracle of Forgiveness,* 212.
5. Frost, "The Road Not Taken," 105.
6. In McKay, *Gospel Ideals,* 13.
7. Donne, "Holy Sonnets VII," 249.
8. Smith, *Doctrines of Salvation,* 1:227.
9. Shakespeare, *Hamlet,* 1.3.78.
10. Kimball, *Teachings of President Spencer W. Kimball,* 88.
11. Ibid., 99.
12. Roberts, *Gospel and Man's Relationship to Deity,* 25.
13. Featherstone, *Generation of Excellence,* 156–59.
14. Dante, *Divine Comedy,* 48.
15. Smith, *Matthew Cowley,* 298.
16. Phillips, "The Tennis Machine," 56–57.
17. Kimball and Kimball, *Spencer W. Kimball,* 197.
18. Coleridge, "The Rime of the Ancient Mariner," in Williams, *Immortal Poems,* 287; emphasis added.
19. Wilde, *Picture of Dorian Gray,* 176; emphasis added.
20. Dante, *Divine Comedy,* 48.
21. Gandhi, *Autobiography,* 23–24; emphasis added.
22. Conference Report, Oct. 1955, 124.
23. The poet John Donne spoke eloquently of Christ's atoning blood and its wondrous power to transform a sinner into a saint:

> *Yet grace, if thou repent, thou canst not lacke;*
> *But who shall give thee that grace to beginne?*
> *Oh make thy selfe with holy mourning blacke,*
> *And red with blushing, as thou art with sinne;*
> *Or wash thee in Christ's blood, which hath this might*
> *That being red, it dyes red soules to white.*

(Donne, "Holy Sonnets IV," 248)

24. Even when we repent, however, we may still suffer from the consequences of our sin—missed opportunities, hurt relationships, and the like.
25. Smith, *Matthew Cowley,* 295.
26. Maxwell, "Overcome . . . Even As I Also Overcame," 72.

CHAPTER 18

THE BLESSING OF PEACE OF MIND

---∝∝∝---

A CONSOLING POWER

Among its many blessings, the Atonement brings peace. It not only cleanses us, but it consoles us. I have found from practical experience that these two blessings do not always come hand in hand. On occasion, I have met with good Saints whom I believe have fully repented and partaken of the cleansing power of the Savior's sacrifice, but who still confess that they live with troubled consciences. They do not see how the Lord can possibly forgive them for what they have done. This forcibly struck me when I was conducting a temple recommend interview with a convert of about fifteen years. He had been faithful and devoted from the day of his baptism, but he wondered if the Lord could truly forgive him for his checkered life before he heard the gospel message. Such forgiveness seemed too much to ask. I do not believe he was alone in those feelings.

While believing in Christ and his Atonement, some people have innocently, but incorrectly, placed limits on his regenerative powers. They have somehow converted an infinite Atonement into a finite one. They have taken the Atonement and circumscribed it with an artificial boundary that somehow falls short of their particular sin. Stephen Robinson made a similar observation:

"I have learned there are many who believe Jesus is the Son of God and that he is the Savior of the World, but they do not believe that he can save them. They believe in his identity, but not in his power to cleanse and to purify and to save. To have faith in his identity is only half the principle. To have faith in his ability and in his power to cleanse and to save, that is the other half."[1]

These Saints are tougher on themselves than even the Savior might be. In a sense they have adopted their own parameters of justice and mercy. C. S. Lewis offered this counsel: "I think that if God forgives us we must forgive ourselves. Otherwise it is almost like setting up ourselves as a higher tribunal than Him."[2] Such an attitude can even engender the wrath of the Lord, as observed by Zenock: "Thou art angry, O Lord, with this people, because they will not understand thy mercies which thou hast bestowed upon them because of thy Son" (Alma 33:16). In short, these Saints are their own bar to peace of mind. That is one reason it is so essential to understand the Atonement and its infinite nature, to seek after the whys and hows, as well as the consequences, for as our understanding of the Atonement increases, our ability to forgive ourselves and others increases as well.

When we more fully understand the depths to which the Savior descended, the breadth to which he reached, and the heights to which he ascended, we can more readily accept that our own sins are within the vast sphere of his conquered domain. We then become believers, not only in the Atonement's infinite expanse, but in its intimate reach. The Savior's loving offer, "My peace I give unto you" (John 14:27), transforms itself from some abstract hope to a profound personal reality. At such a time we receive not only of the cleansing power, but also the consoling power of the Atonement. Paul spoke of this blessing: "Our Lord Jesus Christ . . . hath loved us, and hath given us everlasting consolation and good hope through grace" (2 Thessalonians 2:16). It is through this consoling power that our "burdens may be light, through the joy of his Son" (Alma 33:23). We can then appreciate and accept Jacob's invitation to his people, "Let us remember him, and lay aside our sins, *and not hang down our heads, for we are not cast off*" (2 Nephi 10:20; emphasis added). We can receive the "exceedingly great joy" that comes to those who have received a remission of their sins after having "come to the knowledge of the glory of God" (Mosiah 4:11).

While serving as a priesthood leader, I became acquainted with an exceptionally good man who some years before had committed a transgression that brought him great remorse. His suffering was prolonged and intense. My heart went out to him. In time I believed he was fully prepared to seek renewal of his temple recommend. I encouraged him in this pursuit, but he was reluctant to proceed. Even though I felt he had been forgiven, he could not seem to forgive himself. He may have been cleansed, but he was not convinced, neither was he consoled. As a result he deferred his return to the House of the Lord. His condition weighed on my mind. One day, while reflecting on him, my mind was forcibly struck with this impression: "Brother _____ has paid the uttermost farthing." A short time later the same impression returned with equal force. I shared the experience with this good brother and soon thereafter he found sufficient peace to renew his temple covenants. I have subsequently wondered—why did that impression come to me rather than the man himself? Perhaps his inability to forgive himself proved an impenetrable barrier to spiritual promptings. Perhaps he would have dismissed or rationalized away as self-generated any such impression if it had come directly to him. Maybe the Lord, in his loving kindness, knew the only way to reach him was by a message through an outside source, namely, his priesthood leader, which would be impossible to dismiss as his own wishful thinking. In any event, peace, that peace that heals and comforts and consoles the wounded soul, eventually found its place in another human heart.

The people of King Benjamin struggled for that peaceful, consoling power. They saw "themselves in their own carnal state" and felt "even less than the dust of the earth." In unanimity they pleaded, "O have mercy, and apply the atoning blood of Christ that we may receive forgiveness of our sins." Then came the divine response: "The Spirit of the Lord came upon them, and they were filled with joy, having received a remission of their sins, and having peace of conscience, because of the exceeding faith which they had in Jesus Christ" (Mosiah 4:2–3). The Atonement did not just cleanse them, but it also consoled them.

THE ATONEMENT IS THE ANSWER— THE ONLY ANSWER

Nephi and Lehi, the sons of Helaman, were cast into prison for their missionary efforts among the Lamanites. Many days passed without food. Then came the fateful day when their captors returned to slay them; but this time the Lord would stay his hand no longer. Nephi and Lehi were encircled about "as if by fire." Their assailants "were overshadowed with a cloud of darkness, and an awful solemn fear came upon them." A still, mild voice pierced them to the very soul. Three times it came. The message was clear: "Repent ye, repent ye." The earth shook, the prison walls trembled, and the cloud of darkness hovered with unrelenting tenacity. It would "not disperse" (Helaman 5:23, 28, 29, 31). This cloud of darkness was a physical manifestation of the spiritual cloud that blanketed their unrepentant souls. The symbolism of the moment was clear and unmistakable. Ironically, the unrepentant were now the imprisoned ones, for they were "immovable." The tangible prison walls were a token of the spiritual prison they had built brick by brick for themselves as they indulged in lives of wickedness. They were anything but free. It was as though their spiritual condition, seemingly invisible to the mortal eye for so many years, was now being mirrored in stark reality by physical symbols.

Finally, the Lamanites could take it no longer. They cried unto God, "What shall we do, that this cloud of darkness may be removed from overshadowing us?" It symbolized all that was depressing and debilitating in their lives. Then Aminadab, a

Nephite dissenter, gave with compelling force the answer that would dispel not only the physical cloud but also the spiritual one that clung to them: "You must repent, and cry unto the voice, even until ye shall have faith in Christ, . . . and when ye shall do this, the cloud of darkness shall be removed from overshadowing you."

It matters not the time or place. The solution for the unrepentant is always the same—repent and have faith in Christ. So it was with these Lamanites who "could not flee." In response to the impending crisis, they cried unto God until the cloud dispersed. They were then encircled about, "yea every soul, by a pillar of fire . . . and they were filled with that joy which is unspeakable and full of glory." Then came those soothing words of solace, "Peace, peace be unto you, because of your faith in my Well Beloved" (Helaman 5:34, 40, 41, 43, 44, 47).

The events on that occasion were reminiscent of Alma the Younger's experience. He, too, struggled for peace. He was in the depths of despair. In graphic language he describes his condition: "I was like to be cast off. . . . I was in the darkest abyss. . . . My soul was racked with eternal torment" (Mosiah 27:27, 29). Only when he thought of Jesus Christ and his Atonement did he receive the peace he so desperately yearned for:

"While I was harrowed up by the memory of my many sins, behold, I remembered also to have heard my father prophesy unto the people concerning the coming of one Jesus Christ, a Son of God, to atone for the sins of the world.

"Now, as my mind caught hold upon this thought, I cried within my heart: O Jesus, thou Son of God, have mercy on me. . . . *And now, behold, when I thought this, I could remember my pains no more;* yea, I was harrowed up by the memory of my sins no more. And oh, what joy, and what marvelous light I did behold; yea, my soul was filled with joy as exceeding as was my pain!" (Alma 36:17–20; emphasis added; see also Mosiah 27:29).

In Book of Mormon times, as in our own, the answer to attaining peace of mind is the same—to understand and partake of the Atonement of Jesus Christ. It was the solution that worked for the

Lamanites on more than one occasion. In the days of the Anti-Nephi-Lehies, their king noted that they had been "the most lost of all mankind" (Alma 24:11). Then they repented. The king acknowledged that they had been forgiven, but thanked God, in addition, that "he hath . . . taken away the guilt from our hearts, through the merits of his Son" (Alma 24:10). Enos heard the divine voice say, "Thy sins are forgiven thee," and then rejoiced in the marvelous miracle that followed: "Wherefore, my guilt was swept away" (Enos 1:5–6). Macbeth longed for that same peace for Lady Macbeth, that same guiltless conscience. Perhaps his yearnings ring in the hearts of many today:

> Canst thou not minister to a mind diseased,
> Pluck from the memory a rooted sorrow,
> Raze out the written troubles of the brain,
> And with some sweet oblivious antidote
> Cleanse the stuffed bosom of that perilous stuff
> Which weighs upon the heart?[3]

Rooted sorrows linger in the hearts of many in our day, and the world still looks in vain for the antidote. Many seek solutions through worldly counselors, money, and fame, but to no avail.

The Lord clearly declared the futility of the world's solutions: "In the world ye shall have tribulation" (John 16:33), and "The way of peace they know not" (Isaiah 59:8). Peace can be found in no man; it comes only through the Savior. With particularity the scriptures describe the gruesome consequences of the world's solutions: a man's soul shall be "harrowed up under a conscious-ness of his own guilt" (Alma 14:6), even "seared with a hot iron" (1 Timothy 4:2). "The demands of divine justice do awaken his immortal soul to a lively sense of his own guilt, . . . and doth fill his breast with guilt, and pain, and anguish, which is like an unquenchable fire, whose flame ascendeth up forever and ever" (Mosiah 2:38). Nephi adds the warning: "The guilty taketh the truth to be hard, for it cutteth them to the very center" (1 Nephi 16:2). The wicked are they who "shall flee when none pursueth [them]" (Leviticus 26:17; see also Proverbs 28:1) and who "go mourning all the day long" (Psalm 38:6). Job spoke harshly, but truthfully, of those who had nothing to offer but worldly comfort: "How then comfort ye me in vain, seeing in your answers there remaineth falsehood?" (Job 21:34).

All of Satan's alluring temptations, counterfeit programs, and specious promises, incorporated one way or another into the world's solutions with all their multidimensional appeal, oratory, and glitter, simply collapse under the Lord's time-tested declaration: "There is no peace, saith my God, to the wicked" (Isaiah 57:21). The words of the hymn are sobering:

> *Where can I turn for peace?*
> *Where is my solace*
> *When other sources cease to make me whole?* [4]

The Lord gave the answer, the only sure answer: "My peace I give unto you: not as the world giveth, give I unto you" (John 14:27). That peace of which he spoke is the peace that "passeth all understanding" (Philippians 4:7). It is to be found only as we come to know, appreciate, and accept the Atonement of Jesus Christ. Then "peace [shall] be multiplied unto you through the knowledge of God, and of Jesus our Lord" (2 Peter 1:2; see also Helaman 5:47). Ammon was a living witness of that. He spoke of the hopelessness of those who tried another way: "Behold, this is joy which none receiveth save it be the truly penitent and humble seeker of happiness" (Alma 27:18). David knew the futility of seeking another source of peace: "Lord, what wait I for? my hope is in thee" (Psalm 39:7).

Following the Savior's compelling sermon on the Bread of Life, perhaps the most memorable sermon ever given outside the Sermon on the Mount, many of his disciples forsook him. The Savior then turned to Peter and inquired, "Will ye also go away?" Peter gave an answer that might burn in every heart and hang on every hearth: "Lord, to whom shall we go? thou hast the words of eternal life" (John 6:67–68). One may search the world in vain, he may scour the journals of thought, he may toy with the philosophies of men, but eventually he will learn that there is no hope, no lasting peace outside of Jesus Christ.

The atoning sacrifice of Christ, and our full acceptance of it, is the spiritual antidote that heals the wounded soul. It is such an antidote that replaces despair with hope, darkness with light, and turmoil with peace. It was this antidote that worked for Zeezrom. He lay sick with a burning fever. He recounted his many sins, believing there was "no deliverance" for what he had done. Then Alma posed the tide-turning question, "Believest thou in the power of Christ unto salvation? . . . If thou believest in the redemption of Christ thou canst be healed" (Alma 15:3, 6, 8). The response was positive. The healing that followed was not only physical but spiritual as well. The prerequisite was a belief in the Atonement of Jesus Christ.

Jacob invited his people to "hear the pleasing word of God, yea, the word which healeth the wounded soul" (Jacob 2:8). This invitation was again extended by the Savior during his mortal ministry: "Come unto me, all ye that labour and are heavy laden, and I will give you rest. Take my yoke upon you, and learn of me . . . and ye shall find rest unto your souls" (Matthew 11:28–29). Nephi spoke of those glorious days when "the Son of righteousness shall appear unto them [the righteous]; and he shall heal them, and they shall have peace" (2 Nephi 26:9).

Is it any wonder that the Savior, after giving an autobiographical insight into his own Atonement, should instruct the Saints of the latter days, "Learn of me, and listen to my words . . . and you shall have peace in me" (D&C 19:23). He is indeed the author of peace, "the founder of peace" (Mosiah 15:18), the "Prince of Peace" (Isaiah 9:6), to all those who come unto him. Enos was a witness of this promise: "And I soon go to . . . my Redeemer; for I know that in him I shall rest" (Enos 1:27; see also D&C 54:10).

The Lord anxiously wants us to be at peace. It is one of the gifts of his Atonement. Like any loving father, he longs to shower upon us those gifts that will accrue to our spiritual well-being. Luke records the account of the woman who suffered from "an issue of blood" for twelve years (Luke 8:43). He tells us that she came up behind the Savior, touched the hem of his garment, and was instantly healed. How did she feel? Certainly there was elation at her instantaneous recovery, but one must wonder if there were not some lingering twinge of guilt that her deed had been done in secret. Was there something spiritually incongruent about the act? Did she believe in the Savior's healing powers but feel unworthy to personally make of him the desired request? Whatever the cause for her covert conduct, no sooner had the act occurred than the Savior inquired, "Who touched me?" (Luke 8:45). Peter was amazed. Why should it matter? They were in the midst of a throng; many had pressed about him—but the Savior's spirit had been aroused by one whose touch had not been prompted by chance. With this touch, he knew power had gone out from him. The woman, unable to hide, fell before him trembling and confessed what she had done. Her mortal body was rejuvenated, but her spiritual and emotional tranquility had been left in want. She had peace of body, but not peace of mind. Now the Lord would give her both: "Daughter, be of good comfort: thy faith hath made thee whole; *go in peace*" (Luke 8:48; emphasis added). Oh, what balm those few words must have been to her ailing spirit! The sensitive, tender soul of the Savior knew that this good woman of faith had been only partially healed.

Neither the healing of the body nor the healing of the spirit is complete without peace of mind. That is why the Savior told the man sick of palsy, "Son, be of good cheer; thy sins be forgiven thee" (Matthew 9:2). It was the same message given to Thomas Marsh after his sins had likewise been forgiven: "Let thy heart be of good cheer" (D&C 112:4). To Lyman Sherman, the Lord promised, "Your sins are forgiven you" (D&C 108:1). That was the cleansing part. Then came the words of consolation: "Therefore, let your soul be at rest concerning your spiritual standing" (D&C 108:2). Similar words of comfort were given to the Prophet Joseph and Oliver Cowdery in the Kirtland Temple. First came the cleansing: "You are clean before me." Then came the consoling assurance that all was right: "Therefore, lift up your heads and rejoice" (D&C 110:5). In each instance the Lord placed a capstone on his healings—peace of mind. During the last supper the Lord put it all in perspective: "In me ye might have peace. In the world ye shall have tribulation: but be of good cheer; I have overcome the world" (John 16:33; see also D&C 78:18).

One marvels how on this occasion the Lord could invite "good cheer" when, seemingly, only dark clouds loomed ahead. Gethsemane was imminent. Judas' betrayal was on the horizon. Peter's denial was forthcoming. There was the mockery of a pseudo-trial, the haunting chant of those whom he had come to save—"Crucify him, crucify him!"—and finally, Calvary itself. All this lay ahead, and yet he could say, "Be of good cheer." Why? Because he would overcome the world; he would descend beneath it all. He would make it possible for every person of every age to overcome every obstacle, every weakness, every sin, and every tinge of guilt. Because of the Savior's sacrifice, Alma's experience may be relived by each of us: "I did cry out unto the Lord Jesus Christ for mercy . . . and I did find peace to my soul" (Alma 38:8).

NOTES

1. Robinson, "Believing Christ," 26.
2. Lewis, *Quotable Lewis,* 221.
3. Shakespeare, *Macbeth,* 5.4.40–45.
4. Emma Lou Thayne, "Where Can I Turn for Peace?" in *Hymns,* no. 129; used by permission of the author.

CHAPTER 19

THE BLESSING OF SUCCOR

---∞∞∞---

"THE ULTIMATE COMFORTER"

One of the blessings of the Atonement is that we can receive of the Savior's succoring powers. Isaiah spoke repeatedly of the Lord's healing, calming influence. He testified that the Savior was "a strength to the needy in his distress, a refuge from the storm, a shadow from the heat" (Isaiah 25:4). As to those who sorrow, Isaiah declared that the Savior possessed the power to "comfort all that mourn" (Isaiah 61:2), and "wipe away tears from off all faces" (Isaiah 25:8; see also Revelation 7:17); "revive the spirit of the humble" (Isaiah 57:15); and "bind up the brokenhearted" (Isaiah 61:1; see also Luke 4:18; Psalm 147:3). So expansive was his succoring power that he could exchange "beauty for ashes, the oil of joy for mourning, the garment of praise for the spirit of heaviness" (Isaiah 61:3).

Oh, what hope soars in those promises! Though our life seems empty or pointless, perhaps reduced to nothing more than the scattered ashes of a course bent on self-destruction, there is a miraculous rebirth, a spiritual phoenix that emerges with our acceptance of the Savior and his Atonement. His spirit heals; it refines; it comforts; it breathes new life into hopeless hearts. It has the power to transform all that is ugly and vicious and worthless in life to something of supreme and glorious splendor. He has the power to convert the ashes of mortality to the beauties of eternity. So sweeping is the Savior's healing balm that Isaiah promised, "Sorrow and sighing shall flee away" (Isaiah 35:10).

While the Savior knew all things in the Spirit (Alma 7:13), he also knew the pains, infirmities, and temptations of man as experienced in the flesh. He never allowed godly power to insulate him when he walked the path of mortals. He chose to let every pain and affliction and weakness of man traverse and engulf his physical frame. Paul observed that he became "like unto his brethren, that he might be a merciful and faithful high priest" (Hebrews 2:17). The refiner's fire of human experience confirmed in his godly nature the tenderness of heart, the softness of soul, that made the Savior not only just but merciful, not only omnipotent but compassionate.

Elder Neal A. Maxwell gave this insight into the relationship between the Atonement and the Savior's succoring powers: "His empathy and capacity to succor us—in our own sicknesses, temptations, or sins—were demonstrated and perfected in the process of the great atonement."[1] He also said, "The marvelous atonement brought about not only immortality but also the final perfection of Jesus' empathetic and helping capacity."[2] William Wordsworth offered a consistent thought in his poem "Character of the Happy Warrior":

> More skillful in self knowledge, even more pure,
> As tempted more; more able to endure,
> As more exposed to suffering and distress;
> Thence, also, more alive to tenderness.[3]

The Savior is a God whose miracles were driven by compassion, a God who befriended mortals, a God who wept at human sorrow, a God who lived a life of intimacy, not "distancy," from his mortal counterparts. Our Lord is a personal, loving, caring God who is our friend, our brother, our advocate, and our Savior. What mercy and compassion fill his soul! Isaiah summarized it well: "Sing, O heavens; and be joyful, O earth; . . . for the Lord hath comforted his people, and will have mercy upon his afflicted" (Isaiah 49:13).

The Savior was no ivory-tower observer, no behind-the-lines captain. He was no spectator, no "high priest which cannot be touched with the feeling of our infirmities; but was in all points tempted like as we are, yet without sin" (Hebrews 4:15). Paul further explains, "For in that he himself hath suffered being tempted, he is able to succour them that are tempted" (Hebrews 2:18; see also D&C 62:1). The Savior was a participant, a player, who not only understood our plight intellectually, but who felt our wounds because they became his wounds. He had firsthand, "in the trenches," experience. He knew "according to the flesh how to succor his people according to their infirmities" (Alma 7:12). He could comfort with empathy, not just sympathy, all "those that are cast down" (2 Corinthians 7:6). That is why Peter invited each saint to cast his "care upon him; for he careth for you" (1 Peter 5:7). He was indeed what President Ezra Taft Benson called "the ultimate *Comforter*."[4]

Mormon, in his closing mortal words, addressed his son, Moroni. He cited the atrocities of the Lamanites and then added this striking condemnation of his own people: "Notwithstanding this great abomination of the Lamanites, it doth not exceed that of our people" (Moroni 9:9). Immorality, murder, torture, perversion—they had done it all. Mormon acknowledged they were "like unto wild beasts" (Moroni 9:10). He could not recommend them unto God lest God should smite him. That was the dismal state of affairs. In such dire straits, could Mormon offer any hope to his faithful son Moroni? Listen to these wonderful words of counsel from a sensitive father:

"My son, be faithful in Christ; and may not the things which I have written grieve thee, to weigh thee down unto death; *but may Christ lift thee up,* and may his sufferings and death, and the showing his body unto our fathers, and his mercy and long-suffering, and the hope of his glory and of eternal life, *rest in your mind forever*" (Moroni 9:25; emphasis added).

No matter how lost the world at large may be, no matter how

depraved or degenerate it may become, there is yet a bright light of hope for those individuals who have a faith in Christ. Those who focus on him and his atoning sacrifice, who let these glorious truths rest in their minds continually, will find that Christ's power to lift the human soul transcends even the weightiest burdens the world may thrust upon them. There is a certain spiritual buoyancy that attends a study of, and reflection upon, the Atonement. Such spiritual serenity finally came to Abraham, but only after his troubled spirit was permitted to pierce the veil of history and he was able to see with prophetic eyes "the days of the Son of Man, and [he] was glad, and his soul found rest" (JST, Genesis 15:12). Alma, knowing this source of ultimate comfort, cried out, "O Lord, my heart is exceedingly sorrowful; wilt thou comfort my soul in Christ" (Alma 31:31).

No mortal can cry out, "He does not understand my plight, for my trials are unique." There is nothing outside the scope of the Savior's experience. As Elder Maxwell observed, "None of us can tell Christ anything about depression."[5] As a result of his mortal experience, culminating in the Atonement, the Savior knows, understands, and feels every human condition, every human woe, and every human loss. He can comfort as no other. He can lift burdens as no other. He can listen as no other. There is no hurt he cannot soothe, rejection he cannot assuage, loneliness he cannot console. Whatever affliction the world casts at us, he has a remedy of superior healing power. Truman Madsen spoke forcefully of the Savior's comforting powers:

"No human encounter, no tragic loss, no spiritual failure is beyond the pale of his present knowledge and compassion. . . . And any theology which teaches that there were some thing[s] he did *not* suffer is [a] falsification of his life. He knew them all. Why? That he might succor, which is to say comfort and heal, this people. He knew the full nature of the human struggle."[6]

Man's needs, however onerous or multitudinous they may be, will never outdistance God's succoring powers. That is part of the miracle of his redemption. He is always there. He never tells us not to come back home. He is never found in short supply of anxious concern. He never wants for a remedy. The Savior's love and compassion will always circumscribe every real and imaginable need of man.

We rejoice in his glorious invitation and promise: "Come unto me, all ye that labour and are heavy laden, and I will give you rest" (Matthew 11:28). This, too, is part of the power and blessing of the Atonement—to succor those who stand in need. That was the essence of Alma's message to the Zoramites. He taught them of the Atonement, urged them to "plant this word" in their hearts, and then concluded, "And then may God grant unto you that your burdens may be light, through the joy of his Son" (Alma 33:23).

How much easier to follow and love that leader who has felt all that we have felt and more—who not only sympathizes, but empathizes with our cause. Even though the Savior may have known all things in the Spirit, even the travails of the flesh, the fact that he took upon him a body of flesh and bones, and thereafter suffered the indignities of man, increases both our affection for him and our ability to identify with him. Elder Maxwell quotes G. K. Chesterton in this regard: "No mysterious monarch, hidden in his starry pavilion at the base of the cosmic campaign, is in the least like that celestial chivalry of the Captain who carries his five wounds in the front of the battle."[7] It is such a "wounded" leader we are fortunate to have. It is such a wounded leader who succors us in our wounds.

NOTES

1. Maxwell, *Plain and Precious Things,* 99.
2. Ibid., 42.
3. Clark and Thomas, *Out of the Best Books,* 1:67.
4. Benson, "Jesus Christ," 5.
5. Maxwell, "Enduring Well," 10.
6. Madsen, *Christ and the Inner Life,* 5, 12.
7. Maxwell, *More Excellent Way,* 12.

CHAPTER 20

THE BLESSING OF MOTIVATION

THE POWER TO DRAW MEN UNTO HIM

Another significant blessing flowing from the Atonement is the power to motivate. The primary purpose of the Savior's suffering was to redeem us from the Fall and from the effects of our own sin. In the process of performing that divine deed, however, there was a "divine fallout," some of which was the motivational power that draws men unto him. Some have referred to this as the "moral influence theory" or "love appeal syndrome," but the name is of little import compared to the consequence.

The powers of the Atonement do not lie dormant until one sins and then suddenly spring forth to satisfy the needs of the repentant person. Rather, like the forces of gravity, they are everywhere present, exerting their unseen but powerful influence.

Nephi alluded to the omnipresence of these motivational powers: "He doeth not anything save it be for the benefit of the world; for he loveth the world, even that he layeth down his own life *that he may draw all men unto him*" (2 Nephi 26:24; emphasis added). Following the Savior's resurrection he taught, "For this cause have I been lifted up; therefore . . . *I will draw all men unto me"* (3 Nephi 27:15; emphasis added; see also James 4:10). In this sense, the Savior exerts a form of spiritual gravity that draws and entices all men unto him.

These motivational powers are always extending themselves, reaching out, penetrating every open heart. It is these powers that help fire the desire to repent. It is these powers that can inspire our course of conduct *before* sin is ever committed. Just as reflection upon our mothers' lives and their sacrifices may influence our conduct for good, so too a reflection upon the Savior's life and his sacrifice may inspire our course of conduct before sin is ever committed. Thus, the powers that emanate from the Atonement are not only reactive in nature, but, of equal importance, they are proactive. Suffice it to say, the Atonement is much more than a divine remedy to correct our sins after they are committed. The Atonement is, in fact, the most powerful motivational force in the world *to be good* from day to day and, when necessary, *to repent* when we have fallen short. Elder Charles W. Penrose taught, "If we really do believe in God and in Jesus Christ," then "the desire will enter our hearts to turn away from sin."[1]

Force has never been the Savior's governing scepter. Instead, he teaches that power and godly influence come "by persuasion, by long-suffering, by gentleness and meekness, and by love unfeigned" (D&C 121:41). His modus operandi is to invite and draw all men unto him. Alma taught this gratifying principle: "Behold, he sendeth an invitation unto all men, for the arms of mercy are extended towards them" (Alma 5:33; see also 2 Nephi 26:25). One need not have a vivid imagination to picture a father with outstretched arms welcoming the wayward child back to his home of security and love. There is a certain compelling magnetism to that setting. What child can resist such an invitation? Of course, that is the point: if we are childlike, we will not resist, we will not delay—rather we will run to the open arms that draw us in. Even when we are rebellious, even when we play the part of the prodigal son or daughter, we cannot forget the kindly father who "had compassion, and ran, and fell on his [rebellious son's] neck, and kissed him" (Luke 15:20). Such a forgiving love is hard to resist. It is a powerful invitation to return home. Such is the effect of the Savior's loving sacrifice.

HOW DOES IT WORK?

But how does the Atonement motivate, invite, and draw all men unto the Savior? What causes this gravitational pull—this spiritual tug? There is a certain compelling power that flows from righteous suffering—not indiscriminate suffering, not needless suffering, but righteous, voluntary suffering for another. Such suffering for another is the highest and purest form of motivation we can offer to those we love. Contemplate for a moment: How does one change the attitude or the course of conduct of a loved one whose every step seems bent on destruction? If example fails to influence, words of kindness go unheeded, and the powers of logic are dismissed as chaff before the wind, then where does one turn? Jag Parvesh Chader spoke of exhausting all such nonviolent sources and then added this insight: "When it fails to produce any salutary effect, voluntarily [one] invites suffering in his own body to open the eyes of the person who is determined to see no light."[2]

Fasting has often been employed for just such a purpose. Abstinence does much more than make us hungry; it does more than refine our spirits; it has within it a certain inherent motivational power that can change and soften the hearts of others, particularly when they know we are fasting for them. Therein lies a force that can penetrate the granite walls of pride, replenish the barren reservoirs of humility, and engender increased affection and gratitude for him who so suffers.

In the words of the missionary evangelist, E. Stanley Jones, suffering has "an intense moral appeal." Jones once asked Mahatma Gandhi as he sat on a cot in an open courtyard of Yeravda jail, "'Isn't your fasting a species of coercion?' 'Yes,' he said very slowly, 'the same kind of coercion which Jesus exercises upon you from the cross.'" As Jones reflected upon that sobering rejoinder, he

213

said: "I was silent. It was so obviously true that I am silent again every time I think of it. He was profoundly right. The years have clarified it. And I now see it for what it is: a very morally potent and redemptive power if used rightly. But it has to be used rightly."[3]

Not all suffering motivates for good. There is the suffering of the prison inmate, yet the prison houses continue to overflow. There is the recurring hurt and suffering of war, yet the world resounds with war and conflict. There is the suffering of those who contract contagious diseases from immoral conduct, but thousands continue to follow suit. And then there is the suffering of those pure and noble souls who are able to suffer beyond themselves, whose suffering has more than a purifying power for self; it also brings a redemptive power to others.

This principle is powerfully illustrated in the Book of Mormon. Ammon and his brethren had brought thousands of the Lamanites to a knowledge of the truth. Wanting to distinguish themselves from the nonbelievers, these converts called themselves the "people of Anti-Nephi-Lehi." Unfortunately, the schism between believer and nonbeliever widened until the hatred of the nonbelievers reached a fever pitch, even until "their hatred became exceedingly sore" (Alma 24:2). War was imminent. Then came the ultimate in human sacrifice. The people of Anti-Nephi-Lehi, with full knowledge of an impending attack, buried their weapons of war, "vouching and covenanting with God, that rather than shed the blood of their brethren they would give up their own lives; and rather than take away from a brother they would give unto him." If need be, they "would suffer even unto death" (Alma 24:18–19).

One can almost visualize the heartrending scene that followed. On the one hand were the believers—weaponless, guileless, prostrated upon the ground in the very act of prayer, humbly submitting themselves to God's will; on the other hand, the nonbelievers—vengeful, hateful, armed to the hilt, rushing with blood-curdling cries, like fiends, toward their helpless prey, having only one purpose in mind: "destroying the people of Anti-Nephi-Lehi" (Alma 24:20). The massacre was merciless—1,005 of the believers were hewn down. Through it all there was no resistance, no opposition of any sort, no defensive or strategic countermeasures, only a silent, unyielding resolve to trust in God whatever the consequences might be—and what consequences they were!

Finally, the cumulative suffering of those undaunted saints was so magnified as to work an unforgettable miracle. A force unknown to military ranks swept the battlefield. No doubt an eerie silence hovered over the scene of carnage. It was as though a mass spiritual transfusion were in progress. The pendulum had reversed its course. Hate, vengeance, and pride were being jettisoned while guilt, shame, remorse, and finally repentance filled the void. Alma recounts what happened next:

"When the Lamanites saw [the self-sacrifice of their brethren] they did forbear from slaying them; and there were many whose hearts had swollen in them for those of their brethren who had fallen under the sword, for they repented of the things which they had done. And it came to pass that they threw down their weapons of war, and they would not take them again, for they were stung for the murders which they had committed; and they came down even as their brethren, relying upon the mercies of those whose arms were lifted to slay them. And it came to pass that the people of God were joined that day by more than the number who had been slain. . . . And there was not a wicked man slain among them; but there were more than a thousand brought to the knowledge of the truth; thus we see that the Lord worketh in many ways to the salvation of his people" (Alma 24:24–27).

Suffering of immense proportions had brought salvation. Where reason had failed, family ties had been severed, and cultural heritage had been inadequate to sustain lasting bonds, righteous suffering had succeeded. Suffering proved to be more than a purifying process for the donor; it also brought a redemptive power for the recipient.

Mohandas Gandhi seized upon righteous suffering as a powerful motivational tool for good. Each of his fasts possessed a certain motivational power, but none had more far-reaching effects than the fasts at Calcutta and Delhi. Calcutta was a battleground of hate. Gandhi, a Hindu, stayed at a Muslim home in the heart of the riot district. Some Hindus were incensed at Gandhi's conciliatory conduct towards the enemy. An attempt on his life failed. Various consortiums of hot-headed Hindu youth were sent to Gandhi to convince him of the error of his ways. Each time the youth would return and repeat, "The Mahatma is right." The war continued. Finally, Gandhi announced a fast to the death unless the foes altered their course. It would be peace for them or death for him. After three days of fasting, the suffering of one revered by an entire nation proved too much for the people to bear. The softening and persuasive powers of his suffering melted "hearts of stone." Weapons, from knives to Sten guns, were laid at his feet. Almost overnight the healing occurred. Lord Mountbatten, one of the military leaders present observed, "What 50,000 well-equipped soldiers could not do, the Mahatma has done. He has brought peace."[4] And so he had.

Delhi was his next challenge. The tension was screw-tight. Gandhi proposed eight points on which Hindus and Muslims must reach accord, or again he would fast to the death. All eight points favored the Muslims. The risk was staggering, but his goal was honorable: to unify a divided nation. After six days the pact of peace was signed. E. Stanley Jones, present just before the fast, wrote: "This was no cheap signing of an ordinary peace pact. There was a moral quality here that made it different. His blood and their tears cemented the pact." He also noted: "His method and his aim were right. . . . He shook that nation to its depths— shook it morally."[5] Through the power of righteous suffering a diminutive, seventy-nine-year-old man, waning in life, literally saved a nation by bringing it to its spiritual senses.

While an instructor at Harvard, Truman Madsen learned of an experience shared by the university's president, Charles Eliot, with a student who wanted to quit, to throw it all away. Evidently

President Eliot used all the powers of reason he possessed to dissuade the young man from his course. It was to no avail. The student was intransigent; his destructive course was set. Then a thought flashed through President Eliot's mind. He inquired, "What about your wife and parents who labored and struggled to put you through this far? Does their sacrifice count for nothing?" That thought struck a responsive chord in the young man. Not for himself, but for others who had loved and suffered and sacrificed, he would stick it out. Their suffering would not be spent in vain.[6]

THE ELEMENTS OF SUFFERING THAT REDEEM

Suffering in behalf of another seems to have its major impact for good when at least four elements are present. First, the sufferer is pure and worthy. In this sense there was only one completely without blemish, one worthy of suffering spiritually for all others. Second, the cause for which he suffers is just. There is no worthier cause than that for which the Savior suffered, namely, bringing to pass "the immortality and eternal life of man" (Moses 1:39). Third, the recipient knows and loves the sufferer. And fourth, the recipient appreciates the cause for which the suffering occurs. When these four elements simultaneously exist, the chemistry for human behavioral change is explosive.

In the context of the Atonement the first two elements above are givens. The last two are entirely dependent upon us. This is one reason it is so critical to understand the Atonement, including its whys and hows, as well as its consequences. Imagine the power for good that could be unleashed if we fully understood the breadth of Christ's love and the depth of his suffering. Paul saw this potential. He taught that "the blood of Christ" purges or turns our "conscience from dead works to serve the living God" (Hebrews 9:14). As we expand our knowledge of the Atonement and increase our love for the Savior and the cause for which he suffered, our hearts begin to soften and more readily yield to the motivational powers of his sacrifice. We find new reservoirs of commitment to "serve the living God." Eventually, there emerges a personal burning resolve that his suffering shall not have been in vain.

Just before the Church was organized the Lord gave some instructive counsel to Joseph and Oliver. He forgave them for their shortcomings and encouraged them to be faithful and keep the commandments. In so doing, he gave them a key to spirituality: "Look unto me in every thought. . . . Behold the wounds which pierced my side, and also the prints of the nails in my hands and feet" (D&C 6:36–37). The Savior knew that an honest contemplation of the Atonement turns our thoughts and actions heavenward. That is why we have such great emphasis on remembering the Savior and his Atonement. It is a central component of the sacramental prayers (see D&C 20:77, 79). To "remember" the Savior's sacrifice is a repeated theme of the scriptures (2 Nephi 10:20; Mosiah 4:11, 30). The Lord knows that such reflection is more than a mental exercise—it is, in truth, a precursor to Christlike works.

Years ago Handel composed his masterpiece in choir repertoire—the unparalleled *Messiah*. This composition was not just the product of a gifted man. Flowing from the lyrics are the clear markings of divine intervention. The heavenly voiceprint is unmistakable. For twenty-four days Handel remained a spiritual recluse in his room as he fashioned line after line of music seemingly fit for heavenly choirs. At one point, after having scored the Hallelujah Chorus, he called to his servant and exclaimed, "I did think I did see all Heaven before me, and the great God Himself." Following one of the performances, a friend remarked that he had been entertained. Handel replied, "I should be sorry if I only entertain them. I wish to make them better."[7] Likewise, the Savior is anxious that the Atonement make us better. He must be gravely disappointed if people merely acknowledge his Atonement as a magnificent sacrifice to be viewed in awe, but with no thought of change. The atoning sacrifice was designed to motivate us, to draw us unto him, to lift us to higher ground, and ultimately to assist us in becoming as he is.

NOTES

1. *Journal of Discourses,* 21:85.
2. Jones, *Mahatma Gandhi,* 110.
3. Ibid., 110.
4. Ibid., 116–17.
5. Ibid., 117–18.
6. This experience was shared with the author by Truman G. Madsen.
7. Kavanaugh, *Spiritual Lives of Great Composers,* 3, 6.

CHAPTER 21

THE BLESSING OF EXALTATION

THE POWER TO EXALT

The Atonement was not only a redemption of that which was lost in the Fall; it "added upon" (Abraham 3:26) Adam and Eve and all their descendants, lifting them above their pre-fallen condition. The Atonement is both redemptive *and exalting* in its nature. C. S. Lewis understood this principle: "For God is not merely mending, not simply restoring a *status quo. Redeemed humanity is to be something more glorious than unfallen humanity would have been,* more glorious than any unfallen race now is (if at this moment the night sky conceals any such). . . . And this super-added glory will, with true vicariousness, exalt all creatures."[1] Recognizing the necessity of the Atonement for its perfecting qualities as well as its redemptive features, Lewis added, "It would have occurred for Glorification and Perfection even if it had not been required for Redemption."[2]

How tragic it would be if the Atonement merely restored us to an Edenic state. A literal redemption of Adam's transgression, with nothing more, would mean a return to innocence, to an inability to have children, to a lack of opportunity to choose good or evil, and to frustrated hopes for godhood. Fortunately, the Atonement was far more than a restoration of that which was lost, much more than a return to the starting line. President John Taylor gave some additional insight on this issue:

"The gospel, when introduced and preached to Adam after the fall, through the atonement of Jesus Christ, placed him in a position not only to have victory over death, but to have within his reach and to possess the perpetuity, not only of earthly, but of heavenly life; not only of earthly, but also of heavenly dominion; and through the law of that gospel enabled him (and not him alone, but all his posterity) to obtain, not only his first estate, *but a higher exaltation on earth and in the heavens, than he could have enjoyed if he had not fallen; the powers and blessings associated with the atonement being altogether in advance of and superior to any enjoyment or privileges that he could have had in his first estate.*"[3]

On another occasion, President Taylor stated: "As a man through the powers of his body he could attain to the dignity and completeness of manhood, but could go no further; as a man he is born, as a man he lives, and as a man he dies; but through the essence and power of the Godhead, which is in him, which descended to him as the gift of God from his heavenly Father, he is capable of rising from the contracted limits of manhood to the dignity of a God, and thus through the atonement of Jesus Christ and the adoption he is capable of eternal exaltation, eternal lives and eternal progression. But this transition from his manhood to the Godhead can alone be made through a power which is superior to man—an infinite power, an eternal power, even the power of the Godhead."[4]

Elder Bruce Hafen wrote an insightful article entitled "The Atonement is Not Just for Sinners."[5] The obvious implication of such a title is that the Atonement's circle of influence extends far beyond a cleansing for our willful misdeeds. In fact, the more this doctrine is explored, researched, and analyzed, the further its boundaries seem to expand, almost with endless elasticity. It is as though someone had set a never-ending array of curtains in space. At first, each curtain is lifted with the expectation it is the last, the conclusion of all space; but as one relentlessly pursues his course it finally dawns on him that there is no end to these curtains. Likewise, there is seemingly no end to the blessings the Atonement bestows, no finale to the questions to be asked and answers to be found—at least not in our mortal lifetimes. It is a wonderfully exhilarating, yet humbling pursuit—a finite mind chasing the infinite. At some point one feels he has approached a cloud; he sees the object at hand but somehow lacks the tools to capture it. But this is in no way an indictment of the search, but rather an enticement to renew the quest with increased vigor, knowing that with each new truth, each new insight, even each new question, the quest for truth, that truth which saves souls and builds faith and enlightens our understanding of eternity, is being advanced, however small it may be on the scale of cosmic verities.

King Benjamin envisioned the Atonement's circle of influence as extending far beyond the willful sinner. "His blood," he taught, "atoneth for the sins of those . . . who . . . died not knowing the will of God . . . or who have ignorantly sinned" (Mosiah 3:11; see also 3 Nephi 6:18). Thus, the Atonement's redemptive powers are not just for the knowing sinner; they can redeem the souls of those who have sinned without knowing or understanding the will of God. But what about weaknesses, shortcomings, and inadequacies that are not so much a function of sin or ignorance as a lack of capacity? Can the Atonement fill this void? Can it not only correct but also endow, add to, and enlarge our capacity for godhood? Can it take a deficit spiritual account and not only wipe the slate clean, but transform it to a surplus? Elder Bruce Hafen shares this enlightening conversation he had with Elder Bruce R. McConkie:

"Elder Bruce R. McConkie visited Ricks College to deliver a devotional talk. As we drove together toward the campus from the airport, I asked Elder McConkie if he thought the concepts of grace and the Lord's Atonement had anything to do with the affirmative process of perfecting our nature—apart from the connection of those concepts with forgiveness of sin.

"He said that is what the scriptures teach. Turning to the Doctrine and Covenants, he read aloud from Joseph Smith's description of those in the celestial kingdom: 'These are they who are *just* men *made perfect* through Jesus the mediator of the new covenant, who wrought out this perfect atonement through the shedding of his own blood' (D&C 76:69; emphasis added). . . . Elder McConkie told the Ricks students later that day that the Atonement compensates for *all* the effects of the Fall and makes possible our inheritance of God's quality of life—eternal life."[6]

The definition of grace as set forth in the LDS Bible Dictionary is consistent with Elder McConkie's observation: "This grace is an enabling power that allows men and women to lay hold on eternal life and exaltation after they have expended their own best efforts."[7]

King Benjamin pleaded with his people to put off the natural man and become "a saint through the atonement of Christ the Lord" (Mosiah 3:19). Elder Hafen elaborated on this thought: "As King Benjamin here suggests, the Atonement does more than pay for our sins. It is also the agent through which we develop a saintly nature."[8] That is exactly what Moroni taught: "Yea, come unto Christ, and be perfected in him, . . . that by his grace ye may be perfect in Christ; . . . then are ye sanctified in Christ by the grace of God, through the shedding of the blood of Christ" (Moroni 10:32–33). Elder Hafen continues to develop this concept: "Here we will see that the Lord's grace, unlocked by the Atonement, can perfect our imperfections. . . . While much of the perfection process involves a cleansing from the contamination of sin and bitterness, there is an additional, affirmative dimension through which we acquire a Christlike nature, becoming perfect even as the Father and Son are perfect."[9]

Elder Hafen then adds this further comment: "The Savior's victory can compensate not only for our sins but also for our inadequacies; not only for our deliberate mistakes but also for our sins committed in ignorance, our errors of judgment, and our unavoidable imperfections. Our ultimate aspiration is more than being forgiven of sin—we seek to become holy, endowed affirmatively with Christlike attributes, at one with him, like him. Divine grace is the only source that can finally fulfill that aspiration, after all we can do."[10]

Some have asked, "If we subject ourselves to the laws of justice, will we receive the same fruit as if we had submitted ourselves to Christ and received the blessings of the laws of mercy?" In other words, can we "eat, drink and be merry," and then at the last minute bear the full weight of justice and receive the same reward as the man who has repented? The answer is no. Paying the price of justice alone neither cleanses the soul nor perfects our character. Yet because of Christ, repentance does both.

The man who has served his five-year jail term has satisfied the laws of the land; he has paid the debt of justice—but such compliance, such endurance does not, in and of itself, transform a criminal into a saint. One "becometh a saint" only "through the atonement of Christ the Lord" (Mosiah 3:19). All the justice in the universe, administered through all the eons of time, will not produce one single saint. Sainthood, which leads to godhood, requires repentance; repentance requires mercy; and mercy requires the Atonement of Jesus Christ. It always comes back to the Atonement.

The heavy hand of justice does not change or soften or rehabilitate or reform. Unlike repentance, it is not a spiritual catalyst. To the contrary, it is neutral, always neutral. The Lord spoke of its unyielding, noncleansing nature: "That which breaketh a law, and abideth not by law, but seeketh to become a law unto itself, and willeth to abide in sin, and altogether abideth in sin, cannot be sanctified by law, neither by mercy, justice, nor judgment. Therefore, they must remain filthy still" (D&C 88:35).

The judge with all his mighty sway cannot lower his gavel with purifying power; neither can the iron bars of the most formidable fortress confine with a cleansing catharsis. Justice can be satisfied to the utmost farthing, and yet one can be filthy still. Why? Because the power to cleanse is not bestowed in this manner, but rather by him whose right it is to bestow. Justice is external, repentance internal. A man's soul may stoically endure justice, but justice may cause no more change in a human soul than a hammer on cold steel. In contrast, the repentant soul is malleable and flexible. It is molten steel in the forge of the blacksmith, wet clay on the wheel of the potter, a Stradivarius in the grasp of the virtuoso. Repentance is a broken heart and contrite spirit in the hands of the Great Physician. It is the internal desire of man combined with the external power of God, so merging in miraculous harmony that it enlarges, endows, and enlightens the human spirit with a godlike nature. Repentance is the divinely chosen process that leads to godhood while satisfying justice each step of the way.

The law of justice brings about order and stability in the universe. That is good. But the law of repentance does much more; it brings about godhood. Repentance is more than a passive process to "get us even"; it is the affirmative process to improve us, refine us, and ultimately perfect us. Its purpose goes far beyond the satisfaction of justice. It opens the door to the cleansing and perfecting powers of the Atonement.

Elder Bruce Hafen has written: "I once wondered if those who refuse to repent but who then satisfy the law of justice by paying for their own sins are then worthy to enter the celestial kingdom. The answer is no. The entrance requirements for celestial life are simply higher than merely satisfying the law of justice. For that reason, paying for our sins will not bear the same fruit as repenting of our sins. Justice is a law of balance and order and it must be satisfied, either through our payment or his. But if we decline the Savior's invitation to let him carry our sins, and then satisfy justice by ourselves, we will not yet have experienced the complete rehabilitation that can occur through a combination of divine assistance and genuine repentance. Working together, those forces have the power permanently to change our hearts and our lives, preparing us for celestial life. . . .

"The doctrines of mercy and repentance are rehabilitative, not retributive, in nature. The Savior asks for our repentance not merely to compensate him for paying our debt to justice, but also as a way of inducing us to undergo the process of development that will make our nature divine, giving us the capacity to live the celestial law."[11]

OVERCOMING WEAKNESSES, INADEQUACIES, AND SHORTCOMINGS

It seems that some people lose sight and hope of godhood, not because of major sins, but because of innocent mistakes or weaknesses. "I'm not a bad person," they say. "I just can't seem to overcome the weaknesses that so easily beset me and distance me from God. It's not the sins so much as the lack of talent, the lack of capability, the lack of strength that separate me from God." Those of us who fall within this category need to be reminded of the Atonement's intimate, as well as infinite reach. Regardless of the depth or multiplicity of our individual weaknesses, the Atonement is always there. Therein lies its beauty and genius—it is never beyond our grasp. The Savior is always standing by, anxiously longing to endow us with those powers that will convert our every weakness to a strength. The LDS Bible Dictionary puts every man's need for this power in perspective: "Divine grace is needed by every soul in consequence of the fall of Adam and also because of man's weaknesses and shortcomings."[12]

When our daughter Angela was in the fourth grade, she came home from school one day feeling distraught. Her report card was in her hand. The teacher had placed a check under the column "Handwriting," indicating a need for improvement—an assessment that was hard for her sensitive soul to take. Teary-eyed and despondent, she felt like a failure. We tried to comfort her, but it was to little avail. Finally, a kind Father in heaven prompted us in our struggles. As we discussed possible solutions a scripture came to mind—Ether 12:26–27. We opened the Book of Mormon and read it with our daughter. We read how Moroni, as he abridged the plates of Ether, lamented to the Lord that the Gentiles would mock his writing. He felt comfortable in speaking; in fact, he acknowledged that the Lord had made him "mighty in word," but then added, "Thou hast not made us mighty in writing"

(Ether 12:23). Moroni was feeling a sense of genuine inferiority and insecurity, acknowledging a real weakness that was about to be exposed, perhaps even exploited. Moroni confesses, "When we write we behold our weakness, and stumble because of the placing of our words; and I fear lest the Gentiles shall mock at our words" (Ether 12:25).

In response to Moroni's fears, the Lord gave this magnificent promise: "I give unto men weakness that they may be humble; and my grace is sufficient for all men that humble themselves before me; for if they humble themselves before me, and have faith in me, then will I make weak things become strong unto them" (Ether 12:27).

What power in that promise! The Lord promised much more than an overcoming of our weaknesses—he proclaimed they could become strengths in our lives. What a difference in perspective! What a difference in consequence!

After reading that passage, we discussed Moroni's experience with our daughter. We knew, and she knew, the Lord would not make an idle promise. As the scripture required, we did have faith in his power to strengthen. We knew, however, that the Lord expects us to do all we can to assist in that process. Accordingly, I gave a father's blessing to our daughter. We knew that this alone would not solve the problem, but it would be one of many positive steps we could take. Angela made a poster inscribed with the Lord's promise to Moroni, which she placed in a prominent spot in her room as a constant reminder of her potential and of the Lord's promise. She resolved that each day she would pray for the Lord's help with her penmanship needs. She agreed to let her parents review her homework each night; if her writing was unimproved, she would redo it. My wife bought her a calligraphy set, which further whetted her appetite to improve her writing skills. Time slipped by almost unnoticed until she was in the sixth grade and about to graduate. The principal announced that certificates would be given to the five students with the finest penmanship. One can imagine our elation when he called out the name of Angela Callister to receive her award. What might have been an abstract principle became a very real and personal testimony for this sweet little girl.

Some years later I visited our daughter at BYU. She invited me into her room. I was glancing at the pictures and quotes on her wall when my eyes fell on those words of the Lord to Moroni: "If they humble themselves before me, and have faith in me, then will I make weak things become strong unto them" (Ether 12:27). Angela knew from personal experience this promise was true. So also did Paul of old: "I can do all things through Christ which strengtheneth me" (Philippians 4:13). Jacob made it clear that this strengthening power originates not from self, but from the grace of Christ: "The Lord God showeth us our weakness that we may know that it is by his grace . . . that we have power to do these things" (Jacob 4:7).

The power to convert a weakness to a strength is possible through the grace of Christ, but the Lord has imposed two prerequisites, humility and faith. If these requirements are satisfied, the grace of Christ becomes like a booster rocket that powers and lifts us above our weaknesses. That is what James taught: "God . . . giveth grace unto the humble. . . . Humble yourselves in the sight of the Lord, and he shall lift you up" (James 4:6, 10; see also 1 Peter 5:5). Isaiah likewise wrote of this lifting, soaring power: "He giveth power to the faint; and to them that have no might he increaseth strength. . . . They that wait upon the Lord shall renew their strength; *they shall mount up with wings as eagles*" (Isaiah 40:29, 31; emphasis added).

What an appropriate description. Those who humbly and faithfully wait upon the Lord may, like the eagles, soar above their weaknesses.

Moses felt weighed down by a glaring weakness in his life. He was called as a prophet but nonetheless agonized, "O my Lord, I am not eloquent, . . . but I am slow of speech, and of a slow tongue." It was as though he were saying, "How can I lead this people when I have no fluency of speech, no gift of oratory?" The Lord answered his worries in this classic reply: "Who hath made man's mouth?" In other words, the Lord was reminding him that

God, who created both man and worlds without end, certainly could correct the simple problem inherent in one man's fluency. Then the Lord gave Moses this promise: "Now therefore go, and I will be with thy mouth, and teach thee what thou shalt say."

That should have solved the problem, closed the damper of disbelief. But Moses, great as he was, still lacked in faith on this occasion, for he replied, "O my Lord, send, I pray thee, by the hand of him whom thou wilt send." Moses could not believe his speech problems could be solved by the Lord; instead he sought his own solution—a spokesman. How did the Lord react? "The anger of the Lord was kindled against Moses" (Exodus 4:10–14). The consequence: Moses got his spokesman, but a weakness failed to become the strength it might have become.

Contrast Moses' experience with that of Enoch. The initial facts are almost identical, but here the story diverges. Enoch, too, was called to be a prophet. Enoch, too, had a glaring speech impediment: "Why is it that I have found favor in thy sight, and am but a lad, and all the people hate me; for I am slow of speech; wherefore am I thy servant?" (Moses 6:31). The Lord's response to Enoch was similar to his advice to Moses: "Open thy mouth, and it shall be filled, and I will give thee utterance" (Moses 6:32). To this point the scripts are parallel. It was the same play, same act, same scene. Only the names and dates had been changed. It is here, however, that the scripts part company. There is no suggestion in the scriptural record that Enoch doubted the Lord's promise; rather, he humbled himself in simple obedience and faith. Enoch, in describing this encounter, says, "The Lord spake with me, and gave me commandment [to preach the gospel]; wherefore, for this cause, to keep the commandment, I speak forth these words" (Moses 6:42).

The scriptures then reveal the awesome power of God's grace: "As Enoch spake forth the words of God, the people trembled, and could not stand in his presence" (Moses 6:47). The scriptural record continues: "So great was the faith of Enoch that . . . he spake the word of the Lord, and the earth trembled, and the mountains fled, even according to his command; and the rivers of water were turned out of their course; . . . *and all nations feared greatly, so powerful was the word of Enoch, and so great was the power of the language which God had given him*" (Moses 7:13; emphasis added).

Does that sound like someone slow of speech? To the contrary, his weakness had become a mighty strength. The promise of the Lord, as spoken through the Apostle Paul, was a confirmation of Enoch's experience: "My grace is sufficient for thee: for my strength is made perfect in weakness" (2 Corinthians 12:9).

THE QUEST FOR GODHOOD

To overcome a weakness is a marvelous achievement; to convert it to a strength borders on the miraculous, but to claim it may yet be more, even perfection, crosses the line of heresy for many. Yet in each instance the process is the same. It is a case of "grace for grace" (D&C 93:12). David knew of this perfecting process, for he wrote, "God is my strength and power: and he maketh my way perfect" (2 Samuel 22:33).

Perhaps no doctrine, no teaching, no philosophy has stirred such controversy as has this—that man may become perfect as God is. It is a prime focus of anti-Mormon literature; it was the underlying motivation that caused the Jews, when confronting the Savior, to cry out, "For a good work we stone thee not; but for blasphemy; and because that thou, being a man, makest thyself God" (John 10:33). Ironically, godhood for his children is the crowning goal of the Savior's atoning sacrifice.

We live in a day when this glorious principle advocating man's quest for godhood is being maligned and ridiculed. It is viewed by some as blasphemous, by others as absurd. Such a concept, they challenge, lowers God to the status of man and thus deprives God of both his dignity and divinity. Others claim this teaching to be devoid of scriptural support. "Certainly," they say, "no God-fearing, right-thinking, Bible-oriented person would subscribe to such a philosophy as this"—and the attack goes on and on.

But wherein lies the truth? For our search we turn first and foremost to the testimony of the scriptures; second, to the wisdom of those poets and authors who drink from the divine well; third, to the power of logic; and fourth, to the voice of history. It is these witnesses that can whisper to our souls the quiet but certain truth.

SCRIPTURES

The scriptures are replete with references to man's potential for perfection and thus godhood. As early as the book of Genesis an angel appeared to Abraham and extended to him this heavenly mandate, "Walk before me, and be thou perfect" (Genesis 17:1). What type of perfection was the angel alluding to? As compared to other men? Angels? God? During the Sermon on the Mount the Savior gave the unequivocal answer: "Be ye therefore perfect, *even* as your Father which is in heaven is perfect"[13] (Matthew 5:48; emphasis added). This challenge was consistent with the Savior's high-priestly prayer. Speaking of the believers, he petitioned "that they may be one, even as we are one: I in them, and thou in me, that they may be made perfect in one" (John 17:22–23). Paul taught that a vital reason for the church was "for the perfecting of the saints, . . . till we all come . . . unto a perfect man, . . . unto the measure of the stature of the *fulness of Christ*" (Ephesians 4:12–13; emphasis added). Note the measuring rod— not man, not some form of mini-Christ or quasi-God, but rather "the fulness of Christ." The standard of perfection was not other men, nor angels, but Christ himself.

The scriptures supporting this doctrine continue to roll forth with repeated and powerful testimony. At one point the Savior was about to be stoned by the Jews for blasphemy. To this charge he responded, "Is it not written in your law, I said, Ye are gods?" (John 10:34). He was referring to his own Old Testament declaration, with which the Jews should have been familiar: "I have said, Ye are gods; and all of you are children of the most High" (Psalm 82:6). The Savior was merely reaffirming a prophetic teaching that all men are children of God and thus might become like him. Paul understood this principle, for when speaking to the men of Athens he said: "Certain also of your own poets have said, For we are also his offspring" (Acts 17:28).

Paul knew our potential as offspring of God, for while speaking to the Romans he declared, "The Spirit itself beareth witness with our spirit, that we are the children of God: and if children, then heirs; heirs of God, and joint-heirs with Christ" (Romans 8:16–17)—not subordinate heirs, not junior, not contingent, but joint, equal heirs with Christ, to share in all that he shall receive. President Joseph F. Smith understood the significance of this scripture, for he observed, "The grand object of our coming to this earth is that we may become like Christ, for if we are not like him, we cannot become the sons of God, and be joint heirs with Christ."[14] John the Revelator saw in vision how all-inclusive this inheritance might be, even for a struggling mortal: "He that overcometh shall inherit all things; and I will be his God, and he shall be my son" (Revelation 21:7). There are no qualifiers here. The Lord does not promise "some things" or even "many things," but rather "all things." Timothy knew of this possibility. Paul promised him, "If we suffer, we shall also reign with him" (2 Timothy 2:12). The word *reign* suggests a kingdom, a dominion over which we will have rule. The words *reign with him* suggest a position of *like* power and rule. The Lord was most specific on this issue: "He [God] makes them equal in power, and in might, and in dominion" (D&C 76:95). Again and again, the message is clear and consistent.

Is it any wonder that Paul should write to the saints of Philippi, "I press toward the mark for the prize of the high calling of God in Christ Jesus" (Philippians 3:14)? Paul, who understood this doctrine, was striving for the prize of godhood. He then extended this universal invitation to all saints, "Let us therefore, as many as be perfect, be thus minded" (Philippians 3:15). To the Hebrews he gave the same message, "Therefore not leaving the principles of the doctrine of Christ, let us go on unto perfection. . . . And we will go on unto perfection if God permit" (JST, Hebrews 6:1, 3). Peter, who also knew of these "exceeding great and precious promises" adds his testimony that we "might be partakers of the divine nature" (2 Peter 1:4), meaning recipients of godhood. That is exactly what Jesus commanded: "Therefore, what manner of men ought ye to be? Verily I say unto you, even as I am" (3 Nephi 27:27).

The critic, unable to understand, responds, "But such a concept lowers God to the status of man, and thus robs God of his divinity." "To the contrary," comes the reply, "does it not elevate man in his divine potential?" Paul knew the critic's argument well and gave the answer that should have silenced him once and for all. Speaking to the saints of Philippi he said, "Let this mind be in you, which was also in Christ Jesus: who, being in the form of God, *thought it not robbery to be equal with God*" (Philippians 2:5–6; emphasis added). The Savior knew that for him to be a god would not rob God of his divinity. Paul carries this one step further. He suggests that each of us should view these things as Jesus did, for if we do, we will also know that it is possible for us to become like God without robbing him of his divinity. That is good logic. After all, who is greater, that being who limits, or that being who enhances man's eternal progress? Brigham Young addressed this issue: "[Man's godhood] will not detract anything from the glory and might of our heavenly Father, for he will still remain our Father, and we shall still be subject to him, and as we progress in glory and power, the *more* it enhances the glory and power of our heavenly Father."[15] That is the irony of the critic's argument—godhood for man does not diminish God's status; to the contrary, it elevates it by producing more intelligent, more sensitive, more respectful Saints who have enlarged capacities to understand, honor, and worship him.

The Savior's soul-stirring and thought-provoking injunction to "be ye therefore perfect" was more than the sounding of brass or tinkling of cymbals. It was a heavenly mandate to rise up to our full potential and become like God our Father. C. S. Lewis, an articulate advocate of this simple but glorious truth, wrote:

"The command 'Be ye perfect' is not idealistic gas. Nor is it a command to do the impossible. He is going to make us into creatures

that can obey that command. *He said (in the Bible) that we were 'gods' and He is going to make good His words. . . .* The process will be long and in parts very painful; but that is what we are in for. Nothing less. *He meant what He said. . . .* Those who put themselves in His hands will become perfect, *as He is perfect*—perfect in love, wisdom, joy, beauty, and immortality."[16]

The scriptures teach with repetition and clarity that man may become like God.

POETIC INSIGHT

We may also find a witness of this truth in the wisdom of selected poets and authors who are men and women of integrity and spiritual insight. It was C. S. Lewis who again reaffirmed this divine proposition: *"It is a serious thing to live in a society of possible gods and goddesses,* to remember that the dullest and most uninteresting person you talk to may one day be a creature which . . . you would be strongly tempted to worship, or else a horror and a corruption such as you now meet, if at all, only in a nightmare. All day long we are, in some degree, helping each other to one or other of these destinations. It is in the light of these overwhelming possibilities, it is with the awe and the circumspection proper to them, that we should conduct all our dealings with one another, all friendships, all loves, all play, all politics. *There are no ordinary people.* You have never talked to a mere mortal. Nations, cultures, arts, civilization—these are mortal, and their life is to ours as the life of a gnat. But it is immortals whom we joke with, work with, marry, snub, and exploit—immortal horrors or everlasting splendors."[17]

There are no ordinary people—no ciphers, no zeros, only potential gods and goddesses in our midst. Henry Drummond, a Canadian poet, noted the difference between the simply moral man and the spiritual man: "The end of salvation is perfection, the Christ-like mind, character and life. . . . Therefore the man who has within himself this great formative agent, Life [spiritual life] is nearer the end than the man who has morality alone. The latter can never reach perfection, the former *must.* For the life must develop out according to its type; and being a germ of the Christ-life, *it must unfold into a Christ*."[18]

Victor Hugo, the masterful French author, offered this corollary thought of profound implications: "The thirst for the infinite proves infinity." Perhaps our thirst and drive for godhood likewise proves the possibility of godhood. Would the God of heaven plant the vision and desire for godhood within a man's soul and then frustrate him in his ability to attain it?

Robert Browning, whose vision so often pierced the mortal veil, knew the answer, as disclosed in these lines from his poem "Rabbi Ben Ezra":

> *Life's struggle having so far reached its term.*
> *Thence shall I pass, approved*
> *A man, for aye removed*
> *From the developed brute—a god, though in the germ.*[19]

Do not all Christian churches advocate Christlike behavior? If so, are we better men and women, better Christians, if we desire to be only 90 percent like Christ, rather than 100 percent? If it is blasphemous to think we can become as God now is, then at what point is it not blasphemous to become like him—90 percent, 50 percent, 20 percent, 1 percent? Is it more honorable to seek partial godhood than total godhood? Are we to walk the path of godhood with no hopes of ever reaching the destination? Yet that seems to be the tragic conclusion of many.

Fortunately Lorenzo Snow saw both the path and the promised destination. Before President Snow was a member of the Church, Joseph Smith Sr., then patriarch of the Church, prophesied that Lorenzo would be baptized, and then added this postscript, "You will become as great as you can possibly wish—EVEN AS GREAT AS GOD, and you cannot wish to be greater."[20] Two weeks later Lorenzo was baptized, but the rest of the promise remained a "dark parable" to him until four years later when a burst of revelation came upon him, enlightening his mind on the subject. He tells of his extraordinary experience:

"The Spirit of the Lord rested mightily upon me—the eyes of

my understanding were opened, and I saw as clear as the sun at noonday, with wonder and astonishment, the pathway of God and man. I formed the following couplet which expresses the revelation, as it was shown me, and explains Father Smith's dark saying to me at a blessing meeting in the Kirtland Temple, prior to my baptism, as previously mentioned in my first interview with the Patriarch.

> As man now is, God once was:
> As God now is, man may be."[21]

Lorenzo Snow, both prophet and poet, seized upon this glorious principle and lyricised in one of those poems that are filled with spiritual truth:

> Dear Brother:
> Hast thou not been unwisely bold,
> Man's destiny to thus unfold?
> To raise, promote such high desire,
> Such vast ambition thus inspire?
>
> Still, 'tis no phantom that we trace
> Man's ultimatum in life's race;
> This royal path has long been trod
> By righteous men, each now a God:
>
> As Abra'm, Isaac, Jacob, too,
> First babes, then men—to gods they grew.
> As man now is, our God once was;
> As now God is, so man may be,—
> Which doth unfold man's destiny. . . .
>
> The boy, like to his father grown,
> Has but attained unto his own;
> To grow to sire from state of son,
> Is not 'gainst Nature's course to run.
>
> A son of God, like God to be,
> Would not be robbing Deity;
> And he who has this hope within,
> Will purify himself from sin.[22]

LOGIC

The power of logic also teaches us of our divine potential. Do not the laws of science teach us that like begets like, each after its kind? Science has discovered that a complex genetic code transferred from parent to child is responsible for the child attaining the physical attributes of his parents. If this be so, is it illogical to conclude that spiritual offspring receive a spiritual code giving to them the divine potential of their parent—even God himself? No, it is but a fulfillment of the law that like begets like. This is the same truth taught by Lorenzo Snow, who through personal revelation was so well acquainted with this principle:

"We were born in the image of God our Father; He begat us like unto Himself. *There is the nature of Deity in the composition of our spiritual organization.* In our spiritual birth, our Father transmitted to us the capabilities, powers and faculties which He possessed, as much so as the child on its mother's bosom possesses, although in an undeveloped state, the faculties, powers and susceptibilities of its parent."[23]

Elder Boyd K. Packer tells of coming home one day and being met by his little children, who were anxious to show him some newly hatched chicks. As his little four-year-old daughter picked one of them up Elder Packer said, "That will make a nice watchdog when it grows up, won't it?" His daughter looked at him with an expression that suggested he did not know much. So he said, "It won't be a watchdog, will it?" She shook her head and replied, "No, Daddy." Then he added, "It will be a nice riding horse." His little daughter gave him "that 'Oh, Dad!' look." Then he said, "Even a four-year old knows that a chick will not grow to be a dog, nor a horse, nor even a turkey. It will be a chicken. It will follow the pattern of its parentage."[24] President John Taylor taught this principle by asking a series of rhetorical questions: "What will the boys be when they are grown up? They will be men, will they not? They are now the sons of men. If a man be inducted into the family of God, and becomes a son of God, what will he become when he gets his growth? You can figure that out yourselves."[25]

Who among us can sing that stirring song, "I Am a Child of God," without instinctively sensing our divine potential?

The Gospel of Philip, one of the Nag Hammadi discoveries, makes this simple statement of logic: "A horse sires a horse, a man begets man, a god brings forth a god."[26] That is exactly what John Taylor taught: "As the horse, the ox, the sheep, and every living creature, including man, propagates its own species and perpetuates its own kind, so does God perpetuate His."[27]

The difference between man and God is significant, but it is one of degree, not kind. It is the difference between an acorn and an oak tree, a rosebud and a rose, a son and a father. In truth, every man is a god in embryo, in fulfillment of that eternal law that like begets like. To suggest otherwise is to suggest that God created inferior offspring, in direct conflict with every scientific law known to man. But somehow, most of the world continues to miss the mark. In *Paradise Lost*, John Milton echoes the world's sentiments: "Man hath offended the majesty of God by aspiring to Godhood."[28] But why would the majesty of God be offended? What scriptures support, what logic evidences or what spirit dictates such a proposition as this?

Milton has Satan present the argument for godhood via a dream to Eve, thus suggesting that the divine pursuit is contrary to God's plan. Satan tenders his best case for godhood. Interestingly enough, Milton never successfully refutes it. The key lines are as follows:

> . . . *O fruit divine,*
> *Sweet of thyself, but much more sweet thus cropped,*
> *Forbidden here, it seems, as only fit*
> *For gods, yet able to make gods of men!*
> *And why not gods of men, since good, the more*
> *Communicated, more abundant grows,*
> *The author not impaired, but honoured more?*[29]

The last line is the focal point. Is God impaired, degraded, lessened, dethroned because he has given to others the capacity to become like him? Or, alternatively, is he honored more? Who can honor more or worship with greater impact, a creature of lower or more exalted status? Can a plant offer the same honor or worship with the same feelings as an animal? Can an animal have the same emotional charge and spiritual promptings as a human? Can a mere mortal experience the empyreal feelings or the spiritual fervency of a potential God? One's capacity to honor and worship is magnified with one's intellectual, emotional, cultural, and spiritual enlightenment. Accordingly, the more we become like God, the greater our ability to pay him homage. In that process of lifting men heavenward, God simultaneously multiplies his own honor and thus is "honored more," not less.

God's crowning creation possessed the ultimate power to honor him, and in addition to become like him. The purpose of this creation and the reason for God's sacrifice was obvious to C. S. Lewis: "[God] did not create the humans—He did not become one of them and die among them by torture—in order to produce candidates for Limbo, 'failed' humans. He wanted to make Saints; gods; things like Himself."[30] He expressed similar sentiments on another occasion: "Whatever may have been the powers of unfallen man, it appears that those of redeemed Man will be almost unlimited. Christ, re-ascending from his great dive, is bringing up Human Nature with Him. Where He goes, it goes too. It will be made 'like Him.'"[31]

Joseph Smith spoke of the great purpose of salvation, the ultimate reason behind it all, when he said, "*He [Christ] proposed to make them [men] like unto himself,* and he was like the Father, *the great prototype of all saved beings;* and for any portion of the human family to be assimilated into their likeness is to be saved: . . . and on this hinge turns the door of salvation."[32] If the purpose of salvation is to become like "the great prototype of all saved beings," then it should not seem surprising that God has provided a way to accomplish that very purpose. Joseph Smith so declared: "All those who keep his commandments shall grow up from grace to grace, and become heirs of the heavenly kingdom, and joint heirs with Jesus Christ; possessing the same mind, being transformed into the same image or likeness, even the express image of him who fills all in all; being filled with the fullness of his glory, and become one in him."[33] Such a declaration is in full accord with the scriptural promise: "The saints shall be filled with his glory, and receive their inheritance and be made equal with him" (D&C 88:107). It seems both logical and reassuring that we might become like him who is indeed our literal Father in heaven.

THE VOICE OF HISTORY

The voice of history likewise verifies our godly potential. Perhaps we all feel inadequate when we look at the distance between God and us, but we can take comfort when we contemplate what is accomplished in the short space of a mortal life. B. H. Roberts expressed it in these lofty terms:

"Think for a moment what progress a man makes within the narrow limits of this life. Regard him as he lies in the lap of his mother . . . a new-born babe! . . . There lies a man in embryo, but helpless. And yet, within the span of three score years and ten, by the marvelous working of that wondrous power within that little [child], what a change may be wrought! From that helpless babe may arise one like Demosthenes, or Cicero, or Pitt, or Burke, or Fox, or Webster, who shall compel listening senates to hear him, and by his master mind dominate their intelligence and their will, and compel them to think in channels that he shall mark out for them. Or from such a babe may come a Nebuchadnezzar, or an Alexander, or a Napoleon, who shall found empires or give direction to the course of history. From such a beginning may come a Lycurgus, a Solon, a Moses, or a Justinian, who shall give constitutions and laws to kingdoms, empires and republics, blessing happy millions unborn in their day, and direct the course of nations along paths of orderly peace and virtuous liberty. From the helpless babe may come a Michael Angelo [sic], who from some crude mass of stone from the mountain side shall work out a heaven-born vision that shall hold the attention of men for generations, and make them wonder at the God-like powers of man that has created an all but living and breathing statue. Or a

240

Mozart, a Beethoven, or a Handel, may come from the babe, and call out from the silence those melodies and the richer harmonies that lift the soul out of its present narrow prison house and give it fellowship for a season with the Gods. . . .

"And all this may be done by a man in this life! Nay, it has been done, between the cradle and the grave—within the span of one short life. Then what may not be done in eternity by one of these God-men?"[34]

Contemplate for a moment what can be accomplished in the mere span of a mortal life. Suppose now, that you were to remove from man the barrier of death, grant him immortality and God for his guide—what limits would you then want to ascribe to his mental, moral, or spiritual achievements? Again, B. H. Roberts expressed it well when he said: "If within the short space of mortal life there are men who rise up out of infancy and become masters of the elements of fire and water and earth and air, so that they well-nigh rule them as Gods, what may it not be possible for them to do in a few hundreds or thousands of millions of years? What may they not do in eternity? To what heights of power and glory may they not ascend?"[35]

C. S. Lewis reminds us, "The job will not be completed in this life: but He means to get us as far as possible before death."[36]

A glimpse beyond the veil tells us that our progress does not end at death. Victor Hugo sensed the unlimited possibilities in the afterlife: "The nearer I approach the end the plainer I hear around me the immortal symphonies of the world which invites me. . . . For half a century I have been writing my thoughts in prose and in verse; history, philosophy, drama, romance, tradition, satire, ode and song; I have tried all. But I feel I have not said the thousandth part of what is in me. When I go down to the grave I can say like many others,—'I have finished my day's work.' But I cannot say, 'I have finished my life's work.' My day's work will begin again the next morning. The tomb is not a blind alley; it is an open thoroughfare. It closes on the twilight, it opens on the dawn. My work is only beginning."[37]

The scriptures suggest that the quest is neither easy nor quick at hand. Peter admonished the saints to "humble yourselves therefore under the mighty hand of God, that he may exalt you *in due time"* (1 Peter 5:6; emphasis added). John spoke in a similar vein: "You may come unto the Father in my name, and in *due time* receive of his fulness" (D&C 93:19; emphasis added). As important as is the quest for perfection, the Lord does not require it in a day. He reminds us, perhaps even forewarns us, to "continue in patience until ye are perfected" (D&C 67:13; see also Hebrews 12:1).

Such patience is required even beyond these mortal moorings. The Prophet Joseph spoke of the process: "When you climb up a ladder, you must begin at the bottom, and ascend step by step, until you arrive at the top; and so it is with the principles of the Gospel—you must begin with the first, and go on until you learn all the principles of exaltation. But it will be a great while after you have passed through the veil before you will have learned them. It is not all to be comprehended in this world; it will be a great work to learn our salvation and exaltation even beyond the grave."[38]

The First Presidency of the Church in 1909 reiterated the promise and also the timetable: "Undeveloped offspring of celestial parentage is capable, by experience through ages and aeons, of evolving into a God."[39]

Shortly before his death, President Lorenzo Snow visited Brigham Young University for the purpose of speaking to the assembled student body. On their way to the assembly room, BYU President George H. Brimhall escorted President Snow through one of the kindergarten rooms. There President Snow saw the children making spheres with clay and said:

"President Brimhall, these children are now at play, making mud worlds, the time will come when some of these boys through their faithfulness to the gospel, will progress and develop in knowledge, intelligence and power, *in future eternities,* until they shall be able to go out into space where there is unorganized matter and call together the necessary elements, and through their knowledge of and control over the laws and powers of nature, to organize matter into worlds on which their posterity may dwell, and over which they shall rule as gods."[40]

C. S. Lewis exposed the one obstacle to "absolute perfection" and godhood—ourselves. He teaches the principle by way of a childhood experience. He recalls his repeated toothaches and his desire for relief—but likewise the nagging fear that if he disclosed his pain, his mother would take him to the dentist. He said, "I knew those dentists; I knew they started fiddling about with all sorts of other teeth which had not yet begun to ache. . . . [I]f you gave them an inch, they took an ell." Then he made this comparison: "Our Lord is like the dentists. . . . Dozens of people go to Him to be cured of some one particular sin which they are ashamed of. . . . Well, He will cure it all right: but He will not stop there. That may be all you asked; but if you once call Him in, He will give you the full treatment.

" . . . 'Make no mistake,' He says, 'if you let Me, I will make you perfect. The moment you put yourself in My hands, that is what you are in for. Nothing less, or other, than that. You have free will, and if you choose, you can push Me away. But if you do not push Me away, understand that I am going to see this job through. Whatever suffering it may cost you in your earthly life, whatever inconceivable purification it may cost you after death, whatever it costs Me, I will never rest, nor let you rest, until you are literally perfect—until my Father can say without reservation that He is well pleased with you, as He said he was well pleased with Me. This I can do and will do. But I will not do anything less.'

" . . . You must realize from the outset that the goal toward which He is beginning to guide you is absolute perfection; and no power in the whole universe, except you yourself, can prevent Him from taking you to that goal. That is what you are in for. And it is very important to realize that."[41]

His last observation is telling. He reminds us there is no one in this entire universe that can rob us of perfection, except ourselves.

Unfortunately, some people sell themselves short. In feigned honor of God they auction themselves off as servants, not sons.

Some will blame their failed attainments on abusive parents, inattentive teachers, or wayward friends. Some will seek excuse in the temporal tragedies of life—the death of a loved one, the loss of a job, or a physical handicap. Yet deep down in our quiet reflective moments of oneness with Divinity, we know there is no outside force that can steal away our spiritual strength. Every event, every encounter, every disaster, however despairing it may seem to the outward eye, may be met with spiritual success. A temporal tragedy need never result in a spiritual defeat. To the contrary, such "tragedies" have often proven the springboard for a sublime spiritual victory. One man accepts his deafness by excoriating God; another, Beethoven, scores the Ninth Symphony. One woman with loss of sight sees only darkness; another with greater vision, Helen Keller, becomes a beacon to a blinded world. One man responds to his disease with loss of faith; another, Job, declares, "Though he slay me, yet will I trust in him" (Job 13:15). One man loses his wife and in the process his zest for life; another, Robert Browning, draws ever deeper from the well to pen with compelling passion poetry of divine dimensions. One man may respond to the seemingly disastrous events of life with vengeance and venom; another may respond with humble submissiveness to God's will, an appreciation for life as it is, and a firm resolve to be better. For one, life's challenges and tragedies become stumbling blocks; for the other, they become stepping-stones. So it was with the Nephites after a prolonged and bitter war with the Lamanites. The scriptures reveal that "many had become hardened, because of the exceedingly great length of the war; and many were softened because of their afflictions, insomuch that they did humble themselves before God, even in the depth of humility" (Alma 62:41).

We may not control our temporal setbacks, but we always, always, always control our spiritual destiny. Every temporal tragedy may be countered with a spiritual victory—and the ultimate victory is godhood. In the last analysis, through his grace, God has permitted us to define our own divine destiny.

Scriptures, poetic insight, logic, and history testify not only of the divine possibility, but of the divine reality that man may become as God. Almost two thousand years ago the Lord made this astounding promise to John the Revelator: "To him that overcometh will I grant *to sit with me in my throne,* even as I also overcame, and am set down with my Father in his throne" (Revelation 3:21; emphasis added). What was that throne? Nothing less than the throne of God. A similar promise had been made millennia before to Enoch: "Thou hast . . . given unto me a right to thy throne" (Moses 7:59). Is there any evidence that any mortals have actually obtained such a throne? The Doctrine and Covenants reveals as to Abraham, Isaac, and Jacob, "Because they did none other things than that which they were commanded, they have entered into their exaltation . . . and *sit upon thrones, and are not angels but are gods*" (D&C 132:37; emphasis added; see also D&C 124:19; Moses 7:59). For these men the divine possibility became the divine reality. The promise is certain: "To him who overcometh, and keepeth my commandments unto the end, will I give power over many kingdoms" (JST, Revelation 2:26).

Some might ask, What difference does it make if I really understand this principle of godhood? Elder McConkie wrote, "No doctrine is more basic, no doctrine embraces a greater incentive to personal righteousness . . . as does the wondrous concept that man can be as his Maker."[42] As we better understand this lofty goal, our level of confidence and motivation is greatly heightened. How could we not have increased faith in God and in ourselves by knowing he had planted within our souls the seeds of godhood?

The Atonement is the sun, water, and soil that nourish those seeds. It is the eternal power so essential to our growth. That is what John Taylor taught: "It is for the exaltation of man to this state of superior intelligence and Godhead that the mediation and atonement of Jesus Christ is instituted; and that noble being, man . . . is rendered capable of becoming a God, possessing the power, the majesty, the exaltation and the position of a God."[43] There can be no mistake about it, as Brigham Young observed: "We are created, we are born for the express purpose of growing up from the low estate of manhood, to become Gods like unto our Father in heaven."[44]

If we are not destined for godhood, the critic must answer, "Why not?" Perhaps we could suggest three answers for the critic's consideration.

Maybe man cannot become like God because God does not have the power to create a celestial offspring. It is beyond his present level of comprehension and intelligence. "Blasphemous," responds the critic. "He has all knowledge and all power."

Perhaps God does not create such a divine offspring because he does not love us. "Ridiculous," the critic replies. "'For God so loved the world, that he gave his only begotten Son'" (John 3:16).

Well, perhaps God has not planted within us the divine spark because he wants to retain godhood for himself; he is threatened by our progress; he can retain his superiority only by asserting man's inferiority. "No, no," insists the critic. "Have you ever known a loving, kindly father who did not want his children to become all that he is and more?"

So it is with God, our Father. He has the power, the love, and the desire to make us like him, and for these very reasons has planted within each of us the seeds of godhood. To believe otherwise is to suggest that God does not have the power to make us like him, or worse yet, chooses not to do so. Yet this is the proposition asserted by much of the world. To the contrary, the scriptures, poetic insight, logic, and history combine to teach with power and conviction that there are no ordinary people among God's children, only potential gods and goddesses in our midst. The Atonement is the means of unleashing that divine potential.

NOTES

1. Lewis, *Miracles,* 122–23; emphasis added.

2. Ibid., 123.

3. Taylor, *Gospel Kingdom,* 278; emphasis added.

4. Taylor, *Mediation and Atonement,* 141.

5. Hafen, *Broken Heart,* 1.

6. Ibid., 17.

7. LDS Bible Dictionary, 697.

8. Hafen, *Broken Heart*, 8.

9. Ibid., 16.

10. Ibid., 20.

11. Ibid., 7–8.

12. LDS Bible Dictionary, 697.

13. The word *perfect* as used in this scripture comes from the Greek word *telios*. Some have suggested this might be translated as "finished" or "completed," resulting in a connotation other than moral perfection—perhaps meaning a complete or mature saint. While this might be one interpretation, the scripture does not preclude a reference to moral perfection. In fact, when read in context, this passage seems to *require* moral perfection. It specifically delineates the type of completeness or perfection to which it is referring when it makes the comparison, "*even as your Father which is in Heaven is perfect*" (emphasis added). God is not perfect like a mature saint or in a relative sense. He is absolutely perfect. Furthermore, the corollary passage to Matthew 5:48 as found in the Book of Mormon was not originally in Greek, but rather reformed Egyptian, yet the key word is still translated "perfect." If Joseph had felt inspired to change the word or meaning, he could have easily done so. This is particularly true, since he must have focused on such verse as evidenced by the changing of a few words, to read: "even as I or your Father who is in heaven is perfect" (3 Nephi 12:48). Again, the standard of perfection was God the Father and, in addition, His glorified Son. It was not man or any mortal attribute. This Book of Mormon passage only strengthens the argument that God was inviting us to partake of godly perfection, not some mortal or diluted substitute. (For a further discussion of this point, see Welch, *Sermon at the Temple and the Sermon on the Mount*, 57–62.)

14. Joseph F. Smith, *Gospel Doctrine* 18.

15. *Discourses of Brigham Young*, 20; emphasis added.

16. Lewis, *Mere Christianity*, 176–77; emphasis added.

17. Lewis, *Joyful Christian*, 197; emphasis added.

18. Drummond, *Natural Law in the Spiritual World*, quoted in Smith, *Teachings of the Prophet Joseph Smith*, 346, footnote 3.

19. Clark and Thomas, *Out of the Best Books*, 1:463. C. S. Lewis spoke of this germ as the divine "Fire" that quivers in every soul:

> *That we, though small, might quiver with Fire's same*
> *Substantial form as Thou—not reflect merely*
> *Like lunar angels back to Thee cold flame.*
> *Gods are we, Thou hast said; and we pay dearly.*

("Scazons," in Wain, *Everyman's Book of English Verse*, 614)

20. Snow, *Biography and Family Record of Lorenzo Snow*, 10.

21. Ibid., 46. The ancient Askew Manuscript was explicit about the possibilities of those who keep the law. "There are many mansions, many regions, degrees, worlds, spaces and heavens, but all have but one law. If you keep that law, *you, too, can become creators of worlds*" (quoted in Nibley, *Old Testament and Related Studies,* 142; emphasis added).

22. Snow, *Teachings of Lorenzo Snow,* 8–9.

23. Snow, *Biography and Family Record of Lorenzo Snow,* 335; emphasis added.

24. Packer, *Let Not Your Heart Be Troubled,* 289.

25. *Journal of Discourses,* 24:3.

26. "Gospel of Philip," 145.

27. Taylor, *Mediation and Atonement,* 165.

28. Milton, *Paradise Lost,* 91.

29. Ibid., 146–47.

30. Lewis, *Quotable Lewis,* 308.

31. Ibid., 525.

32. Smith, *Lectures on Faith,* 79; emphasis added.

33. Ibid., 60.

34. Roberts, *"Mormon" Doctrine of Deity,* 33–34.

35. Ibid., 35.

36. Lewis, *Mere Christianity,* 175.

37. Quoted by Hugh B. Brown, in Conference Report, Apr. 1967, 50. Robert Browning likewise knew the perfecting process continues beyond the grave:

> *But, I need, now as then,*
> *Thee, God, who moldest men; . . .*
> *So, take and use Thy work:*
> *Amend what flaws may lurk,*
> *What strain o' the stuff, what warpings past the aim!*
> *My times be in Thy hand!*
> *Perfect the cup as planned!*
> *Let age approve of youth, and death complete the same!*
> (Clark and Thomas, *Out of the Best Books,* 1:466)

38. Smith, *Teachings of the Prophet Joseph Smith,* 348.

39. Smith, "The Origin of Man," 81.

40. Snow, "Devotion to Divine Inspiration," 658–59; emphasis added. Brigham Young likewise promised that those who keep "their first and second estate" and are "worthy to be crowned Gods . . . will be ordained to organize matter" (*Journal of Discourses,* 15:137). C. S. Lewis concurred, "Christ has risen, and so we shall rise. St. Peter for a few seconds walked on the water, and the day will come when there will be a remade universe, infinitely obedient to the will of glorified and obedient men,

when we can do all things, when we shall be those gods that we are described as being in Scripture" (Lewis, *Grand Miracle*, 62).

41. Lewis, *Joyful Christian*, 77–78.
42. McConkie, *Promised Messiah*, 133.
43. Taylor, *Mediation and Atonement*, 140–41.
44. *Journal of Discourses*, 3:93.

CHAPTER 22

THE BLESSING OF FREEDOM

—∞∞—

WHAT IS FREEDOM?

Nephi spoke of yet another consequence, another blessing, that flows from the seemingly endless spring of the atoning well: "Because that they are redeemed from the fall they have become free forever" (2 Nephi 2:26). Elder James E. Talmage understood that without the Atonement, there could be no freedom: "We proclaim the atonement wrought by Jesus Christ . . . is to all people; it is the message of deliverance from sin and its sorrow, the decree of liberty, the charter of freedom."[1] As with each of the other blessings of the Atonement, this one does not stand alone. It complements, supplements, and overlaps others.

The power to become like God, the crowning blessing of the Atonement, is integrally related to the power to be free, for in truth, the freest of all beings is God himself. President David O. McKay noted that "God could not make men like himself without making them free." He then quoted Dr. Iverach, a Scottish philosopher, who shared this additional insight: "It is a greater manifestation of divine power to make beings that can make themselves than to make beings that cannot, for the former are men and the latter are puppets, and puppets after all are only things."[2]

If the Atonement makes us free, we might appropriately ask, "What does it mean to be free?" To be free is to be like God. Gods are the freest of all beings because "all things are subject unto them . . . [and] they have all power" (D&C 132:20). They "act for themselves" rather than being "acted upon" (2 Nephi 2:26). That is what Alma was trying to tell us about Adam and Eve, that in some things they became "as gods." Why? Because they knew "good from evil" and were "placed in a state to act according to their wills and pleasures" (Alma 12:31).

The lives of gods are driven internally, rather than externally. Their freedom springs from their power to act according to their will without restraint from an outside source. There is no external force that controls their destiny, no spiritual or physical limitation that restricts their desired expression. If they desire to travel at the speed of thought, it seems they can. If they want to comprehend every thought of every living creature, they may (perhaps they automatically do). Gods act, rather than being acted upon. They control every element in every sphere. They are not subject to disease or inclement weather. To the contrary, all forms of life, even the elements themselves, yield in homage to the gods. The scriptures reveal that "all things are subject unto them" and, therefore, they are "above all" (D&C 132:20). Gods do not live oblivious of laws, but through obedience have mastered the laws so that they might use them to accomplish their purposes.

Freedom is achieved through a step-by-step process of obedient compliance to God's will. Consequently the more we become like God, the freer we become. Freedom and godhood are parallel paths; in fact they are the same road.

GOD MAKES MEN FREE

Man could never enjoy the full powers of agency without the intervention of God. Samuel told the people of Zarahemla, "Ye are free; ye are permitted to act for yourselves," and then he added, "He [God] hath made you free" (Helaman 14:30). The latter phrase is one utilized by the prophets on both hemispheres throughout the ages. King Benjamin taught, "Under this head [Christ] ye are made free." He then makes it clear that there is no alternative source of freedom: "And there is no other head whereby ye can be made free" (Mosiah 5:8). The Savior taught that true freedom comes "if the Son . . . shall make you free" (John 8:36). Paul urged the saints of Galatia to retain their "liberty wherewith Christ hath made us free" (Galatians 5:1). And in the latter days the Lord has declared without equivocation, "I, the Lord God, make you free, therefore ye are free indeed" (D&C 98:8; see also D&C 88:86). John Donne envisioned this relationship between Christ and freedom:

> *Take me to you [Christ], imprison me, for I,*
> *Except you enthrall me, never shall be free.*[3]

Freedom is described as the power or agency to act for oneself. Repeatedly the Lord revealed the source of such agency. Lehi taught, "The Lord God gave unto man that he should act for himself" (2 Nephi 2:16). In latter days similar scriptural language was used: "I gave unto him that he should be an agent unto himself" (D&C 29:35; see also Moses 4:3).

THE FOUR COMPONENTS OF FREEDOM

But how does God endow us with agency, and what part does the Atonement play in making us free? This is best understood by dissecting freedom into its four principal components, namely the need for an intelligent being, a knowledge of good and evil, the availability of choices, and the power to execute or carry out such choices.

First is the need for an intelligent being. If freedom is being able to act for ourselves and "not to be acted upon" (2 Nephi 2:26), as suggested by Lehi, then at some point we must have the innate capacity to make decisions upon which our actions are predicated. Simply stated, there can be no freedom without a decision maker, an intelligent being. Man is a conscious, thinking entity, thus fulfilling the first requirement for freedom.

Second is the need for a knowledge of good and evil. This is an indispensable element of freedom. President Joseph F. Smith wrote: "No man is or can be made free without possessing a knowledge of the truth and obeying the same."[4] Moses recorded, "It is given unto them to know good from evil; wherefore they are agents unto themselves" (Moses 6:56). The causal relationship between freedom on one hand and a knowledge of good and evil on the other is a common theme addressed by many of the ancient prophets. One such prophet, Samuel the Lamanite, declared that the people were free because God "hath given unto you that ye might know good from evil" (Helaman 14:31; see also 2 Nephi 2:18, 23; Alma 12:31–32).

Man's initial knowledge of good and evil was triggered at the time of the Fall. The Lord said, "Behold, the man is become as one of us, to know good and evil" (Genesis 3:22). Eve spoke that truth when she said, "Were it not for our transgression we . . . never should have known good and evil" (Moses 5:11). Absent that grant of knowledge, Adam and Eve would have been confined to a state of innocence.

At first glance, one might be led to believe that the Fall, independent of Christ's atonement, was the deliverer of that knowledge sufficient to make man free. In truth, it was a vital link, but it was only the beginning—the gateway to knowledge. The Fall opened doors that had previously been sealed and eyes that had previously been shut. As to Adam and Eve, the scriptures reveal that "the eyes of them both were opened" (Genesis 3:7). This was essential, but it was only the commencement, not the end of the road. With increased knowledge comes the opportunity for increased freedom. This was the Savior's testimony to the scribes and Pharisees: "Know the truth, and the truth shall make you free" (John 8:32). Once again these hypocrites failed to grasp his message. They retorted, "We . . . were never in bondage to any man" (John 8:33). How wrong they were. They had secular knowledge, but not the spiritual truth that makes a man free. They were masters at missing the point. Once again they were tuned to the wrong channel, and so the Savior spoke with unmistakable clarity, "If the Son therefore shall make you free, ye shall be free indeed" (John 8:36). That is the essence of freedom, to know the Savior and obey his truths. As we do so, we become free from prejudice, falsehood, sin, contention, and every other injurious practice or evil nature known to man.

While the Fall opened the gate to the road of knowledge, it was the Atonement that provided the vehicle to proceed. Through the Atonement we are cleansed in the waters of baptism, making us eligible for the gift of the Holy Ghost. It is such a gift that "will guide you into all truth" (John 16:13). As we come to know the Savior and his truths we enlarge our capacity for freedom. This is so because knowledge is power; and power, in its consummate expression is godhood; and godhood is the quintessence of freedom.

The third element of freedom is the availability of choices. President David O. McKay observed: "Only to the human being did the Creator say: ' . . . thou mayest choose for thyself, for it is given unto thee . . . ' (Moses 3:17). As God intended man to become as he, it was necessary that He should first make him free."⁵ Were it not for the Atonement, there would have been no choice between eternal life and eternal damnation. The Fall would have opened the gate to one road and one road only. Our "flesh must have laid down to rot and to crumble to its mother earth, to rise no more. . . . Our spirits must become subject to . . . the devil, to rise no more" (2 Nephi 9:7–8)—a bleak picture, to say the least. Without the Atonement everyone would be compelled to participate in this no-option program. The Fall, without the Atonement, would lead us to a downhill plunge from which there was no escape. Jacob explained this troubling prospect and then rejoiced, "O how great the goodness of our God, who prepareth a way for our escape from the grasp of this awful monster; yea, that monster, death and hell, which I call the death of the body, and also the death of the spirit" (2 Nephi 9:10). Jacob went on to say that "because of the way of deliverance of our God" that "hell must deliver up its captive spirits, and the grave must deliver up its captive bodies" (2 Nephi 9:11–12).

The Atonement is the means of deliverance, the means of

freeing our bodies from the grave and our spirits from hell, of offering another road, another choice, another option. Elder McConkie recorded in verse that same truth:

I believe in Christ; he ransoms me.
From Satan's grasp he sets me free.[6]

Lehi taught that because men "are redeemed from the fall they have become free forever, . . . free to choose liberty and eternal life, through the great Mediator of all men, or to choose captivity and death" (2 Nephi 2:26–27). Lehi then pled with his sons to "look to the great Mediator . . . and choose eternal life"; otherwise, he warned, the devil will have "power to captivate" you and "reign over you" in his kingdom (2 Nephi 2:28, 29).

The message is clear. We can accept the Atonement, a choice that leads to eternal life (the ultimate in freedom); or we can choose the way of the Evil One, a choice that leads to destruction, chains, and captivity (the ultimate in bondage). As we choose the Lord, he gives us more rope; as we choose Satan, he tightens the noose until we are in his grasp. Charles Dickens vividly illustrated this truth. In Dickens' *A Christmas Carol*, Scrooge, seeing his ghost-like partner bound with chains, inquired, "You are fettered. . . . Tell me why?" Jacob Marley's answer was sobering: "I wear the chain I forged in life. . . . I made it link by link, and yard by yard; I girded it on of my own free will, and of my own free will I wore it."[7]

The prophet Jacob concluded his beautiful discourse on the Atonement by encouraging his people to "cheer up." After all, he explained, "Ye are free to act for yourselves—to choose the way of everlasting death or the way of eternal life" (2 Nephi 10:23). That freedom of choice comes through the Atonement of Jesus Christ. That is what Lehi taught: "The Lord God gave unto man that he should act for himself. Wherefore, man could not act for himself save it should be that he was enticed by the one or the other" (2 Nephi 2:16).

One element is yet lacking for a fulness of freedom. It is the power to execute or to carry out the choices before us. We may have knowledge of good and evil; we may even have choices placed before us; but unless we have power to execute, the power to fulfill, then our freedom is but a facade. We are somewhat like an astronomer who with his naked eye looks into the starry sky with the intent of spotting Neptune. However long he scans the heavens, however intent his gaze may be, he will look in vain. Now give him a telescope and what vision he beholds! The issue is not knowledge, for he knows with precision the celestial siting. The issue is not choice, for he has the option to look or not to look without obstruction. The issue is simply power—the power to see. God has a vast inventory of spiritual telescopes, hearing aids, time capsules, and power-enhancing tools to enrich our lives and make us free to see and hear and do without restraint.

All men have some power from God. The Lord declared, "Men should be anxiously engaged in a good cause, and do many things of their own free will, and bring to pass much righteousness; for the power is in them, wherein they are agents unto themselves" (D&C 58:27–28). How can we enhance this power? History has long confirmed that knowledge is the precursor of power. It is knowledge that has expanded space, conquered disease, hastened the speed of travel, and revolutionized our means of communication. God does not belittle these powers acquired from secular learning; he encourages such pursuits. He invites our mastery "of things both in heaven and in the earth" (D&C 88:79) and our study "out of the best books" (D&C 88:118). He offers inspiration to assist us in these pursuits.

While God is certainly a proponent of earthly knowledge, he also wants us to know that powers of a higher source flow from the acquisition of spiritual truths. It is this spiritual power that parted the Red Sea, that caused the sun to "stand still," rivers to change their course, and mountains to flee (Exodus 14:21–29; Joshua 10:12–14; Moses 7:13). This unseen force has calmed the angry sea, quelled the reckless storm, compelled the drought-stricken skies to disgorge their hidden pearls of dew, and, in short, controlled, directed, and governed every native element of the universe (Matthew 8:23–27; 1 Kings 18:41–46; Moses 7:13–14).

Where science has faltered, even fallen short, this divine power has taken up the slack and, when it was God's will, healed those who could find no temporal relief. This power is of such magnitude that it has penetrated and softened even the hearts of those who were known to be "a wild and a hardened and a ferocious people" (Alma 17:14).

Both earthly and spiritual power (which ultimately are but one power) constitute the power of godhood, for gods "have *all* power" (D&C 132:20; emphasis added). With each new power acquired, we develop greater control not only of the elements but of our destiny. In this way, we become the driver, not the driven—the cause rather than the effect. We act for ourselves rather than being "acted upon" (2 Nephi 2:26); and in this manner we become free.

While knowledge is essential to the acquisition of power, there is yet another ingredient, often ignored, and sometimes even ridiculed, that is a prerequisite to receiving the "higher" powers—those powers necessary to enjoy a fulness of freedom. It is obedience.

OBEDIENCE—A KEY TO FREEDOM

Some might contend that freedom comes when there are no laws or restraints. They contend that freedom in its purest form is the right to do anything, anytime, anywhere, without consequence. About twenty-five hundred years ago Nephi prophesied of those misguided souls who would teach, "Eat, drink, and be merry, for tomorrow we die; and it shall be well with us" (2 Nephi 28:7; see also Mormon 8:31). Does it not seem ironic that such a philosophy is authored by the master slave himself? It was he who was cast out of heaven, who was deprived of a body, who will be bound a thousand years, and who will ultimately be banished to outer darkness. The freedom he promises is illusory; it is a mirage on the desert; it is the very condition that has always eluded his grasp. It was the same lie promulgated by Cain after he slew his brother Abel: "I am free," he said (Moses 5:33). In truth, he was never in more bondage. He was the servant, even the slave of sin.

The scriptures describe again and again the true state of those who adopt this worldly philosophy. They, too, become the slaves of sin, bound with everlasting chains and subject to captivity, death, and hell, hardly a blissful state of freedom (2 Nephi 1:13; Alma 12:11).

How then does the Lord propose to make us free? The answer is obedience. In fact, Brigham Young indicated there is no other way: "In rendering . . . strict obedience, are we made slaves? No, *it is the only way on the face of the earth* for you and me to become free."[8]

Contrary to the belief of many, obedience is not the antithesis of freedom, but the foundation of it. Charles Kingsley distinguished between the world's view of freedom and the Lord's: "There are two freedoms, the false where one is free to do what he likes, and the true where he is free to do what he ought."[9] Lehi was speaking of the latter when counseling his sons, Laman and Lemuel: "Hearken unto his great commandments" (2 Nephi 2:28), he said—and if you do, the devil will have no power to "reign over you" (2 Nephi 2:29). The Doctrine and Covenants tells us the same thing: "The law [or it might have said, the commandments] also maketh you free" (D&C 98:8). Jacob told his people, "Ye are free to act for yourselves" (2 Nephi 10:23). Then he taught them the means, not only for maintaining their freedom, but enhancing it: "Reconcile yourselves to the will of God" (2 Nephi 10:24). The Lord announced that he had made Adam "an agent unto himself" and then shared the divine sequel to maintaining and developing such agency: "And I gave unto him commandment[s]" (D&C 29:35). In other words, if there were no commandments and no obedience to them, man would soon see his newly acquired agency in irreversible decline.

Commandments are no more restrictive to the spiritual man than street signs are to the motorist. Neither prohibits our progress; to the contrary, they enhance it by serving as guideposts or directional signs to help us find and reach our destination. The Lord spoke to the Prophet Joseph of "a new commandment," and then added, "Or, in other words, I give unto you *directions* how you may act before me, that it may turn to you for your salvation" (D&C 82:8–9; emphasis added). The great movie producer, Cecil B. De Mille, famous for *The Ten Commandments,* understood the relationship between law and freedom:

"We are too inclined to think of law as something merely restrictive . . . something hemming us in. We sometimes think of law as the opposite of liberty. But that is a false conception. . . . God does not contradict himself. He did not create man and then, as an afterthought, impose upon him a set of arbitrary, irritating, restrictive rules. *He made man free—and then gave him the commandments to keep him free.* We cannot break the Ten Commandments. We can only break ourselves against them—*or else, by keeping them, rise through them to the fulness of freedom under God.*"[10]

There are a number of spiritual truths that must seem like irreconcilable ironies to the secular world—humility breeds strength, faith nurtures vision, and obedience brings freedom. There is a simple test, however, by which we can learn the veracity of these spiritual precepts for ourselves. The Lord revealed it. "If any man will do his will, he shall know of the doctrine, whether it be of God, or whether I speak of myself" (John 7:17). Simply put, if we are obedient to God's will, we will experience newfound freedoms in our life; if we are disobedient, freedom will be the star we can never reach.

As discussed, freedom requires a knowledge of good and evil, the availability of choices, and the power to execute or carry them out. Each of these is enhanced by obedience to God's will.

As we obey God's laws we receive increased knowledge of God's plan, and with increased knowledge comes increased capacity for freedom. Isaiah taught that as we hearken unto the Lord we receive "precept upon precept; line upon line" (Isaiah 28:10). The promise made to those who obey the Word of Wisdom is that they "shall find wisdom and great treasures of knowledge" (D&C 89:19). The Lord made it clear that the acquisition of knowledge was not solely an intellectual pursuit, for he said, "He that keepeth his commandments receiveth truth and light, until he is glorified in truth and knoweth all things" (D&C 93:28; see also D&C 93:39). Obedience brings that kind of knowledge that is indispensable for godly freedom. That is why the Lord promised that "if a person gains more knowledge and intelligence in this life through his diligence and obedience than another, he will have so much the advantage in the world to come" (D&C 130:19). Obedience unlocks the doors of knowledge; knowledge is a prerequisite of godhood; and godhood is the apogee of freedom.

Obedience also broadens the list of our choices. If we are not obedient we have no option to be baptized, no option to receive the priesthood, no option to be endowed or sealed in the temple, all of which are necessary in our transformation into the freest of all beings, namely, gods.

But obedience does even more. It also generates power, another vital link to freedom. A number of years ago at a youth conference I called a young man forward and invited him to sit on the piano bench. I took from my wallet a number of crisp twenty dollar bills and offered them to him if he would play any song in the hymn book he desired. As he looked at the crisp twenty dollar bills and then the piano, he became frustrated. "I can't play," he said. "Why not?" I responded. "You have the music, the piano, the fingers, seemingly all the ingredients necessary to play." "But I don't know how!" he answered. He had everything he needed except for one thing—the power to execute, which is an indispensable element of freedom. Power comes by obedience. We gain power to play the piano as we obey the law of practicing. We gain mastery over a language as we learn and follow the rules of linguistics. We gain power over the elements as we obey the laws of God. That is why the Lord said to the obedient, "Then shall they be gods, because they have all power." Then he divulged the secret to that achievement, "Except ye abide my law ye cannot attain to this glory" (D&C 132:20, 21). Obedience is one of the prime keys that unlock the power of godhood, bringing freedom in its fullest and grandest measure. Obedience is not an enemy of freedom; to the contrary, it is freedom's best friend.

The Lord so observed: "Hear my voice and follow me, and you shall be a free people" (D&C 38:22). The Prophet Joseph identified the link between the Atonement, godhood, and obedience in the third article of faith: "We believe that through the Atonement of Christ, all mankind may be saved, by obedience to the laws and ordinances of the Gospel" (see also D&C 138:4).

The end product of an obedient life is power, not the scepter-swaying power of the dictator, not the emotionally charged power of the demagogue, not the irreverent, decadent power of the charlatan, but the pure, benevolent power of a god. Ironically, if we want that power we must follow the commandments with exactness. As to the disobedient, the Lord prophesied of their predicament: "Where I am they cannot come, for they have *no power*" (D&C 29:29; emphasis added).

Obedience to the laws and ordinances of the gospel brings increased knowledge, a multiplicity of choices, and an enhanced power to execute, all of which result in added freedom. It is the Atonement, however, that gives substance and meaning to those laws and ordinances. Of what vitality would the principles of faith and repentance be without the Savior's mission? What cleansing power would the baptismal waters bestow if there were no Atonement? What healing powers would the sacrament have if there were no redemption? What would the longevity of the sealing powers be if the Savior had never condescended? Obedience to these ordinances and laws without the Atonement would be an empty gesture.

The Atonement of Jesus Christ opened the floodgates of spiritual knowledge through baptism and the gift of the Holy Ghost. It provides a range of choices from captivity and the devil on one hand, to eternal life and godhood on the other. It unleashes power upon power to those humble saints who keep the laws and ordinances of the gospel, each of which finds its sustaining strength in the atoning sacrifice. The Atonement of Jesus Christ is the nurturing force for each of those elements that fosters freedom.

Brigham Young taught, "The difference between the righteous and the sinner, eternal life or death, happiness or misery, is this, to those who are exalted there are no bounds or limits to their privileges."[11] Now that is freedom! Lehi understood this glorious truth. He declared that, because of Christ's redemption, men would "become free forever" (2 Nephi 2:26).

NOTES

1. Talmage, *Essential James E. Talmage,* 89.
2. McKay, "Whither Shall We Go?", 3.
3. Donne, "Batter My Heart," in Untermeyer, *Treasury of Great Poems,* 367.
4. Smith, *Gospel Doctrine,* 211.
5. Conference Report, Oct. 1963, 5.
6. McConkie, "I Believe in Christ," in *Hymns,* no. 134.
7. Dickens, *Christmas Stories,* 28.
8. *Journal of Discourses,* 18:246; emphasis added.
9. In Wallis, *Treasure Chest,* 47.
10. Quoted by Richard L. Evans, Conference Report, Oct. 1959, 127; emphasis added.
11. Young, *Discourses of Brigham Young,* 63.

CHAPTER 23

THE BLESSING OF GRACE

———❧———

THE POWER TO EXALT US

One might appropriately wonder how the Atonement can be effective in the lives of mortals. Even though we seek to be worthy and to repent of our sins, in the end we are all, in one way or another, unprofitable servants (see Mosiah 2:21). Given our weakness and our recurring failings, how are we able to receive the many blessings of the Atonement in our lives? How are we able to receive of its cleansing powers, or peace, or succor, or freedom? How does the perfection and exaltation of an imperfect being come about? Nephi gave the answer: "We know that it is by grace that we are saved, after all we can do" (2 Nephi 25:23). This might have read, "We know that it is by grace that we are *exalted,* after all we can do." Some have misunderstood this scripture, supposing that the Atonement provides the cleansing power, while our works alone provide the perfecting power; thus, working hand in hand, exaltation is achieved. But such an interpretation is not correct. It is true that the Atonement provides the cleansing power. It is also true that works are a necessary ingredient of the perfecting process. But without the Atonement, without grace, without the power of Christ, all the works in the world would fall far short of perfecting even one human being. Works

263

must be coupled with grace both to perfect and to cleanse a person unto exaltation. In other words, grace is not only necessary to cleanse us, but also to perfect us.

The LDS Bible Dictionary defines grace as a "divine means of help or strength" made possible through the Atonement. It then adds that grace is a means of "strength and assistance to do good works that [men] otherwise would not be able to maintain if left to their own means." And finally it asserts that grace is "an enabling power" necessary to lift men above their weaknesses and shortcomings, so that they might "lay hold on eternal life and exaltation after they have expended their own best efforts."[1] In essence, grace is a gift of divine power, made possible by the Atonement, that can transform a mere mortal with all his failings into a god with all his strengths—provided we have done "all we can do" (2 Nephi 25:23). That is exactly what Peter taught: "[Christ's] divine power hath given unto us *all things* that pertain unto life *and godliness*" (2 Peter 1:3; emphasis added).

The divine principle to be learned is this: that God will use his heavenly powers to exalt us, but only if we have done all within our power to accomplish that end. The brother of Jared learned this principle when he petitioned the Lord to light the Jaredite barges. The Lord could have instantaneously given him the solution. Instead, he responded: "What will ye that I should do that ye may have light in your vessels?" (Ether 2:23). With that divine challenge the brother of Jared devised and implemented an ingenious plan—he melted out of rock sixteen transparent stones that he took to the Lord, requesting the Lord to touch them, "that they may shine forth in darkness" (Ether 3:4). When the brother of Jared had done his best, the door to heavenly powers swung wide open.

The raising of Lazarus from the dead dramatically illustrates this same celestial law. The Savior approached the grave or cave where Lazarus had lain for four days. He instructed those who were nearby to remove the stone cover. Then in a loud voice he cried out, "Lazarus, come forth" (John 11:43), and the scriptures record that "he that was dead came forth, bound hand and foot with graveclothes: and his face was bound about with a napkin" (John 11:44). At that point Jesus commanded the onlookers to unbind him. One might ask, "Why didn't Jesus remove the stone with a show of power? Why didn't Jesus unwrap the revived corpse?" His response was a demonstration of the divine law of economy, namely, that we must do all we can, and when we have reached our limits, when we have asserted all our mental, moral, and spiritual energies, then the powers of heaven will intervene. Man could remove the stone and unwrap the corpse, so he must do it, but only the power of God could call the dead to life. Accordingly, it was only the latter event that was divinely dictated. It is this same principle that governs our exaltation.

There are certain occasions when our best efforts, as extraordinary as they may be, are simply inadequate. It is not simply a function of time and effort (meaning, if we had enough time and were willing to put forth the effort, we would eventually become gods); it is more than that. It is also a matter of capacity. Can we in and of ourselves, unaided by any artificial means, fly through the air? We may have the compelling urge to do so. We may jump off the cliff and attempt the enterprise with an unrelenting determination; we may have biceps of extraordinary proportion; we may rotate our arms with astounding speed; we may have a Ph.D. in aerodynamics—but we will fall just the same. If we desire to travel as God does, some external power must transform our physical body to one of celestial material.

Can we of our own accord acquire the wisdom of God? What if in the course of eternity we were to read every book, master every mathematical equation, and conquer every language? Would we then be God's intellectual equal? The answer is a resounding no! We would still be restricted to a finite mind, to a limited number of thoughts at a given moment. The Lord made reference to this disparity: "For my thoughts are not your thoughts, neither are your ways my ways. . . . For as the heavens are higher than the earth, so are my ways higher than your ways, and my thoughts than your thoughts" (Isaiah 55:8–9). King Benjamin echoed the same sentiments: "Believe that man doth not comprehend all the things which the Lord can comprehend" (Mosiah 4:9). Sometime, somehow, somewhere, we must be "added upon." We must receive a divine endowment to be able to entertain multiple, even infinite thoughts, concurrently. Only then can our mind begin to become like God's.

We cannot become like God without such an endowment—in essence, a manifestation of grace. And that grace comes because of the Atonement of Jesus Christ. That was the promise Enoch understood and expressed to God: "Thou hast made me, and given unto me a right to thy throne, and not of myself, but through thine own grace" (Moses 7:59).

Our embrace of the Atonement opens up a new cache of spiritual powers that "add upon" and endow man with godly traits that he cannot generate from internal sources alone. It is then that the ultimate purpose of the Atonement is achieved—we become both "at one" with God (the redemptive quality) and "at one" like God (the exalting quality). That was the promise of John to the "sons of God," that "when he shall appear, *we shall be like him*" (1 John 3:2; emphasis added), *not just with him.*

Certain powers of the Atonement cleanse us and thus make us worthy to stand in God's presence and be at one with him. Such cleansing powers purge our souls and leave us innocent (meaning without sin), but innocence is not perfection. Innocence is the *entrance* to the straight and narrow path; perfection is the *destination.* A newborn baby is pure and innocent, but it is certainly not perfect in the sense of possessing all the powers of godliness. The Savior was pure and innocent at birth, but even he grew from grace to grace until he achieved the fulness of godhood. The scriptures record that the Savior "received not of the fulness at first, but continued from grace to grace, until he received a fulness" (D&C 93:13). Joseph F. Smith spoke of Christ's progressive journey: "Even Christ himself was not perfect at first; he . . . received not a fulness at the first, but increased in faith, knowledge, understanding and grace until he received a fulness."[2]

It is by grace that those enabling, endowing, exalting powers of the Atonement, provided measure upon measure and line upon line, transform a man into a god. The Savior bore record of this. He admonished us to listen to John's message on grace, so that we might come unto the Father in his name "and in due time receive of his fulness" (D&C 93:19). He then described how the fulness is achieved for each of us: "If you keep my commandments you shall receive of his fulness, and be glorified in me as I am in the Father; therefore, I say unto you, you shall receive grace for grace" (D&C 93:20). Line upon line, measure upon measure, grace upon grace we become one, as he and the Father are one. That is exactly what the Prophet Joseph taught: "You have got to learn how to be Gods yourselves, . . . the same as all Gods have done before you, namely, by going from one small degree to another, and from a small capacity to a great one; from grace to grace, from exaltation to exaltation, until you . . . are able to dwell in everlasting burnings, and to sit in glory, as do those who sit enthroned in everlasting power."[3]

HOW DOES A MORTAL RECEIVE GRACE?

But how is this grace transferred to us? How does God transmit divine qualities and powers to a mere mortal? The medium for the infusion of godlike powers and enabling traits from a divine being to an ordinary man is the Holy Ghost. In a classic statement, Elder Parley P. Pratt describes its refining and perfecting power: "The gift of the Holy Ghost . . . quickens all the intellectual faculties, increases, enlarges, expands, and purifies all the natural passions and affections, and adapts them, by the gift of wisdom, to their lawful use. It inspires, develops, cultivates, and matures all the fine-toned sympathies, joys, tastes, kindred feelings, and affections of our nature. It inspires virtue, kindness, goodness, tenderness, gentleness, and charity. It develops beauty of person, form, and features. It tends to health, vigor, animation, and social feeling. It invigorates all the faculties of the physical and intellectual man. It strengthens and gives tone to the nerves. In short, it is, as it were, marrow to the bone, joy to the heart, light to the eyes, music to the ears, and life to the whole being."[4]

All of these divine qualities, so eloquently expressed by Elder Pratt, are scripturally labeled "spiritual gifts" or "gifts of the Spirit."

WHAT ARE THE GIFTS OF THE SPIRIT?

Gifts of the Spirit are in fact endowments of godly traits; and thus, as we acquire these gifts, we become partakers of the divine nature. Each of these gifts is a manifestation of some celestial quality. Through the medium of the Holy Ghost, each such gift may be bestowed upon an imperfect being and thus aid him in his pursuit of godhood. Elder Orson Pratt taught that these gifts were not only given to assist in the conversion of the gentiles—but also for the perfecting of the Saints:

"It is altogether a mistaken idea to suppose that these gifts were merely given for the convincing of unbelievers. Paul says expressly, that the gifts which were given by our Lord after His ascension were intended for other purposes. . . . These, together with numerous other gifts, were given, not merely to establish the truth of Christianity, but as Paul says, 'For the perfecting of the Saints, for the work of the ministry, for the edifying of the body of Christ.' . . .

"By these declarations we discover the objects which the Lord has in view, by giving gifts unto men. One object is declared to be *'for the perfecting of the Saints. . . . ' The only plan which Jesus has devised for the accomplishment of this great object, is through the medium of the spiritual gifts. When the supernatural gifts of the Spirit cease, the Saints cease to be perfected,* therefore they can have no hopes of obtaining a perfect salvation. . . .

"Has Jesus anywhere in His word told us that His plan of perfecting the Saints should cease, and that mankind would introduce a better one? If not, why then should we not prefer our Savior's plan in preference to all others? Why do away [with] the powers and gifts of the Holy Ghost, which were intended, not merely for the convincing of unbelievers, but for the perfecting of believers? In every nation and age, where believers exist, there the gifts must exist to perfect them, otherwise they would be altogether unprepared for the reception of the still greater powers and glories of the eternal world. If there were no unbelievers on the earth, still there would be the same necessity for the miraculous gifts that there was among early Christians; *for if the whole world were believers in Christ they could not possibly be perfected without these gifts.*"[5]

The gifts of the Spirit are discussed at length in 1 Corinthians 12–14, Doctrine and Covenants 46, and Moroni 10. Evidently they are of such import that God is anxious for this message to be taught with repetition in each of the various works of holy writ. The prophets made it clear that such gifts in their fulness are restricted to members of the Church. Paul commenced his discourse on the gifts by saying, "Now concerning spiritual gifts, brethren, I would not have you ignorant" (1 Corinthians 12:1). Paul was addressing this letter to the saints at Corinth and hence the reference to "brethren." The chapter heading supports this conclusion: "Spiritual gifts are present among the saints" (1 Corinthians 12). Doctrine and Covenants 46 teaches the same principle. It begins, "Hearken, O ye people of my church" (D&C 46:1). This section reveals that the gifts are for those who "keep all my commandments" (D&C 46:9) and then adds this comforting postscript, "and him that seeketh so to do" (D&C 46:9). The Savior also informs us that these gifts are *given unto the church*" (D&C 46:10; emphasis added). Consistent with this understanding, the bishop is then described as the one who is given the power of discernment over all the gifts so as to avoid confusion among those who falsely lay claim to these spiritual treasures. Consistent with these scriptural accounts, Moroni confirms that these sacred gifts are only "dispensed to the faithful" (Moroni 10, chapter heading), again referring to active, devoted members of the Church. All this seems reasonable because these gifts "are given by the manifestations of the Spirit" (Moroni 10:8), meaning the Holy Ghost. That is why they are called gifts of the Spirit, because their origin, sustaining influence, and enabling qualities all emanate from the Holy Ghost.

Since the gift of the Holy Ghost is given only to members of the Church, it follows that the fruits and gifts of this Spirit are given in their fulness only to Church members. Elder Bruce R. McConkie taught this same principle: "Men must receive the gift of the Holy Ghost before that member of the Godhead will take up his abode with them and begin the supernal process of distributing his gifts to them. . . . Thus the gifts of the Spirit are for believing, faithful, righteous people; they are reserved for the saints of God."[6]

This is not to suggest that others do not have faith to be healed, or wisdom or love, for those qualities can be developed to some extent by the light of Christ, which illuminates every soul, and likewise by those manifestations of the Holy Ghost that may temporarily descend upon an unbaptized person. There are many good and honorable people outside Christ's church who demonstrate godlike virtues. But faith in its fullest and most enduring measure, that faith that moves mountains, stops the mouths of lions and quenches the violence of fire; that wisdom that duplicates the mind and will of the Lord; and that charity that resembles the pure love of Christ—these and all other divine attributes in their grandest and consummate expression, in their full and unrestricted godlike proportions, come only through the gift of the Holy Ghost. They come to those who have embraced the Savior and his atoning sacrifice and who have so witnessed by baptism and receipt of the Holy Ghost. To reason otherwise would suggest that we, without the gift of the Holy Ghost, could develop a virtue to absolute perfection, and if one such virtue were developed, then arguably all virtues could be attained in like manner. If such a state existed, we could achieve the status of God without the gift of the Holy Ghost—a spiritual impossibility.

Whether or not the Atonement itself is the source of these spiritual gifts seems not yet to have been revealed in the scriptures, but certainly the availability of these gifts is conditioned on our faith in and demonstrated acceptance of that divine act. Our reception of the Atonement is the key to unlock these gifts and all their enabling powers, for it is the Atonement that purifies us and prepares us to be eligible recipients.

The doctrinal discourses in 1 Corinthians 12–14, Doctrine and Covenants 46, and Moroni 10 each itemize various gifts of the Spirit. They refer to the gift of wisdom, the gift of exceeding great faith, the gift of healing, the gift of charity, the power to work mighty miracles, the gift of tongues, the gift of administration, and others. The enumeration of certain gifts by the prophets was never intended as an exhaustive list but rather as a representative sampling. Elder McConkie taught, "These gifts are infinite in number and endless in their manifestations because God himself is infinite and endless."[7] Certainly divine qualities such as patience, humility, integrity, kindness, and unselfishness, which are unmentioned by the prophets in the foregoing chapters, are also spiritual gifts worthy of pursuit. Elder Marvin J. Ashton described some of these "gifts not so evident but nevertheless real and valuable" as the "gift of listening," the "gift of caring for others," and the "gift of being able to ponder."[8]

A stake president has the responsibility to periodically review the patriarchal blessings issued by the patriarch in his stake. In performing this duty, I discovered that these blessings were filled with gifts not specifically designated by Paul or Moroni. These included, among others, the gift of compassion, the gift of music, and the gift of noncontentiousness. Paul references only certain of the spiritual gifts and then concludes that the greatest of all is the gift of charity: "And now abideth faith, hope, charity, these three; but the greatest of these is charity" (1 Corinthians 13:13). Mormon defines charity as "the pure love of Christ" (Moroni 7:47; see also Moroni 8:17). Such a quality is the quintessence of godhood. No wonder Mormon pleads with us to "pray unto the Father with all the energy of heart, that ye may be filled with this love." Why? "That ye may become the sons of God; that when he shall appear we shall be like him" (Moroni 7:48). That is the whole purpose of life, the prime objective of the Atonement, to help us return to him and become like him. As we acquire the gifts of the Spirit, that gap between man and God is narrowed, for with each gift acquired we advance along the path toward godhood. Is it any wonder that the Lord wants us to pursue these gifts with unrelenting determination?

GIFTS OF THE SPIRIT OVERCOME WEAKNESSES

Benjamin Franklin created a systematic plan whereby he pursued perfection. Although he tried diligently to follow it, he recalled his frequent relapses to old ways, his lack of progress and finally the near resolution "to give up the attempt, and content myself with a faulty character." Such a train of thought reminded him of the man who brought an ax to a blacksmith and "desired to have the whole of its surface as bright as the edge. The smith consented to grind it bright for him if he would turn the wheel; he turned, while the smith pressed the broad face of the ax hard and heavily on the stone, which made the turning of it very fatiguing. The man came every now and then from the wheel to see how the work went on, and at length would take his ax as it was, without farther [sic] grinding. 'No,' said the smith, 'turn on, turn on; we shall have it bright by-and-by; as yet, it is only speckled.' 'Yes,' says the man, *but I think I like a speckled ax best.*'"[9]

Perhaps there are some who have reconciled themselves to a speckled life, who have found it easier to accept a spiritual status quo than exert the required effort to make the whole of their lives bright. No doubt there are some who believe they possess irrevocable weaknesses and shortcomings—spiritual defects that are incurable, tempers that are insurmountable, ill feelings that are irrepressible, or a lack of faith that is unconquerable. Many such good souls may have "plateaued out" spiritually. "It is my nature," they say. But the words of the Lord to Moses echo in our minds again and again, "Who hath made man's mouth?" (Exodus 4:11). Cannot God, the creator of all, fashion, shape, add to, modify and help overcome any weakness of any faithful, humble person? Was that not the promise from the Holy One himself?

President George Q. Cannon spoke of man's shortcomings and the divine solution. He recognized the link between spiritual gifts and godhood. He eloquently and fervently pleaded with the saints to overcome each manifested weakness through the acquisition of a countermanding gift of strength, known as a gift of the Spirit. He spoke as follows:

"No man ought to say, 'Oh, I cannot help this; it is my nature.' He is not justified in it, for the reason that God has promised to give strength to correct these things, and to give gifts that will eradicate them. . . .

"He wants His Saints to be perfected in the truth. For this purpose He gives these gifts, and bestows them upon those who seek after them, in order that they may be a perfect people upon the face of the earth, notwithstanding their many weaknesses, because God has promised to give the gifts that are necessary for their perfection. . . .

"If any of us are imperfect, it is our duty to pray for the gift that will make us perfect. Have I imperfections? I am full of them. What is my duty? To pray to God to give me the gifts that will correct these imperfections. If I am an angry man, it is my duty to pray for charity, which suffereth long and is kind. Am I an envious man? It is my duty to seek for charity, which envieth not. So with all the gifts of the Gospel. They are intended for this purpose."[10]

HOW DO WE ACQUIRE GIFTS OF THE SPIRIT?

If the gifts of the Spirit are the medium by which we perfect ourselves, how can we accelerate our acquisition of such gifts? Paul delivers his discourse on spiritual gifts and then highlights the manner in which they might be obtained: "Covet earnestly the best gifts" (1 Corinthians 12:31). In other words, do not be satisfied with one gift alone (for every member is given at least one gift), but seek all the "best" gifts of the Spirit, and as we do so in an orderly, persistent pursuit, at the same time diligently seeking the other blessings of the Atonement, the Lord will lead us along the divine path of godhood. Elder McConkie acknowledged the absolute necessity of this pursuit: "Faithful persons are expected to seek the gifts of the Spirit with all their hearts."[11] Paul, who was himself striving "for the prize of the high calling of God" (Philippians 3:14), reemphasizes this theme: "Follow after charity, and desire spiritual gifts" (1 Corinthians 14:1). Moroni, speaking directly and candidly to our generation, reiterates the mandate: "And again I would exhort you that ye would come unto Christ, and lay hold upon *every* good gift" (Moroni 10:30; emphasis added). The same counsel was given to the Prophet Joseph for our dispensation: "Seek ye earnestly the best gifts, always remembering for what they are given" (D&C 46:8).

The Lord in his unbounded kindness anxiously seeks to shower these spiritual gifts upon us. It is his way of bestowing upon us some of the attributes of godhood. In some respects these gifts are like a spiritual gold mine at our disposal that remains untapped if we fail to pursue the mining process. But how do we tap into the gold mine and acquire these gifts of the Spirit that may presently elude our grasp—these gifts that refine us, ennoble us, and ultimately even perfect us? Certainly, obedience to God's word is necessary, but alone it is insufficient. There is yet another, perhaps more subtle prerequisite—we must ask. We must want the gifts so fervently that this pursuit is a constant, unending struggle.

Mormon knew that a casual request would never suffice. Speaking of the gift of charity, he said that we must "pray unto the Father with all the energy of heart, that ye may be filled with this love" (Moroni 7:48). It reminds one of the student who had graduated number one in his class from a leading university. There were others with higher I.Q.'s, others with greater creative genius. Asked why he excelled them all, he replied, "As for the others I cannot say, I only know that I cared like blazes." Somewhere, sometime, that level of caring must surface. Pure obedience and silent endurance are not enough. There must be a burning desire, a reaching out, a seeking, in short, an exhaustive exercise of our combined spiritual, intellectual, and emotional energies, all focused on obtaining these divine gifts.

The Savior promised again and again, "Ask, and it shall be given you" (Matthew 7:7). After teaching the Nephites about faith, repentance, baptism, and the sanctifying power of the Holy Ghost, Jesus gave them this divine mandate: "What manner of men ought ye to be? Verily I say unto you, even as I am." This was his invitation for them to become perfect. Then he identified the means to attain such lofty heights: "Whatsoever things ye shall ask the Father in my name shall be given unto you. Therefore, ask, and ye shall receive" (3 Nephi 27:27–29). Ask for what? For help with all our needs, including those things that refine and perfect, chief among which are the gifts of the Spirit. Hugh Nibley made this salient observation: "The [spiritual] gifts are not in evidence today, except for one gift, which you notice the people ask for—the gift of healing. They ask for that with honest intent and with sincere hearts, and we really have that gift, because we are desperate and nobody else can help us. . . .

"As for these other gifts—how often do we ask for them? How earnestly do we seek for them? *We could have them if we did ask, but we don't. 'Well, who denies them?' Anyone who doesn't ask for them.*"[12]

The consequences of righteous, persistent asking are staggering. Who could have had more faith than the Savior's original Twelve—yet they came to him and implored, "Lord, increase our faith" (Luke 17:5). What a marvelous petition. It was a simple, honest request for the gift of which Moroni spoke—"exceedingly great faith" (Moroni 10:11). And what faith came by the asking!

When David, the mighty king of Israel, died, his son Solomon fell heir to the throne. Solomon, probably in his early twenties, was distraught with the responsibility thrust upon him. He felt inadequate. In such a state, he cried out to the Lord, "I know not how to lead them, to go out, or come in before them, and I, thy servant, am as a little child, in the midst of thy people whom thou hast chosen, a great people that cannot be numbered, nor counted for multitude. . . . For who is able to judge this thy people, so great a people?" (JST, 1 Kings 3:8–9).

The overwhelming weight of the crown pressed heavily upon him. No doubt there were many in this favored nation who were older and wiser than he. How could he govern so great a people as this? And so he pled with the Lord for an understanding heart. How did the Lord react to this request? "The speech pleased the Lord, that Solomon had asked this thing" (1 Kings 3:10). Because he righteously desired and asked for this gift, he was rewarded. The Lord gave him a wise and understanding heart. The scriptures record, "God gave Solomon wisdom and understanding exceeding much, and largeness of heart, even as the sand that is on the sea shore. . . . For he was wiser than all men" (1 Kings 4:29, 31). With the gift of wisdom, Solomon's mind began, in part, to partake of the mind of God, and thus the workings of the Atonement—that process of making "at one" both man and God—became operative. The gifts of the Spirit, available only because of the Atonement, became the means of facilitating that spiritual enhancement.

THE RELATIONSHIP AMONG GRACE, GIFTS, AND GODHOOD

Moroni 10 is Moroni's concluding message, his "last lecture," to the generations of this dispensation. He saw our day with 20/20 foresight: "Behold, I speak unto you as if ye were present, and yet ye are not. But behold, Jesus Christ hath shown you unto me, and I know your doing" (Mormon 8:35). With that vision, what would be his final farewell to this generation he knew so intimately? What counsel could he give them that would help them, save them, even exalt them? Moroni 10 is the answer. Moroni spells out certain gifts of the Spirit, and then concludes with the spiritual formula that will make us like God:

"I would exhort you that ye would come unto Christ, and *lay hold upon every good gift* [meaning the gifts of the Spirit and the other blessings of the Atonement]. . . .

"Yea, come unto Christ, and be perfected in him, and deny yourselves of all ungodliness; and if ye shall deny yourselves of all ungodliness, and love God with all your might, mind and strength, *then is his grace sufficient for you, that by his grace ye may be perfect in Christ.* . . .

"And again, if ye by the grace of God are perfect in Christ, and deny not his power, *then are ye sanctified in Christ by the grace of God, through the shedding of the blood of Christ,* which is in the covenant of the Father unto the remission of your sins, that ye become holy, without spot" (Moroni 10:30, 32, 33; emphasis added).

Moroni 10 is the Book of Mormon's concluding doctrinal dissertation. It defines the relationship among grace, gifts, and godhood. The grace that flows from the Savior's atoning sacrifice opens the gate to the divine road, the gifts are the vehicle, and godhood is the destination. By the grace of God the gifts come, and with the acquisition of the gifts, godhood emerges.

NOTES

1. LDS Bible Dictionary, 697.
2. Smith, *Gospel Doctrine,* 68.
3. Smith, *Teachings of the Prophet Joseph Smith,* 346–47.
4. Pratt, *Key to the Science of Theology and a Voice of Warning,* 61.
5. Pratt, *Orson Pratt's Works,* 1:96–97; emphasis added.
6. McConkie, *New Witness,* 370, 371. Orson Pratt taught the same: "We here give [honest inquirers of truth] an infallible sign by which they may always know the kingdom of God from all other kingdoms. Wherever the miraculous gifts of the Holy Ghost are enjoyed, there the kingdom of God exists[;] wherever these gifts are not enjoyed, there the kingdom does not exist" (Pratt, *Orson Pratt's Works,* 1:76).
7. McConkie, *New Witness,* 270.
8. Ashton, *Measure of Our Hearts,* 17.
9. Franklin, *Benjamin Franklin,* 83.
10. In Ashton, *Measure of Our Hearts,* 24–25; emphasis added.
11. McConkie, *Mormon Doctrine,* 314.
12. Nibley, *Of All Things,* 5; emphasis added.

CHAPTER 24

HOW DO THE ORDINANCES RELATE TO THE ATONEMENT?

———— ⊗⊗⊗ ————

THE SPIRITUAL SUBSTANCE OF EVERY ORDINANCE

Some years ago the manager of our law office mistakenly deposited two of my payroll checks into my secretary's account. It was not long before I received an embarrassing phone call from the bank. My checks were "NSF," meaning, of course, "Not Sufficient Funds." As well-meaning as my intentions were, there was simply no money in my checking account at the necessary time to cover the amounts written. In like manner, if there were no Atonement, every baptism, every marriage, every ordinance would be like a check written on an empty account. There would simply be insufficient funds to pay the required price necessary to cleanse us at the time of baptism, to seal us at the moment of marriage, or to resurrect us at the Second Coming. Without the Atonement, each of the ordinances of the gospel might have stamped across it in bold, black letters—"NSF." The Atonement is what gives life and breath and substance to every gospel principle and ordinance. It is the spiritual bank, the letter of credit upon which we draw the ransom funds necessary to pay the demands of justice. In this regard Elder George F. Richards taught: "The ordinances of the Gospel have virtue in them by reason of the atoning blood of Jesus Christ, and without it there would be no virtue in them for salvation."[1] Accordingly, if we want to better understand a saving ordinance and its symbolism, we might appropriately ask, "How does this ordinance relate to the Atonement of Jesus Christ?"

SACRIFICE AND OFFERINGS

The first ordinance instituted among man was animal sacrifice. Adam had been commanded to offer up the firstlings of his flock. This ordinance was designed to direct man's thoughts and attention to the central point in history—the Atonement. The angel declared to Adam, "This thing is a similitude of the sacrifice of the Only Begotten of the Father" (Moses 5:7). The Lord wasted no time in focusing man's spiritual, emotional, and intellectual efforts on that event that mattered most. The sacrifice of animals was among God's first commands to mortal man.

The underlying intent of the sacrificial ordinance was to direct man's thoughts and reflective powers toward the Atonement. This was "the whole meaning of the law, every whit pointing to that great and last sacrifice; and that great and last sacrifice will be the Son of God, yea, infinite and eternal" (Alma 34:14; see also Alma 13:16). Jacob taught, "We keep the law of Moses, it pointing our souls to him" (Jacob 4:5).

As the hosts of Israel offered their sacrifices, however, one wonders how many truly understood the divine meaning behind the mechanical process. Unfortunately, many in Israel never did understand the ordinances and sacrifices relating to the mission of the Savior. They apparently thought that the ordinances themselves brought salvation, without the sacrifice of a redeemer. Abinadi so testified: "There was a law given them, yea, a law of performances and of ordinances. . . . And now, did they understand the law? I say unto you, Nay, they did not all understand the law; and this because of the hardness of their hearts; for they understood not that there could not any man be saved except it were through the redemption of God" (Mosiah 13:30, 32; see also Alma 33:19–20).

Some misguided souls knew of the need for a Redeemer, but incorrectly believed that Abel's blood, not Christ's blood, was the cleansing agent. The Lord spoke of such heresy to Abraham: "And God talked with [Abraham], saying, My people have gone astray from my precepts, and have not kept mine ordinances, which I gave unto their fathers; . . . and have said that the blood of the righteous Abel was shed for sins; and have not known wherein they are accountable before me" (JST, Genesis 17:4, 7; emphasis added).

With hindsight it seems incredible that a people could understand the necessity of the atoning sacrifice but fail to know the sacrificial lamb.

King Benjamin came to the same tragic conclusion: "Many signs, and wonders, and types, and shadows showed he unto them, concerning his coming; and also holy prophets spake unto them concerning his coming; and yet they hardened their hearts, and understood not that the law of Moses availeth nothing except it were through the atonement of his blood" (Mosiah 3:15).

The Lord asked a key question of apostate Israel: "To what purpose is the multitude of your sacrifices unto me? . . . I delight not in the blood of bullocks, or of lambs, or of he goats" (Isaiah 1:11). In other words, sacrifices in and of themselves are meaningless. They are not an end. They become purposeful only if they serve to focus the mind and heart of the giver upon the Savior's atoning sacrifice. Short of that, they are a slaughter, not a sacrifice; they are repulsive, not pleasing to the Lord.

One wonders how so many could fail to understand the Atonement when day after day, year after year, numberless animals were sacrificed as prototypes of the Atoning One. Did not the masses see in this divinely prepared ordinance a simple and clear prototype of the redemption? Similarly, why was it that Daniel alone saw the divine manifestation, "for the men that were with me saw not the vision" (Daniel 10:7)? When the multitude of heavenly hosts burst forth from the celestial realm singing "Glory to God in the highest" (Luke 2:14), why did only a select band of hillside shepherds hear those glorious truths (Luke 2:8–11)? The star likely was visible to all, but why was it only the wise men who followed from the East? Why not multitudes from these distant horizons? There was Saul on the road to Damascus, but why among his fellow travelers did he stand alone as full witness of the resurrected Lord? Because spiritual events can be discerned only by spiritual senses.[2] Again and again this sterling, age-old truth is reaffirmed: prophetic events and spiritual ordinances can be understood only through spiritual means. Any attempt to understand without the Spirit, regardless of cerebral capacity, college degree, or worldly experience, is simply futile.

Fortunately, there were some who understood the spiritual significance of sacrifices. For four thousand years every believer who raised his knife to slay the firstborn of his flock might momentarily identify with the Father of us all. Which of these pastors could thrust his blade with glacial emotion into the warm flesh of a lamb he had lovingly nurtured—and perhaps on occasion defended from both element and enemy—and not wince when the pulsating blood stained his cold steel? On such an occasion the hearts of both sheep and shepherd were pierced. As significant as was the symbolism of this moment, however, the lasting lesson was not of the mind, but of the heart. We can never understand the passionate symbolism of this event by cold logic alone; it must be felt. Every herdsman who looked forward to a Redeemer would undergo his own spiritual catharsis, his own broken heart. By such experience, he would begin to feel, however small those swellings might be, the depth of sacrifice yet to be made in the meridian of time.

The ancient ordinance of sacrifice contained all the elements and symbols necessary to teach the basic truths of the Atonement. The firstlings of the flock represented the firstborn of Deity. The Savior, like the offering required in ancient Israel, would be without blemish (Exodus 12:5; 1 Peter 1:19). No bone would be broken (Exodus 12:46). The sacrifice must "be perfect to be accepted" (Leviticus 22:21). The offering would be voluntary. Moses declared, "He shall offer it of his own voluntary will" (Leviticus 1:3; see also Exodus 35:5). The blood of both sacrifices (animal and Christ) would be shed (1 Peter 1:19). Aaron was commanded to "make an atonement upon the horns of [the sacrificial altar] . . . with the blood of the sin offering." The Lord then pronounced his benediction upon the offering: "It is most holy unto the Lord" (Exodus 30:10). The underlying purpose of these ordinances was plainly taught—"that ye may be clean from all your sins before the Lord" (Leviticus 16:30). Lest anyone fail to remember the spiritual meaning underlying these ancient ordinances, Paul helped to bring things into their proper perspective:

"For it is not possible that the blood of bulls and of goats should take away sins. By the which will [God's will] we are sanctified through the offering of the body of Jesus Christ once for all. And every priest standeth daily ministering and offering oftentimes the same sacrifices, which can never take away sins. But this man, after he had offered one sacrifice for sins for ever, sat down on the right hand of God" (Hebrews 10:4, 10–12).[3]

The nature of the Atonement's redeeming powers was twofold: first, to overcome physical death; and second, to overcome spiritual death. The sacrificial ordinance was symbolic of Christ's shedding of his blood so spiritual death could be conquered. But was there an ancient ordinance or offering that was symbolic of the Savior's prospective conquering of physical death? The ancients' offering of the firstfruits of their land may have been such a symbol.[4]

Moses commanded, "The first of the firstfruits of thy land thou shalt bring into the house of the Lord thy God" (Exodus 23:19; see also Exodus 22:29). Solomon and Nehemiah, as spokesmen for the Lord, would later give similar instructions to their people (Proverbs 3:9; Nehemiah 10:35). This symbolism was perfect for a pastoral society. Each season was a reminder of death and life. Each herb, each plant, each living thing would eventually yield to its mortal nature. With absolute certainty the earth would claim her own and then each new season with unbroken repetition would yield new life. The firstfruits were symbolic of that new life. In similar fashion the earth would have but a temporary lease to, but not permanent ownership of, our mortal clay. In due season, our mortal tabernacles would rise from the ground just as the firstfruits spring forth in their proper season. Paul, acutely aware of this symbolism, spoke of the Savior's resurrection in related terms: "Now is Christ risen from the dead, and become the firstfruits of them that slept" (1 Corinthians 15:20). Modern scripture confirms that the ancient practice of offering firstfruits had even broader implications. Those who honor and obey God will likewise be honored as firstfruits as they come forth in the morning of the first resurrection. The scriptures so record: "They are Christ's, the first fruits, they who shall descend with him first, and they who are on the earth and in their graves, who are first caught up to meet him" (D&C 88:98).

The ordinance of sacrifice, coupled with the offering of the firstfruits of the field, were forms of theological drama designed to teach every spiritually sensitive soul that Christ would come to lay his life upon the altar and thereafter rise from the grave. These ancient offerings were frequent, and their symbolism profound. They were stirring and passionate reminders that the cost of salvation could be paid only in the sacrifice of a God.

BAPTISM

The dual consequences of the Atonement, namely the conquering of physical and spiritual death, are symbolized in tandem-like fashion in the remarkable ordinance of baptism. With all its apparent simplicity, it nonetheless radiates with deep symbolic richness. Baptism is symbolic of the death, burial, and resurrection of Christ. Paul taught that we are "baptized into his death" (Romans 6:3). As we stand in the waters of baptism we represent the sinful man who must die, or as Paul puts it, "Our old man is crucified with him, that the body of sin might be destroyed" (Romans 6:6). The analogy is then expanded further: "We are buried with him by baptism into death" (Romans 6:4;

see also Colossians 2:12). Our immersion in the water correlates to the burial of Christ—the transition period between the old man and the new man. We are "baptized after the manner of his burial, being buried in the water in his name" (D&C 76:51). As we rise from the watery grave, we come forth to "walk in newness of life" (Romans 6:4), for "we shall be also in the likeness of his resurrection" (Romans 6:5). The death, burial, and resurrection of Christ are symbolized in perfect harmony. To change the mode of baptism from immersion to sprinkling, pouring, or any other form is to undermine the simple, but profound symbolism of this sacred ordinance. That is why true baptism can be performed in no other way than immersion.

There are two natural cleansing agents known to man, water and fire. The Gospel of Philip, one of the Nag Hammadi finds, espouses this truth: "It is through water and fire that the whole place is purified."[5] These elements are integral parts of baptism and its companion ordinance, the bestowal of the Holy Ghost. Upon Paul's conversion he was instructed, "Arise, and be baptized, and wash away thy sins" (Acts 22:16). The waters of baptism were symbolic of that washing. Fire is likewise recognized as a purifying, refining, and cleansing agent. Nephi taught, "Then cometh a remission of your sins by fire and by the Holy Ghost" (2 Nephi 31:17). Through Joseph Smith, the Lord further taught of the interrelationship between these two ordinances and their respective symbols: "Thou shalt declare repentance and faith on the Savior, and remission of sins by baptism, and by fire, yea, even the Holy Ghost" (D&C 19:31). Thus we see two cleansing elements, water and fire, joining in symbolic unison to make one clean. But we must not let symbols distort reality: water does not wash away sin; and the "fire" of the Holy Ghost is not the ultimate cause of purification. These are powerful symbols, but symbols nonetheless. Speaking to Adam and his posterity, the Lord gives the correct understanding: "Ye must be born again into the kingdom of heaven, of water, and of the Spirit, *and be cleansed by blood, even the blood of mine Only Begotten;* that ye might be sanctified from all sin" (Moses 6:59; emphasis added; see also Revelation 1:5). So taught John: "The blood of Jesus Christ his Son cleanseth us from all sin" (1 John 1:7).

It always comes back to the blood of Christ, Gethsemane, the Atonement. Orson F. Whitney put the elements of baptism into proper perspective: "There are three elements in baptism, the Water, the Spirit and the Blood; though only two—water and spirit—are usually mentioned. Without Christ's atoning blood there could be no baptism of a saving character."[6] It is the Atonement of Jesus Christ that gives profound meaning and spiritual substance to the ordinance of baptism; without it, all the symbolism in the world would be to no avail.

THE SACRAMENT—IN REMEMBRANCE OF HIM

Four thousand years before Christ, the ancients offered sacrifice in anticipation of the Savior's promised Atonement. But during his last week, with Gethsemane and Golgotha nigh at hand, the Savior introduced the sacrament in place of sacrifice. This ordinance was to be symbolic of the blood he would shed and the body he would give. It was then instituted among the Nephites and later to the Saints of the restored Church with the instruction that they should partake of those symbolic emblems often.

Brigham Young declared, "No matter how many generations come and go, believers in him are required to eat bread and drink wine in remembrance of his death and sufferings."[7] In a sense, the sacrament is a weekly memorial service held in honor of the Savior who died for us. It is almost as though Kipling spoke scripture when he penned:

The tumult and the shouting dies—
The Captains and the Kings depart—
Still stands Thine ancient sacrifice,
An humble and a contrite heart.
Lord God of Hosts, be with us yet,
Lest we forget—lest we forget![8]

So that we will not forget, we partake of his emblems often. This is what Brigham Young taught: "Is this custom [the sacrament] necessary? Yes; because we are so liable to forget."[9] History proves him right. In but one generation's time, following the death of Joshua, the scriptures note that the people had already forgotten "the works which [the Lord] had done for Israel" (Judges 2:10). The scriptures further record that only a short time later "the children of Israel remembered not the Lord their God, who had delivered them out of the hands of all their enemies on every side" (Judges 8:34). How soon our memories fade. That was the observation of Mormon while abridging the plates of Nephi: "Thus we see how quick the children of men do forget the Lord their God" (Alma 46:8).

In the sacred waters of baptism we covenant to take upon us the name of Jesus Christ. But the Lord knows that mortals have a tendency to forget their covenants unless they are constantly reminded. In Old Testament times one did not make a singular sacrifice that lasted for a lifetime—instead, he sacrificed repeatedly throughout his life. Why? Paul gave the answer: "In those sacrifices there is a *remembrance again* made of sins every year" (Hebrews 10:3; emphasis added). This was the message of the Savior to ancient Israel, "Remember, and forget not" (Deuteronomy 9:7; see also Psalm 105:5; 106:7). The sacrament table is a place where there is "a remembrance again" of baptismal covenants. The Lord knows that one of our mortal frailties is that our memories lapse.

The Lord was anxious that the children of Israel not forget his parting of the Jordan River. As a reminder, each tribe was commanded to take one stone from the river and place it at a designated spot in their encampment. The Lord then decreed that "these stones shall be for a memorial unto the children of Israel for ever" (Joshua 4:7). Every time they or their descendants looked upon that monument of stones, it was a physical reminder that God had delivered them in their hour of need.

Such monuments keep alive the heroism of past deeds. It may be the towering shaft of the Washington Monument, the marble rotunda of the Jefferson Memorial, or the simple white crosses of Arlington Cemetery, but in each there is cause for deep reflection and solemn reverence for the past. Likewise, the sacrament is a memorial of Christ's Atonement.

The feast of the Passover was instituted in part to remind the Israelites of the destroying angel that passed them by because of the lamb's blood upon the doorposts. This was a token of the Messiah's blood, which could save them spiritually. So that they would not forget this life-saving episode in Egypt and the event it prefigured, the Lord commanded them: "This day shall be unto you for a memorial; and ye shall keep it a feast to the Lord throughout your generations" (Exodus 12:14).

Likewise, the sacrament is designed to be a physical reminder of God's love and saving power for all generations. As we partake of it meaningfully, it draws, channels, and focuses our spiritual thoughts on the essence of the gospel—the Atonement—symbolized by the bread for his body and the water for his blood. The Savior taught this truth: "This do in remembrance of me. . . . For as often as ye eat this bread, and drink this cup, ye do shew the Lord's death till he come" (1 Corinthians 11:24, 26). It is for this reason the sacramental prayers read, "that they may eat in remembrance of the body of thy Son," and subsequently, "that they may do it in remembrance of the blood of thy Son" (D&C 20:77, 79; see also D&C 27:2).

Elder Spencer W. Kimball observed: "When you look in the dictionary for the most important word, do you know what it is[?] It could be 'remember.' Because all of you have made covenants—you know what to do and you know how to do it— our greatest need is to remember. That is why everyone goes to sacrament meeting every Sabbath day."[10]

Such intense focusing on the life of the Savior, and in particular his Atonement, is designed to produce a supreme spiritual feast. Brigham Young declared, "The Lord has planted within us a divinity; and that divine immortal spirit requires to be fed. . . . That divinity within us needs food from the Fountain from which it emanated."[11] That food may be found at the sacrament table. But Elder Melvin J. Ballard cautions, "We must come . . . to the sacrament table hungry."[12] Some come to the banquet table each week with pitchers, ready to catch and drink every drop of eternal life that is offered. Others come with cups—and still others with yet smaller receptacles. Jedediah M. Grant observed: "A great many people partake of the Sacrament, and at the same time are thinking, 'How many teams can I get to-morrow to haul stone? I wonder if that sister has a bonnet like mine, or if I can get one like hers? I wonder if it is going to be a good day to-morrow, or whether it will rain or snow?' . . . You can sit in this stand and read such thoughts in their faces."[13] I imagine that if we could see the heavenly barometer that reads and records the secret thoughts of each person during this holy ordinance, we would have a pretty good measure of the spirituality of that person.

As a young man, S. Dilworth Young was attending a conference at which a number of priesthood leaders were present. During the course of this meeting he noticed an older brother on one of the last pews. He was sound asleep, with his head back, his mouth wide open. Brother Young then noticed a skylight immediately above this older gentleman's head. The thought went through his mind that if he could climb to that skylight, he could drop wads of paper into the man's mouth and give him the shock of his life. The idea was so intriguing that it preoccupied his mind for the rest of the meeting. Finally the meeting ended, the benediction was offered, and all arose to leave. Elder Young found himself behind a man who was obviously touched. This brother turned to the man by his side and said, "Wasn't that a spiritual feast we had today." Elder Young then said to himself, "Dilworth, where were you when the feast was being served?"[14]

Each week a feast is served at sacrament meeting. Speakers, music, and prayers are integral parts of this meeting, but they are not the main course. The music might be discordant, the speakers monotonous—and yet those who come to the sacrament table hungry still can be filled. Any man or woman who comes to sacrament meeting hungering and thirsting for spiritual food will find refreshment and nourishment for his or her soul. The Savior promised the Nephites, "If ye do always remember me ye shall have my Spirit to be with you" (3 Nephi 18:7). Later, by way of reemphasis, he promised each person who partakes of his emblems properly, "His soul shall never hunger nor thirst, but shall be filled" (3 Nephi 20:8).

As we remember the Atonement and genuinely reflect upon his sacrifice and his love, our souls are filled with appreciation, peace, and a feeling of self-worth that comes from being one with the Savior. President Brigham Young taught, "It is one of the greatest blessings we could enjoy, to come before the Lord, and before the angels, and before each other, to witness that we remember that the Lord Jesus Christ has died for us."[15] The Lord reminded Joseph and Oliver of the constant need to so reflect: "Look unto me in every thought. . . . Behold the wounds which pierced my side, and also the prints of the nails in my hands and feet" (D&C 6:36–37).

Somehow the very act of remembering the Savior and reflecting upon his life is, in and of itself, a catalyst for goodness. It must be difficult if not impossible to genuinely reflect upon the Savior's life and simultaneously do evil. That would be tantamount to asking someone to step forward and backward at the same time. Each time we pause to meditate upon the Savior, we take a spiritual step forward.

Someone once said, "Remembering is the seed of gratitude." Peter wrote his second epistle to the beloved saints in hopes he might "stir up" their "pure minds by way of remembrance" (2 Peter 3:1; see also 2 Peter 1:13). Alma, recognizing the converting force of spiritual reflection, asked the passive saints of Zarahemla, "Have you sufficiently retained in remembrance his mercy . . . ?" (Alma 5:6). King Benjamin, after his sermon on the Atonement, pled with his people, "And now, O man, remember, and perish not" (Mosiah 4:30). Elder Marion G. Romney recalled it being said of President Wilford Woodruff "that while the sacrament was being passed, his lips could be observed in silent motion as he repeated to himself over and over again, 'I do remember thee, I do remember thee.'"[16]

Helaman, a wise father, understood the simple but profound power of remembering. He gave his sons the names of Nephi and Lehi; then, at the age of their maturity he explained the underlying reason behind it all: "Behold, I have given unto you the names of our first parents who came out of the land of Jerusalem; and this I have done that when you remember your names ye may remember them; and when ye remember them ye may remember their works; and when ye remember their works ye may know . . . that they were good. Therefore, my sons, I would that ye should do that which is good, that it may be said of you, and also written, even as it has been said and written of them" (Helaman 5:6–7).

Helaman knew that as his sons reflected upon the lives and good works of their namesakes, there would swell within their hearts a desire to do likewise. Helaman then invited his sons to remember something of even greater import: "Remember that there is no other way nor means whereby man can be saved, only through the atoning blood of Jesus Christ . . . ; yea, remember that he cometh to redeem the world" (Helaman 5:9). Helaman concluded his sermon to his sons with a double reminder, "Remember, remember that it is upon the rock of our Redeemer, who is Christ, the Son of God, that ye must build your foundation . . . a foundation whereon if men build they cannot fall" (Helaman 5:12). Mormon, who abridged these records, read the life of these two fine sons and then concluded with this fitting tribute, "And they did *remember* [Helaman's] words" (Helaman 5:14; emphasis added).

Gerald Lund shared the account he read of a climbing instructor, Alan Czenkusch, who ran a mountain climbing school in Colorado. By way of background Brother Lund explained that "belaying" is the safety system used by climbers wherein one climber anchors the rope and himself so he might be better prepared to hold his partner should he fall. Brother Lund then quoted the original account of Czenkusch's near demise:

"Belaying has brought Czenkusch his best and worst moment

in climbing. Czenkusch once fell from a high precipice, yanking out three mechanical supports and pulling his belayer off a ledge. He was stopped, upside down, ten feet from the ground when his spread-eagled belayer arrested the fall with the strength of his out-stretched arms.

"'Don saved my life,' says Czenkusch. 'How do you respond to a guy like that? Give him a used climbing rope for a Christmas present? No, *you remember him. You always remember him.*'"[17]

What a simple but poignant thought—to always remember him. As Brother Lund observed, "Those very words are the words of the sacramental covenant."[18]

THE SACRAMENT—A TIME FOR INTROSPECTION AND COMMITMENT

The sacrament is also a time of deep introspection and self-examination. Paul exhorted, "Let a man examine himself, and so let him eat of that bread, and drink of that cup" (1 Corinthians 11:28). The sacrament is a time when we not only remember the Savior, but we match our life against that of the Great Exemplar. It is a time to put aside all self-deception; it is a time of absolute sublime truth. All excuses, all facades must fall by the wayside, allowing our spirit, as it really is, to commune spirit to Spirit with our Father. At this moment we become our own judge, contemplating what our life really is and what it really should be. David must have felt this way when he pleaded, "Search me, O God, and know my heart: try me, and know my thoughts: and see if there be any wicked way in me, and lead me in the way everlasting" (Psalm 139:23–24).

Elder David O. McKay isolated the two key elements of worship as instruction and meditation, but "of the two, the more profitable introspectively is the meditation."[19] It is during the sacrament that we are presented with the supreme opportunity for meditation, introspection, and self-examination. It is a time to "commune with your own heart" (Psalm 4:4). It is during such solemn, sacred moments that the sacrament becomes a place of commitment wherein we can resolve to put our lives in order with the divine standard from which we have deviated.

Not only is the Savior the master teacher and the master leader, but he is also the master psychologist. He knows that in our weakness we need to commit not just once at baptism, but frequently thereafter. Each week, each month, each year as we stretch forth our hand to partake of his emblems we commit with our honor, for whatever it is worth, to serve him, keep his commandments, and put our life in harmony with the divine standard.

In one sense, we become like the Israelites of old, of whom Joshua said, "Ye are witnesses against yourselves that ye have chosen you the Lord, to serve him." Then the scriptures record the response of the people: "And they said, We are witnesses" (Joshua 24:22). During the sacrament we become witnesses against ourselves each time we proceed with outstretched hand. There can be no rationalizations, at a later date, that we contemplated, we considered, but we did not commit. The physical act supersedes any excuses we might offer. It is our binding signature on the heavenly contract.

The sacrament is a time to meaningfully reflect upon the life of the Savior, to examine and match our own life against his perfect example, and then to resolve to narrow the gap. But it is not easy. Fortunately, there is a divine power to assist us in these resolves—it is the power of the Savior's love, which was so visibly manifested in his Atonement. His love is like a spiritual magnet that draws us upward. Nephi wrote, "He doeth not anything save it be for the benefit of the world; for he loveth the world, even that he layeth down his own life *that he may draw all men unto him*" (2 Nephi 26:24; emphasis added). Indeed, the Atonement has a drawing power. Elder Joseph F. Smith observed, "The ordinance [i.e., the sacrament] has a tendency to draw our minds from the things of the world and to place them upon things that are spiritual, divine, and heavenly."[20]

In those sacred, reflective moments of the sacrament, when our spirits strain for increased spiritual understanding and acceptance, we better glimpse the meaning of his sacrifice and his love. As our thoughts turn to him, there is a certain "gravitational" pull from spirit to Spirit that draws us heavenward. Such are golden moments of resolution and commitment to be at one with him.

THE SACRAMENT—A TIME FOR HEALING

The sacrament is also a time for spiritual healing. Elder Melvin J. Ballard pondered, "Who is there among us that does not wound his spirit by word, thought, or deed, from Sabbath to Sabbath? We do things for which we are sorry and desire to be forgiven."[21] There may be occasions when we have offended others, spoken words we would like to recall, slipped in the payment of our tithes and offerings, neglected our home teaching, or rendered less than our best in Church service. There are some who have strayed from the Word of Wisdom or from that standard of morality that they know to be right. To each of us who has fallen short in one way or another Elder Ballard has offered this glorious hope:

"If there is a feeling in our hearts that we are sorry for what we have done . . . that we would like to be forgiven, then . . . repair to the sacrament table where, if we have sincerely repented and put ourselves in proper condition, we shall be forgiven, and spiritual healing will come to our souls. . . . I am a witness that there is a spirit attending the administration of the sacrament that warms the soul from head to foot; you feel the wounds of the spirit being healed, and the load being lifted."[22]

At such moments the words of Isaiah come to life: "With his stripes we are healed" (Isaiah 53:5). The sacrament provides a healing balm to the spiritually wounded.

TEMPLE ORDINANCES

The ordinance of baptism opens the gate to the celestial kingdom. Nephi spoke of this gate when he said, "For the gate by which ye should enter is repentance and baptism by water" (2 Nephi 31:17). It is the ordinances of the temple, however, that open the gate of exaltation. President Brigham Young so declared:

"Let me give you a definition in brief. Your endowment is, to receive all those ordinances in the house of the Lord, which are necessary for you, after you have departed this life, to enable you to walk back to the presence of the Father, passing the angels who stand as sentinels, . . . and gain your eternal exaltation."[23]

Joseph Fielding Smith added his witness: "You cannot receive an exaltation until you have made covenants in the house of the Lord and received the keys and authorities that are there bestowed and which cannot be given in any other place on the earth today."[24]

Moses taught the children of Israel that without the temple ordinances they could not "see the face of God, even the Father, and live" (D&C 84:20–22). He then sought to sanctify his people through these higher ordinances. Unfortunately, their hearts were hardened and they forfeited that privilege. The Lord did, however, grant to the Israelites the privilege of building a "temple" in the form of a portable tabernacle, where the lesser ordinances could be administered. The Apostle Paul taught that the lesser law, called the law of Moses, was a "schoolmaster to bring us unto Christ" (Galatians 3:24). Accordingly, the tabernacle was so designed that, as taught by the Church Educational System (CES) in a special slide presentation on temples, "its placement, the furniture, the clothing—each item was specified by the Lord to bear witness, in typology, symbolism and similitude of Jesus Christ and his atoning sacrifice."[25]

The gate of the outer court of the tabernacle was made of fine-twined linen colored in white, blue, purple, and scarlet. White was symbolic of purity, blue was representative of the heavens, purple was symbolic of Christ's kingship, and scarlet symbolized the blood he would shed in Gethsemane. Inside the courtyard stood an altar with a wooden horn (like an animal's horn) attached to each corner, representing the four corners of the earth. This was to remind the people of the global saving power of Christ, who himself was referred to as the "horn of salvation" (Luke 1:69). As the blood of the sacrifice was smeared on the horns it suggested the power of the atoning blood of Christ.

Aaron was commanded to "make an atonement upon the horns of it" (Exodus 30:10).

As one approached the tabernacle it became apparent that the structure was draped with three layers of fabric. The underlying layers were the same color scheme as that found in the gate of the outer court and thus were similarly symbolic. The third or outside covering was of scarlet wool. The CES presentation explained: "The significance of this curtain seems connected to the idea that the Lamb of God (wool) and his atoning blood (the scarlet color) thus covered the sins of Israel, which were atoned for within that sacred house."[26]

Within the holy of holies was found the ark of the covenant. The wooden lid of the ark was covered with a single sheet of gold. Two cherubs, covered with the same sheet of gold, had wings providing a protective panoply over the ark itself. The wings were not meant to be seen as literal, but rather were a "representation of power" (D&C 77:4), symbolizing the saving power of the Atonement. This lid was known as "the mercy seat" (Exodus 25:17–22; alternative Hebrew translation is "atonement-cover"[27]), because here, the CES presentation said, "blood was sprinkled and atonement or payment (propitiation) was made for the sins of Israel."[28]

This "temple experience" for the ancient Israelites was designed to rivet their minds on their prospective redemption by the Savior. Accordingly, it should not seem surprising that the Atonement is a focal point of modern temple worship, just as it was in ancient times.

The ancient Christians also had temple rites, as has been noted by such scholars as Hugh Nibley. In Nibley's research he discovered these observations by Cyril about ancient washings and anointings: "The baptism in question, Cyril explains, is rather a washing than a baptism, since it is not by immersion. It is followed by an anointing, which our guide calls 'the antitype of the anointing of Christ himself,' making every candidate as it were a Messiah. . . . Furthermore, the candidate was reminded that the whole ordinance 'is in imitation of the sufferings of Christ,' in which 'we suffer without pain by mere imitation his receiving of the nails in his hands and feet: the antitype of Christ's sufferings.'"[29]

Hugh Nibley observed, "It has often been claimed that the Book of Mormon cannot contain the 'fullness of the Gospel,' since it does not have temple ordinances." He then responds, "As a matter of fact they are everywhere in the book if we know where to look for them, and the dozen or so discourses on the Atonement in the Book of Mormon are replete with temple imagery."[30]

An integral part of the temple experience is the making of covenants. Why? Because faithful observance of those covenants can help to bring about the broken heart and contrite spirit that allow us to more fully enjoy the infinite blessings of the Atonement. Brother Nibley reminds us that the Atonement was "the supreme sacrifice made for us, and to receive it we must live up to every promise and covenant related to it—the Day of Atonement was the day of covenants, and the place was the temple."[31]

Temples are designed to endow us with power so as to enable us to return to God's presence and be like him. As we understand and embrace the full impact of the Atonement, that power is magnified. When temples are dedicated, the Hosanna shout reminds us, in this holy setting, of Christ's role. The word *hosanna* means "O save us," alluding to Christ's power to save us by his atoning act. It is our privilege, in the sanctity of these holy places, to commune and reflect more meaningfully upon the Savior and his vicarious act of love for each of us, and then to receive of that endowing power that lifts us heavenward. As one enters the celestial room, he is reminded that he might become one with God. But as he looks to the nearby sealing rooms, he is reminded that within those sacred walls are administered the exalting ordinances that can extend to him the power to become like God, and thus, in the temple rests the power and the means to achieve the consummate purpose of the Atonement.

The Atonement is the focal point of each saving ordinance.

296

Elder Dallin Oaks described a gospel ordinance as "a sacred act prescribed by our Savior Jesus Christ as one of the conditions upon which we receive the purifying and exalting blessings of his atonement."[32] Thus it seems appropriate that the ordinances, which are the floodgates to the blessings of the Atonement, should also be symbolic of that supernal act.

NOTES

1. In Madsen, "Temple and Atonement," 72.
2. Of course, heavenly manifestations require not only spiritual sensitivity but they also must be in accordance with God's will.
3. Using Paul's sermon as a springboard, Milton spoke of the relationship between the law of sacrifice and faith in Christ:

   Law can discover sin, but not remove,
   Save by those shadowy expiations weak,
   The blood of bulls and goats, they may conclude
   Some blood more precious must be paid for Man,
   Just for unjust, that in such righteousness,
   To them by faith imputed, they may find
   Justification towards God, and peace
   Of conscience, which the law by ceremonies
   Cannot appease, nor Man the moral part
   Perform, and, not performing, cannot live.

   (Milton, *Paradise Lost*, 333)
4. The author recognizes that his feelings on this subject should be weighed in light of the following thoughts of Elder James E. Talmage: "It is a fact that we look around in nature vainly for any analogy of the resurrection. . . .The bursting forth of the buds in the spring time, the putting on of their foliage again by the trees, has been strained by some and pressed into service as another instance of a resurrection from the dead; but I believe that this is equally faulty, for the tree that is dead does not put forth leaves in the spring, and the plant that is dead does not again bear blossoms" (Talmage, *Essential James E. Talmage*, 95. See, however, John 12:23–24).
5. "Gospel of Philip," 135.
6. Whitney, *Baptism*, 11.
7. Young, *Discourses of Brigham Young*, 172.
8. Kipling, "Recessional," in Cook, *Famous Poems*, 40.
9. *Journal of Discourses*, 6:195.
10. Kimball, "Circles of Exaltation," 3.

11. Young, *Discourses of Brigham Young*, 165.

12. Ballard, *Melvin J. Ballard*, 132.

13. *Journal of Discourses*, 2:277.

14. This story was told by Elder S. Dilworth Young at a stake conference session in the Glendale California Stake, which the author attended.

15. Young, *Discourses of Brigham Young*, 172.

16. Romney, "Reverence," 3.

17. Lund, *Jesus Christ*, 45.

18. Ibid.

19. Conference Report, Apr. 1946, 113.

20. *Journal of Discourses*, 12:346.

21. Ballard, *Melvin J. Ballard*, 132.

22. Ibid., 132–33.

23. Young, *Discourses of Brigham Young*, 416.

24. Smith, *Doctrines of Salvation*, 2:253.

25. Church Educational System, "The Tabernacle," Slide #74.

26. Ibid., Slide #45.

27. See LDS edition of the Bible, Exodus 25:17, footnote a.

28. Church Educational System, "The Tabernacle," Slide #62.

29. Nibley, *Mormonism and Early Christianity*, 364.

30. Nibley, *Approaching Zion*, 567.

31. Ibid., 589.

32. Quoted by Elder John Madsen at a Los Angeles Temple Devotional on 13 Dec. 1998.

CHAPTER 25

HOW DO JUSTICE AND MERCY RELATE TO THE ATONEMENT?

―—∞∞∞――

THE IMMUTABLE LAWS OF THE UNIVERSE

Justice and mercy are difficult concepts to explore, not because there is an absence of scriptural references, but because these concepts exhaust our intellectual resources long before divulging all the answers. Elder McConkie wrote, "We know that in some way, incomprehensible to us, his suffering satisfied the demands of justice."[1]

The scriptures frequently refer to "justice" and the demand for its satisfaction. What, then, is justice, and who requires it? Dictionary definitions are many—"fairness," "righteousness," and "the administration of that which is right." These are only a few. But who determines what justice is? Who demands it? What are the consequences of violating or complying with that which is just?

There are certain laws of the universe that are immutable, that are without beginning of days or end of years. They were not created by an intelligent being, nor are they the product of moral thought, rather they are eternal, co-existent realities with the intelligences of the universe. These laws are immutable in that they cannot be altered or modified in any form. They are unchangeable from eternity to eternity. They are self-existing, self-perpetuating laws to which even God himself is subject. B. H. Roberts spoke of the "eternal existences" that govern even Gods: "[There] are things that limit even God's omnipotence. What then, is meant by the ascription of the attribute omnipotence to God? Simply that all that may or can be done by power conditioned by other eternal existences—duration, space, matter, truth, justice, reign of law, God can do. But even he may not act out of harmony with the other eternal existences which condition or limit even him."[2]

Brigham Young taught the same truth: "Our religion is nothing more nor less than the true order of heaven—the system of laws by which the Gods and the angels are governed. Are they governed by law? Certainly. There is no being in all the eternities but what is governed by law."[3]

Certain of these immutable laws affect the physical or natural world. For example, the Prophet Joseph taught that the "pure principles of element . . . can never be destroyed: they may be organized and re-organized but not destroyed. They had no beginning, and can have no end."[4] Likewise, the Doctrine and Covenants teaches, "The elements are eternal" (D&C 93:33). In other words, the universe contains basic, elemental matter that cannot be created or destroyed, or as Brigham Young said, "[It] cannot be annihilated."[5] There is no exception to this natural law. Even God is not exempt. The Prophet Joseph confirmed this when he taught, "Intelligence . . . was not created or made, *neither indeed can be*" (D&C 93:29; emphasis added).

In and of themselves, the laws of the physical or natural world seem to have no moral implications. They do not affect our spiritual growth. We cannot sin by breaking these laws, because it is not possible to break them. We would not drop a ball from a tower and deduce, "This ball will always fall in this way, because the laws of gravity are just." Justice and mercy have no meaning in these circumstances; fairness or rightness are not issues when it comes to the physical, natural laws; they do not allow for obedience by choice, but rather require uncompromising, involuntary compliance.

There appear to be other immutable laws in the universe, however, that offer both a choice and a consequence, and hence, in this sense, they are spiritual laws. These spiritual laws govern all intelligent beings in the universe—and also govern their progress. For these purposes, progress means an increase in eternal power. In other words, there seem to exist certain immutable laws that will bring power if they are followed or "obeyed," but if they are neglected or "disobeyed" they may trigger the opposite result. For example, it may be that an individual cannot progress without acquiring knowledge. President John Taylor noted that even the gods submit to these immutable laws: "There are certain eternal laws by which the Gods in the eternal worlds are governed and which they cannot violate, and do not want to violate. These eternal principles must be kept, and one principle is, that no unclean thing can enter into the Kingdom of God."[6]

Thus, certain laws govern even the gods. President Taylor does not seem to be suggesting that these laws cannot be violated or broken under any set of circumstances, but rather that they cannot be violated by gods who desire to remain as such.

The Savior observed every spiritual law with undeviating exactness. Apparently because of his compliance with each one, he received power upon power until he acquired the attributes of God, even in premortal times. Such progress was a natural consequence of his exacting compliance. His godhood thus seemed to result not from a creation of these laws, but rather from compliance with them. But what of the rest of us, who do not comply with each and every immutable law? Could we not just try and try and try again until we finally got it right, and then become gods, even though it might be on a delayed timetable? The answer is no. Evidently these immutable spiritual laws offer no leniency or mercy or second chances. If we do not comply, we have lost forever that opportunity for increased power that naturally flows from compliance. Aaron taught that once "man had fallen he could not merit anything of himself" (Alma 22:14). In other words, he could not pull himself up by his own bootstraps, regardless of how much time he had to try to do so. The Savior taught the Nephites the same principle: "While ye are in prison can ye pay even one senine? Verily, verily, I say unto you, Nay" (3 Nephi 12:26). The message was clear—once we sinned, violating the laws of eternity, there was no means of escape without outside help.

If someone falls from an airplane, he will plummet to the ground. The law of gravity will not change to accommodate his dire circumstances. There will be no slowing of the descent or softening of the earth to cushion the fall, however good a fellow he may be. He cannot say just before impact, "Let me take that last step one more time." No, there is only the automatic application of the law, hard and fast and uncompromising. Why does it work this way? There is no answer to that question. It is like asking, "Why does matter exist?" or "Why is the sky endless?" "Why" is not a question that can be asked of something that was never created. It exists because it exists.

THE JUSTICE OF GOD

One might refer to these immutable spiritual laws that govern our progression as justice. Yet such "justice" as this is simply the natural consequence that flows from uncreated law. It exists co-eternally with and independent of the uncreated intelligences of the universe. In this regard, one might ask, "Do these laws constitute or determine justice? Does justice, as a concept of fairness and righteousness, exist only as determined and created by a moral being?" If the answer is yes, then justice would not be a self-existing law, but rather a principle of morality that is the product of intelligent thought. If this is the case, then what being or beings determine and demand justice? Is it God alone? Mankind? The intelligences of the universe? All or part of the above?

The scriptures make it clear that God has a system of justice. It is often referred to as "the justice of God" (Alma 41:3; 42:14, 30; D&C 10:28) or "his justice" (2 Nephi 9:26) or "divine justice" (Mosiah 2:38); but clearly the prophets confirm that God provides a moral system by which man is governed. But how does this moral system relate to the immutable, uncreated laws of which we have just spoken? God understood that our failure to comply with these immutable laws would forever bar us from godhood unless there was another source of power that could be available to man—not because he earned it, not because he had a right to it through worthiness, but because another being with more power was so loving and kind that he was willing, even anxious, to propose and implement a plan that would provide the necessary power to exalt man. God instituted such a plan, known as the "plan of salvation" (Alma 42:5; Moses 6:62), the "plan of redemption" (Alma 12:25, 33; 22:13; 34:16), "the plan of mercy" (Alma 42:15), and "the great plan of happiness" (Alma 42:8). As Jacob reflected upon "the merciful plan of the great Creator" (2 Nephi 9:6), he rejoiced with exclamation, "O how great the plan of our God!" (2 Nephi 9:13). Joseph Smith spoke of the purpose of this plan:

"God himself, finding he was in the midst of spirits and glory, because he was more intelligent, saw proper to institute laws whereby the rest could have a privilege to advance like himself. . . . He has power to institute laws to instruct the weaker intelligences, that they may be exalted with himself, so that they might have one glory upon another."[7]

These laws "to instruct the weaker intelligences" are referred to as "his law" (2 Nephi 9:17) or "the laws of God" (D&C 107:84).

Elder Erastus Snow wrote of the immutable laws of the universe: "I understand that what has exalted to life and salvation our Father in heaven and all the Gods of eternity will also exalt us, their children[.] And what causes Lucifer and his followers to descend to the regions of death and perdition will also lead us in the same direction; *and no atonement of our Lord and Saviour Jesus*

Christ can alter that eternal law, any more than he can make two and two to mean sixteen."[8]

That "eternal law" of which he spoke is the immutable law that governs the path to godhood. God's law can never violate it, circumvent it, or "shortchange" it, but it can complement and supplement it. Perhaps it is not unlike the conditions under which Nephihah operated as chief judge. He was given "power to enact laws according to the laws which had been given" (Alma 4:16). In other words, he could create "smaller" laws, provided they did not violate the principles of any existing "larger" laws. It is a well-known legal principle that individual states may create any law that is not expressly prohibited by the federal constitution. This gives each state wide latitude in determining a system of justice that will govern its citizens, provided such laws never violate our national charter. Perhaps, in a similar way, God may establish any law he desires, provided it does not violate one of the immutable laws of the universe. These laws established by God, if obeyed, will endow his children with added power, even that power necessary to become gods.

By way of illustration, God might not be able to rob a man of his agency to jump from a plane (i.e., to prevent him from sinning), but he might be able to put a parachute on the man's back before he leaps (i.e., provide a means to repent). As the dire consequences of this man's foolish decision quickly unfold, he still has a chance to land safely: He can pull the rip cord. In such a circumstance no law is violated or circumvented. The law of gravity is still in full force and effect. No justice is robbed; yet the sinner is given power to land safely if he will just pull the rip cord (i.e., repent and rely on the protective life-preserving power of the Atonement). Nephi spoke of those who relied on the "tender mercies of the Lord" as those who were "mighty even unto the power of deliverance" (1 Nephi 1:20).

What constitutes the basis, the underlying rationale, for God's laws? God has certain inherent, eternal qualities that never change. He can never act inconsistent with or contrary to those qualities, not because he lacks the power to do so, but he has no desire to do so. Perhaps the brother of Jared was alluding to this fact when he said, "O Lord, . . . thou hast all power, *and can do whatsoever thou wilt*" (Ether 3:4; emphasis added). God's consistent compliance with these inherent qualities is a form of justice (i.e., the administration of that which he deems to be fair and right) because his own moral sense demands compliance. This leads to the next question: Is it possible that God demands justice not only to satisfy his own inherent moral sense, but also to satisfy all the other moral beings in the universe who have a similar standard of morality? In other words, could it be that God has in common with every man who has chosen to be a citizen of his kingdom a set of moral values by which they are desirous of being governed?

THE PEOPLE ALSO DESIRE JUSTICE

Justice in the secular sense is the administration of those laws that are established and consented to by the citizens of a nation or a kingdom. Such justice is demanded by the people. Without this form of justice, chaos rather than order would reign. Likewise, justice in the divine dimension is the administration of those laws that are established and consented to by the people who comprise the kingdom of God. No doubt, in the great primeval council such divine laws were discussed and eventually agreed to. The Prophet Joseph explained, "It has been a doctrine taught by this church that we were in the Grand Council amongst the Gods when the organization of this world was contemplated and that *the laws of government were all made and sanctioned by all present.*"[9] We the people, who would be subject to such laws, had a voice in their adoption.

No doubt the Grand Council in Heaven consisted of far more than a divine proposal immediately followed by a sustaining vote. More likely such a council (or perhaps councils) would have included ample time for discussion, debate, questions, the exchange of feelings, and the sharing of testimonies. This is not to suggest that the plan of salvation was in any way altered or refined, for the Father's plan, as presented, would have been perfect in every way. But the participants, other than the Father and Son, were not perfect. No doubt many of us had an anxious desire to explore every facet of the plan, to understand the consequences of moral agency and the risks inherent with mortal birth. All knew there would be pitfalls, crossroads, high roads, low roads, and sometimes seemingly no road at all. Surely we did not receive the plan in a spirit of casualness. No doubt this was a time of rapt attention and intense inquiry. We were profoundly interested and concerned, for our eternal destinies were at stake. Elder Joseph F. Smith taught: "[We] were in the councils of the heavens before the foundations of the earth were laid. . . . We were, no doubt, there, and took a part in all those scenes; we were vitally concerned in the carrying out of these great plans and purposes; we understood them, and it was for our sakes they were decreed and are to be consummated."[10]

At some point Satan and his followers must have raised objections and competing issues. God certainly had the power to silence such opposing arguments and suppress every contrary thought with his compelling logic and commanding spiritual presence, but he seemed to have temporarily withheld—perhaps for the sake of agency he allowed the events to run their course. If the Grand Council was similar to councils today, each man who so desired would have had the opportunity, the "equal privilege" (D&C 88:122), to discharge the honest feelings of his heart. The noble and great ones probably stepped forward to courageously and boldly defend the plan. Just as the Gods "counseled among themselves" (Abraham 5:3), so too the members of this council may have counseled with each other, not to improve the plan, but to more fully understand and embrace it. Then, after all questions had been answered and testimonies borne, the decisive question was most likely put to a vote.

Among the most basic of all gospel principles is the law of common consent. Mosiah taught this law to his people: "It is not common that the voice of the people desireth anything contrary to that which is right; but it is common for the lesser part of the people to desire that which is not right; therefore *this shall ye observe and make it your law—to do your business by the voice of the people*" (Mosiah 29:26; emphasis added; see also Alma 1:14; Mosiah 22:1).

This fundamental principle of governance by consent was announced upon the formation of the Church in the latter days, and similar counsel was repeated twice thereafter within the short space of six months. Each time the message was similar: "And all things shall be done by common consent in the church" (D&C 26:2; see also D&C 28:13).

This law is fundamental not only in mortality, but in all spheres of our existence. Brigham Young taught: "The eternal laws by which he [God] and all others exist in the eternities of the Gods, decree that *the consent of the creature must be obtained before the Creator can rule perfectly.*"[11] Even when the voice of the people goes contrary to God's will, he has respected their agency. Israel desired an earthly king in lieu of their heavenly king. God told Samuel to explain to the people the consequences of a king, so there would be no misunderstanding about their political future. Then he instructed Samuel to "hearken unto their voice" (1 Samuel 8:9), and make them a king.

Would it seem reasonable that God would violate this basic principle of common consent, so emphasized by him, and impose upon his subjects laws not approved by the voice of the people? To the contrary, it seems no one was more anxious and more willing to promote and foster an environment of agency and common consent than God himself. Unfortunately, "the lesser part of the people" (i.e., Satan and a third part of the host of heaven) desired "that which is not right" (Mosiah 29:26) and therefore were cast out of God's presence. This seemed an appropriate consequence, since they chose not to be bound by the laws that would govern God's kingdom. Unbelievably, they chose chaos over order, contention over harmony, war over peace. By rejecting the Father's plan, they could not become the beneficiaries of those very laws that had the power to exalt them. Why they chose Satan over the Savior is the great enigma of the ages. Was it a lack of faith in the Savior's ability to undergo the atoning sacrifice? Was it lack of faith in their own ability to keep the terms and conditions of God's law? Was it pride, ambition, selfishness—all of these weaknesses combined? Whatever the cause, the heavens wept over their wickedness—but honored each person's right to be disobedient.

The two-thirds who remained accepted the laws given us by the Father. "The voice of the people" (Mosiah 29:26) sanctioned the divine laws he proposed through the Son. That is what the Prophet Joseph taught: "At the first organization in heaven we were all present, and saw the Savior chosen and appointed and the plan of salvation made, and we sanctioned it."[12] If we sanctioned the laws by which we would be governed, it seems that we did so with full understanding of their corresponding blessings and punishments. These laws, with their attendant consequences, were considered just. No one forced us to consent. We voluntarily chose to accept these laws that would govern our spiritual lives so that order rather than chaos would reign.

WHO ADMINISTERS THE LAWS?

The administration, supervision, and execution of these laws, punishments, and blessings by which we chose to be bound is what we know to be "justice." The person responsible for administering these laws is the judge. Mosiah urged his people to "appoint wise men to be judges, that will judge this people according to the commandments of God" (Mosiah 29:11). Those in the great primeval council consented that the wisest of all the Father's children—the Savior—should be judge. We did so with the comforting assurance that he would be absolutely fair and just and merciful in the administration of the law. Enoch called him the "righteous Judge, who shall come in the meridian of time" (Moses 6:57). Not only could the Savior sympathize with our cause, but he could empathize. He would suffer the full spectrum of mortality. No one would know the laws better than he who had been our lawgiver. No one was wiser, for he was "more intelligent than they all" (Abraham 3:19). And no one was more merciful, more kind, more loving or concerned than the Savior himself.

The Savior possessed all the qualifications needed and desired in a perfect judge. The "voice of the people" (Mosiah 29:26) wanted him and approved him and rejoiced in him as their judge. No one at a later date could claim exemption from his decrees. No one could claim he did not understand. No one could claim he was unacceptable, for he had our approval, our consent, our vote in advance of the final judgment. David recognized this: "God is the judge" (Psalm 75:7). Isaiah knew it: "The Lord is our judge" (Isaiah 33:22). And Moroni spoke of the Savior as "the Eternal Judge of both quick and dead" (Moroni 10:34). Jesus also testified of this truth: "The Father judgeth no man, but hath committed all judgment unto the Son" (John 5:22).

MERCY AND GRACE—GIFTS FROM GOD

As crucial as are the laws of justice, they cannot save us. Lehi spoke of man's fate if justice alone were the governing scepter: "By the law men are cut off" (2 Nephi 2:5). Jacob, a son of Lehi, knew there was only one spiritual remedy that could prevent a permanent separation from God: "It is only in and through the grace of God that ye are saved" (2 Nephi 10:24; see also 2 Nephi 2:8). Paul taught the same: "According to [God's] mercy he saved us" (Titus 3:5). There are no exceptions—without mercy and grace there is neither salvation nor exaltation. With his usual insight Shakespeare wrote of that spiritual truth:

> *Though justice be thy plea, consider this,*
> *That in the course of justice none of us*
> *Should see salvation. We do pray for mercy.*[13]

Mercy and grace are gifts from God. In essence, they are companion doctrines. The LDS Bible Dictionary defines grace as a "divine means of help or strength, given through the bounteous mercy and love of Jesus Christ."[14] In other words, the merciful nature of God prompts him to lovingly provide us with gifts and powers (i.e., his grace) that will enhance our godly nature.

Sometimes we have a tendency to shy away from the word *grace* and instead to emphasize works (while certain others take the opposite approach)—but in truth, these two concepts go hand in hand. When the lifeguard stretches out a pole to the drowning swimmer, the swimmer must reach out and hold on if he desires to be rescued. Both the lifeguard and the swimmer must fully participate if the swimmer's life is to be saved. Likewise, works and grace are not opposing doctrines, as is so often portrayed. To the contrary, they are indispensable partners in the process of exaltation.

The word *grace* occurs 252 times in the standard works, while the word *mercy* occurs 396 times. It is apparent that these words are not descriptive of fringe gospel principles. They lie at the core of LDS doctrine, flowing directly from the Atonement of Jesus Christ. Elder McConkie taught: "As justice is the child of the fall, so mercy is the offspring of the atonement."[15] We might further add that grace is the offspring of mercy.

Grace, which denotes divine help or gifts from God, is, as the LDS Bible Dictionary tells us, "made possible by [Jesus'] atoning sacrifice."[16] Each of these gifts is a form of "enabling power"[17] designed to strengthen or assist us in our pursuit of godhood. The terms mercy and grace describe both God's loving nature and the actual gifts endowed upon us by God. By definition, these gifts are unearned by the recipient. Paul referred to grace as "the free gift" (Romans 5:15). Lehi made it clear that "salvation is free" (2 Nephi 2:4), and Nephi echoed the sentiments of his father when he preached that salvation was "free for all men" (2 Nephi 26:27). In certain circumstances these gifts are bestowed without any required action on the part of the recipient; in other circumstances the beneficiary must satisfy certain conditions, not as a means of earning the gift, for there is no equal *quid pro quo*, but because the giver will not bestow the gift until certain minimum conditions are satisfied.

Stephen E. Robinson tells of his little daughter, who anxiously pled for a bicycle. He promised her that if she saved all her pennies, she could one day have one. Motivated by her father's promise, she anxiously engaged in chores around the house, carefully saving every penny she earned. One day she returned to him with a jar full of pennies, anxious to now buy her bicycle. Good to his word, Brother Robinson took his elated daughter to the store where she soon found the perfect bike. Then came the moment of truth—the price tag was more than one hundred dollars. Despondent, she counted her sixty-one pennies. She quickly realized that at this rate she would never have enough to buy her dream. Then Brother Robinson lovingly came to the rescue. "I'll tell you what, dear. Let's try a different arrangement. You give me everything you've got, the whole sixty-one cents, and a hug and a kiss, and this bike is yours."[18] The bicycle was certainly not totally earned by the young girl, but nonetheless, it was gladly given by a father who recognized she had given her all.

This is the spirit in which Nephi counseled, "For we know that it is by grace that we are saved, after all we can do" (2 Nephi 25:23). In other words, we contribute to our salvation, but we do not earn it. That was also the spirit of Paul's message: "For by grace are ye saved through faith; and that not of yourselves: it is the gift of God: not of works, lest any man should boast" (Ephesians 2:8–9). Thus works alone cannot save us; grace is an absolute prerequisite. But a certain amount of works (i.e., the best we have to offer) are necessary to trigger God's grace and mercy. No matter how hard we work, how diligently we serve, or how righteously we live, we will never deserve more than we receive. We will never be too qualified for our kingdom of glory. Brigham Young taught this principle with his usual brevity: "There never was any person over-saved; all who have been saved, and that ever will be in the future, are only just saved, and then it is not without a struggle to overcome, that calls into exercise every energy of the soul."[19]

Alma revealed that only the repentant, meaning those who have given of their spiritual best, "have claim on mercy through mine Only Begotten Son" (Alma 12:34). In this way, works and grace are complementary companions. In fact, they are insepa-rable partners in our pursuit of perfection. While discussing the superiority of faith or works, C. S. Lewis responded in his char-acteristically pragmatic fashion, "It does seem to me like asking which blade in a pair of scissors is most necessary."[20] Perhaps Brigham Young summarized the relationship between grace and works as well as it can be said: "It requires all the atonement of Christ, the mercy of the Father, the pity of angels and the grace of the Lord Jesus Christ to be with us always, and then to do the very best we possibly can, to get rid of this sin within us."[21]

God's mercy, both conditional and unconditional, is manifest in abundant fashion. It was demonstrated by our spirit birth, by our physical birth, and by the creation of the world. These out-pourings of mercy seem to be independent of the Atonement, yet each of them added power to our lives. Certain other acts of mercy or grace flow directly from the atoning sacrifice. In each instance they are manifestations of gifts or enabling powers con-ferred upon man. Evidences of these powers or blessings have been discussed in previous chapters.

MERCY—COMPASSION AND LENIENCY

In one sense mercy is the father of grace (and all the powers that flow therefrom), as discussed above. In another sense, mercy means leniency and clemency; it is compassion shown to an offender. In its highest form, it is love and compassion and wis-dom all mixed in divine proportion. Portia pled with an earthly tribunal to exercise this quality that is so quintessentially godlike in nature:

> *The quality of mercy is not strain'd,*
> *It droppeth as the gentle rain from heaven*
> *Upon the place beneath. It is twice blest:*
> *It blesseth him that gives and him that takes.*
> *'Tis mightiest in the mightiest; it becomes*
> *The throned monarch better than his crown. . . .*
> *It is an attribute to God himself.*[22]

That attribute was fully operative in the Savior at all times. He could have called upon his vast reservoir of celestial power, removed himself from the cross, and avenged himself of his persecutors with fiery indignation; to this he was justly entitled—but mercy, not retribution, was his governing scepter.

Nehemiah spoke of this boundless benevolence of God: "Thou art a God ready to pardon, gracious and merciful" (Nehemiah 9:17; emphasis added). David used the same imagery: "Thou, Lord, art good, and ready to forgive; and plenteous in mercy" (Psalm 86:5; emphasis added). One can almost visualize the imagery of those scriptures—God, anxiously and tenderly watching over his creations, so as to detect every righteous act or benevolent thought that he might reward in abundant measure. He is constantly seeking for the good—"his bowels of mercy are over all the earth" (Alma 26:37; see also D&C 101:9). It is he who "delight[s] to bless with the greatest of all blessings" (D&C 41:1). To the tender Saints of the newly restored Church, the Savior said, "I will have compassion upon you. . . . [F]or mine own glory, and for the salvation of souls, I have forgiven you your sins" (D&C 64:2–3). Even in God's day of wrath, he has said, "with everlasting kindness will I have mercy on thee" (Isaiah 54:8; see also D&C 101:9). All of God's faculties, all of his inclinations are poised and bent on blessing at the slightest provocation. Oh, how God loves to be merciful and bless his children! Perhaps that is his greatest joy. It is that inherent quality that drives him with tireless vigilance to save his children. Lehi so observed: "Because thou are merciful, thou wilt not suffer those who come unto thee that they shall perish!" (1 Nephi 1:14). Indeed, our God "is mighty to save" (Alma 34:18).

Mercy was an attribute that Abraham Lincoln possessed in magnificent measure. Robert Ingersoll penned this tribute of him: "Nothing discloses real character like the use of power. It is easy for the weak to be gentle. Most people can bear adversity. But if you wish to know what a man really is, give him power. This is the supreme test. It is the glory of Lincoln that, having almost absolute power, he never abused it, except on the side of mercy."[23]

Lincoln was entitled to this tribute—Christ infinitely more so.

HOW DOES JUSTICE RELATE TO MERCY?

At one end of the law is mercy in all its compassionate splendor, at the other is justice in all its stern reality. The Atonement is the one act in recorded history that demonstrated the maximum mercy, yet never robbed justice of one ounce of payment. The Atonement ran the full gamut of the law, end to end, mercy to justice. It was all-inclusive, infinite, so to speak, in its compliance with the law. Lehi explained this doctrine: "He offereth himself a sacrifice for sin, to answer the ends of the law, unto all those who have a broken heart and a contrite spirit; and unto none else can the ends of the law be answered" (2 Nephi 2:7; see also 2 Nephi 2:10).

Those who do not repent will suffer everything, Brigham Young said, that "justice can require of them; and when they have suffered the wrath of God till the utmost farthing is paid, they will be brought out of prison."[24] Elder Marion G. Romney also spoke of the awful consequences of those who fail to repent: "Without complying with these requirements and the other principles and the ordinances of the gospel, one is left beyond the reach of the plan of mercy, to rely upon the law of justice, which will require that he suffer for his own sins, even as Jesus suffered."[25] Justice will exact its full penalty, every ounce of its crushing weight, upon the unrepentant; from this there is no escape.

But what of the repentant? Is there any leniency on their behalf? Elder Bruce R. McConkie gave the answer: "It is through repentance and righteousness that men are freed from the grasp of that justice which otherwise would impose upon them the full penalty for their sins."[26] Amulek taught that the unrepentant are "exposed to the whole law of the demands of justice" (Alma 34:16), thus implying that the repentant suffer something less. In pursuing this thought Amulek concludes, "Only unto him that has faith unto repentance is brought about the great and eternal plan of redemption" (Alma 34:16). Alma taught of this sequential relationship between repentance and mercy: "Whosoever repenteth, and hardeneth not his heart, he shall have claim on mercy through mine Only Begotten Son, unto a remission of his sins; and these shall enter into my rest" (Alma 12:34).

The unrepentant person is like the criminal who is forced to serve every year, every month, every day of his ten-year term. On the other hand, the repentant person is like the prisoner who is released for good behavior after five years of his ten-year term. Both paid the legal price; both satisfied the laws of justice; but one received a "reduced sentence" by availing himself of the laws of mercy.

In the process of leniency, the Lord has not exempted the repentant from all suffering. Orson F. Whitney taught, "Men and women still suffer, notwithstanding Christ's suffering and atonement but not to the extent that they would have to suffer if such an atonement had not been made."[27]

Repentance still requires remorse of conscience and godly sorrow, but the Lord does allow the repentant to escape the type and depth of suffering he experienced. Thus, mercy has its claim and the repentant are not "exposed to the whole law." Leniency and clemency are extended to their fullest, but no further, and by so doing are able "to appease the demands of justice, that God might be a perfect, just God, and a merciful God also" (Alma 42:15).

This principle is beautifully illustrated in a parable shared by Elder Boyd K. Packer. He tells of a man who incurred substantial debt in order to acquire some coveted goods. The man was warned against incurring the debt, but he felt he could not wait for the luxuries of life. He must have them now. He signed a contract to pay the obligation in what then seemed to be the distant future. The date of payment seemed to be a long time off, but as the days passed the thought of the creditor loomed in the back of the debtor's mind. Eventually, as it always does, the day of reckoning came. The debtor did not have the means to pay. The creditor threatened foreclosure on the debtor's goods if payment were not made. The debtor pled for mercy, but to no avail. The creditor demanded justice—stern, unflinching justice, to which he was entitled. The creditor reminded the debtor that he had signed the contract and agreed to the consequences. The debtor responded that he had no means of repayment and begged for forgiveness. The creditor was not swayed. There would be no justice if the debt were forgiven. Just at the moment when all apparent avenues of escape had vanished, a deliverer appeared on the scene. Elder Packer continues the parable as follows:

"The debtor had a friend. He came to help. He knew the debtor well. He knew him to be shortsighted. He thought him foolish to have gotten himself into such a predicament. Nevertheless, he wanted to help because he loved him. He stepped between them, faced the creditor, and made this offer.

"'I will pay the debt if you will free the debtor from his contract so that he may keep his possessions and not go to prison.'

"As the creditor was pondering the offer, the mediator added, 'You demanded justice. Though he cannot pay you, I will do so. You will have been justly dealt with and can ask no more. It would not be just.'

"And so the creditor agreed.

"The mediator turned then to the debtor. 'If I pay your debt, will you accept me as your creditor?'

"'Oh yes, yes,' cried the debtor. 'You save me from prison and show mercy to me.'

"'Then,' said the benefactor, 'you will pay the debt to me and I will set the terms. It will not be easy, but it will be possible. I will provide a way. You need not go to prison.'

"And so it was that the creditor was paid in full. He had been justly dealt with. No contract had been broken.

"The debtor, in turn, had been extended mercy. Both laws stood fulfilled. Because there was a mediator, justice had claimed its full share, and mercy was fully satisfied."[28]

The debtor of this story was not fully forgiven of his debt, but through the intercession of the friend, the terms of payment were made more palatable, and when those terms were satisfied the debt was erased. Likewise, the Savior made it possible for us to pay our debt on more merciful terms through the divine principle of repentance. He is always offering the maximum mercy without ever encroaching on the demands of justice.

President John Taylor spoke of the engaging relationship between justice and mercy in the gospel setting: "Justice, judgment, mercy and truth all harmonize as the attributes of Deity. 'Justice and truth have met together, righteousness and peace have kissed each other.'"[29] Eliza R. Snow has taught in lyric form that same celestial truth:

> *How great, how glorious, how complete,*
> *Redemption's grand design,*
> *Where justice, love, and mercy meet*
> *In harmony divine!*[30]

CHRIST BECOMES OUR ADVOCATE

The Savior pleads our case for mercy. He is our advocate.[31] He is the champion of our cause as no other can be. We have seen advocates of law before earthly tribunals—mere mortals who have argued their cases with spellbinding suspense, whose logic was flawless, mastery of the laws disarming, and powerful petitions compelling. Before such mortals, juries have sat in awe, almost with breathless wonder, moved and swayed by every glance, every crafted word, every passionate plea. Yet such advocates, almost Herculean heroes to their patrons, are no match to Him who pleads our case on high. He is the perfect proponent "to appear in the presence of God for us" (Hebrews 9:24). How fortunate we are that he is our "advocate with the Father" (1 John 2:1).

On more than one occasion, a devoted mother pleaded with Abraham Lincoln for the life of a son who had committed a serious offense while serving in the Union forces. Often, touched by that mother's own sacrifice for her country, Lincoln granted the pardon. Perhaps he thought, "Not for your son's sake, but for your sake I will pardon him." Likewise, God the Father must have been deeply moved by the incomparable sacrifice of the Savior. Like the mother who pleaded for the life of her son, the Savior pleads for the spiritual lives of his spiritual children. Not because of their own worthiness, but because of the Savior's sacrifice, they will be spared. This is the Son's plea to the Father:

"Listen to him who is the advocate with the Father, who is pleading your cause before him—saying: Father, behold the sufferings and death of him who did no sin, in whom thou wast well pleased; behold the blood of thy Son which was shed, the blood of him whom thou gavest that thyself might be glorified; wherefore, Father, spare these my brethren that believe on my name, that they may come unto me and have everlasting life" (D&C 45:3–5; see also Hebrews 7:25; D&C 38:4; 110:4).

For the Savior's sake, the Father of us all granted the necessary pardon. Zenos readily acknowledged this truth: "Thou hast turned thy judgments away from me, because of thy Son" (Alma 33:11).

The Prophet Joseph noted these influential powers of the Savior. While offering the inspired dedicatory prayer at the Kirtland Temple, he made reference to the Savior's power to influence the Father: "Thou . . . wilt turn away thy wrath when thou lookest upon the face of thine Anointed" (D&C 109:53). It seems that there was something so noble in the Savior's countenance, so moving and powerful in reflection upon his sacrifice, that it profoundly affects the Father.

Christ's advocacy was not meant to change the nature of an already perfect God, any more than Moses' plea to save Israel (Deuteronomy 9:13–29; Exodus 32:10–14) or Abraham's "bargaining" with the Lord to spare Sodom (Genesis 18:23–33) transformed God into a more merciful or compassionate being. The scriptures plainly state, "Notwithstanding their sins, my bowels are filled with compassion towards them" (D&C 101:9; see also Isaiah 54:8). Regardless of man's wickedness, God's bowels are *already filled* with compassion, *before* any pleading or advocacy commences.

If God's nature is not altered by such actions, then why does Christ advocate and plead our case? Such pleading may open doors for God that would otherwise be closed under the laws of justice. For example, faith opens the door to miracles. Moroni declared, "For if there be no faith among the children of men *God can do no miracle*" (Ether 12:12; emphasis added; see also Mark 6:5–6; 3 Nephi 19:35). Asking opens the door to revelation: "If thou shalt ask, thou shall receive revelation upon revelation" (D&C 42:61). In a similar manner, perhaps advocacy, when combined with the Savior's sacrifice, opens the door to divine pardons. It may be that under the laws of justice, advocacy is a necessary prerequisite to invoking God's mercy—a manifestation of that eternal principle that all available resources must be exhausted before harnessing the powers of heaven.[32] In other words, it may be that man, or his divine advocate, must plead his best case before divine pardons are dispensed.

Thus it may be that the ardor of the Savior's request for mercy—coupled with his infinite sacrifice—permits the God of heaven, under the laws of justice, to respond in like fashion. It is a fulfillment of the scriptural truth that "mercy hath compassion on mercy" (D&C 88:40). Faith precedes miracles, asking precipitates revelation, and pleading prompts pardons.

There may be yet another reason for advocacy, particularly Christ's: it brings about a spiritual bonding between Christ and his children that cannot be achieved in any other way. It is the thread that knits our hearts and souls together. Who among us could watch him plead our case with fervent passion, listen to him rehearse the grueling events of Gethsemane, hear his expressions of unbridled love, and not feel a spiritual kinship with him?

As a result of the Savior's Atonement and advocacy, at the judgment day, when the eternal fate of all hangs in the balance, the Savior will stand "betwixt them and justice" (Mosiah 15:9). He will then "make intercession for the children of men" (Mosiah 15:8). He will plead the perfect balance between mercy and justice. He will be each man's advocate and hope for salvation.

NOTES

1. McConkie, "Purifying Power," 9.
2. Roberts, *The Truth, The Way, The Life,* 418.
3. *Journal of Discourses,* 14:280.
4. Smith, *Teachings of the Prophet Joseph Smith,* 351–52.
5. *Journal of Discourses,* 3:356.
6. *Journal of Discourses,* 25:165–66.
7. Smith, *Teachings of the Prophet Joseph Smith,* 354.
8. *Journal of Discourses,* 7:354; emphasis added.
9. Smith, *Words of Joseph Smith,* 84; emphasis added.
10. *Journal of Discourses,* 25:57.
11. *Journal of Discourses,* 15:134; emphasis added.
12. Smith, *Teachings of the Prophet Joseph Smith,* 181.
13. Shakespeare, *Merchant of Venice,* 4.1.198–200.
14. LDS Bible Dictionary, 697.
15. McConkie, *Promised Messiah,* 245.
16. LDS Bible Dictionary, 697.
17. Ibid., 697.
18. Robinson, *Believing Christ,* 30–32.
19. Young, *Discourses of Brigham Young,* 387.
20. Lewis, *Mere Christianity,* 131.
21. *Journal of Discourses,* 11:301.
22. Shakespeare, *Merchant of Venice,* 4.1.184–89, 195.
23. Ingersoll, *Works of Robert G. Ingersoll,* 3:172.
24. Young, *Discourses of Brigham Young,* 382.
25. Romney, "Resurrection of Jesus," 9.
26. McConkie, *Promised Messiah,* 326.
27. Whitney, *Baptism,* 4.
28. Packer, *That All May Be Edified,* 319.
29. Taylor, *Mediation and Atonement,* 171–72.
30. Snow, "How Great the Wisdom and the Love," in *Hymns,* no. 195.
31. We have previously discussed that Christ is our judge. If that is the case, one might wonder how he can also be our advocate. Does it make sense that he would plead with himself for leniency on our behalf? The scriptures are clear that the Savior is not pleading with himself, but rather is our "advocate *with the Father*" (D&C 45:3; emphasis added; see also 1 John 2:1; D&C 38:4; 110:4). If that be the case, then the Father must also be a judge. The Doctrine and Covenants confirms this assertion: "God and Christ are the judge of all" (D&C 76:68; see also 2 Timothy 4:1). This is consistent with John's observation that the Father "hath given [the Son] authority to execute judgement *also*" (John 5:27; emphasis

added). Evidently, the Father is somewhat like a "presiding judge"—the other judges, the trial judges (i.e., the Savior and his apostles), hear the evidence and render the verdict, but each such trial judge is ultimately accountable to the presiding judge for his actions. The Father delegated judicial powers to his Son (who delegated certain powers to his apostles), but the Son still accounts to the Father. John helps us understand the role of each in the judgment process: "As I [the Son] hear, I judge: and my judgment is just; because I seek not mine own will, but the will of the Father which hath sent me" (John 5:30). In the process of advocating, the Father's will is made manifest in the most favorable circumstance to man, which will the Son then carries out through his judgments.

32. This principle is taught by the Lord in Section 101 of the Doctrine and Covenants. Mobs had driven many of the Saints from their homes in Missouri; they had threatened and persecuted many others. The Lord instructed the Prophet Joseph as to the order of redress the Saints should take. First they should importune the judge, and then the governor, and then the president. If none of those worked "then will the Lord arise and come forth out of his hiding place, and in his fury vex the nation" (D&C 101:89).

CHAPTER 26

WAS THE ATONEMENT NECESSARY OR WAS THERE ANOTHER WAY?

———— ∞∞ ————

THE ABSOLUTE NECESSITY OF THE ATONEMENT

Amulek taught the compelling need for the Atonement: "It is *expedient* that an atonement should be made; for according to the great plan of the Eternal God there *must* be an atonement made, or else all mankind must unavoidably perish" (Alma 34:9; emphasis added; see also Alma 42:15). At the conclusion of the Savior's life, he reaffirmed the absolute necessity of the impending redemption. When the chief priests and elders confronted him in the Garden, the Savior instructed Peter to put up his sword and then reminded Peter of his ability to call forth "more than twelve legions of angels" if necessary. Then came the Savior's reason for restraint: "But how then shall the scriptures be fulfilled, that thus it must be?" (Matthew 26:53–54).

Aaron knew that once a man sinned, he could not spiritually pull himself up by his own bootstraps. He taught, "Since man had fallen he could not merit anything of himself" (Alma 22:14). Alma explained that without the redemption "there was no means to reclaim men from this fallen state" (Alma 42:12). Elder

James E. Talmage shared a like testimony: "We affirm that man stands alone in absolute need of a Redeemer, for by self-effort alone he is utterly incapable of lifting himself from the lower to a higher plane."[1] To some extent, we are like the man who cannot climb out of the pit he has dug for himself until he first acquires a ladder. But there is the "catch": where does he find a ladder? Regardless of physical strength or intellectual prowess, his condition is hopeless if left to himself. He must rely on some third party (i.e., the Savior) to provide the means of escape. The Atonement is that spiritual ladder. David sang of the Messianic moment of rescue: "I waited patiently for the Lord. . . . He brought me up also out of an horrible pit, out of the miry clay, and set my feet upon a rock" (Psalm 40:1–2).

Zeezrom must have sensed man's dilemma, for he pointedly asked Amulek if God could "save his people in their sins" (Alma 11:34). This was a key question. He was asking if God, by divine decree, can pardon sinners regardless of their failure to repent, simply because he wills it and wants it. Amulek was direct in his response: "Ye *cannot* be saved in your sins" (Alma 11:37; emphasis added). Some years earlier, Abinadi had spoken of those who died "in their sins," and of their subsequent fate—"neither can the Lord redeem such; for he cannot deny himself; for *he cannot deny justice when it has its claim*" (Mosiah 15:26, 27; emphasis added). In other words, God could not redeem men in their sins because the laws of justice, which he honors, do not so permit. John Taylor gave the reason for this divine compliance: "It would be impossible for [God] to violate law, because in so doing he would strike at His own dignity, power, principles, glory, exaltation and existence."[2]

King Benjamin spoke of the Atonement and then, in language as exacting as language can be, detailed the absolute need for the atoning sacrifice: "This is the means whereby salvation cometh. And there is none other salvation save this which hath been spoken of; *neither are there any conditions whereby man can be saved* except the conditions which I have told you" (Mosiah 4:8; emphasis added).

King Benjamin was certain on this point—there is no other means of salvation than the Savior—no other conditions, no alternative ways. Some might suggest that there are no alternative ways solely because God in premortal times chose this way (i.e., the Atonement). Should the Atonement fail, they claim, God could still resort to one of the other options that existed in premortal times. The language of King Benjamin, however, seems to contain no such "fall back" position. He clearly states that except for the Savior and his Atonement, there are not "any conditions whereby man can be saved" (Mosiah 4:8). This seems not to be an issue of God choosing the best alternative, but rather the only alternative for man's redemption. Simply speaking, there was no easier way, nor any alternative to the Atonement of Jesus Christ.

But why was an atonement necessary? Perhaps it was necessary to comply with some immutable law (i.e., one of those laws that has always existed and remains unchanged throughout eternity). Or perhaps it was necessary because it was dictated by God's perfect attributes. He knew there was something in that act, and only that act, that would maximize the progress of his children. It was a reflection of his basic nature and hence mandatory in that sense. B. H. Roberts addresses these first two possibilities: "The absolute necessity of the Atonement as it stands would further appear by the confidence one feels that if milder means could have been made to answer as an Atonement, or if the satisfaction to justice could have been set aside, or if man's reconciliation with the divine order of things could have been brought about by an act of pure benevolence without other consideration, it undoubtedly would have been done; for it is inconceivable that either God's justice or his mercy would require or permit more suffering on the part of the Redeemer than was absolutely necessary to accomplish the end proposed. Any suffering beyond that which was absolutely necessary would be cruelty, pure and simple, and unthinkable in a God of perfect justice and mercy."[3]

Elder Roberts suggests the improbability of God having put his Son through such excruciating pain if an easier means were available. Such a conclusion strongly suggests there was no equally viable alternative, or God would have chosen it and thus spared the Shepherd without sacrificing the sheep.

Some have proposed a third possibility for the necessity of an atonement. They suggest that the spirits who chose to become part of God's kingdom may have possessed a sense of morality that was similar to God's, and thus, like him, they "felt" the inherent need for an atoning act before the cleansing and exalting powers could be realized. Perhaps in some way these kindred spirits joined with God in sanctioning the necessity of the Atonement. It may have been part of the law of common consent. This concept suggests that the shared sense of fairness or equity held by the members of God's kingdom may help give support to the laws of justice in the universe.

A fourth possibility is centered in the motivational part of the Atonement. Perhaps this event was necessary because it was the only event in the universe that had the motivational power to draw men to godhood. Anything less would be simply inadequate to accomplish such an end. The "dropout" rate would have been even more horrendous without some cosmic force to lift us heavenward. Accordingly, God may have chosen the Atonement because it was the most persuasive power in the universe to bring us back home. B. H. Roberts quoted Sabine Baring-Gould in this regard: "There was no necessity, some theologians have taught, for Christ to have died, but as S. Bernard says, 'perhaps that method is best, whereby in a land of forgetfulness and sloth we might be more powerfully and vividly reminded of our fall, through the so great and so manifold sufferings of Him who repaired it.'"[4]

There is at least a fifth possibility for the necessity of this atonement. It may have been the only event that could sufficiently appeal on a universal basis to the instinctual sense of fairness in God's children, who might otherwise complain under the laws of justice that some had come to exaltation without "earning" their thrones. In other words, it was the only event of such compelling magnitude that it could facilitate exaltation for the repentant without destroying order and harmony among the remainder of God's children.

With the Atonement, it seems the Father could respond to the Son's plea for mercy without any of the citizens of his kingdom objecting. Why? Because they had a similar sense of morality and similar strains of compassion that may have caused them to say, "It is true that this man has not merited salvation through his own works, but because of the Savior's incomparable sacrifice in his behalf and because of our immense love and reverence for Him, we will acquiesce to his request for mercy."

Whether or not the Atonement is a "must" for one or more of the reasons expressed above, we do not know. For the time being there seems to be a sacred and impenetrable veil protecting our intrusion into the infinite. But what we do know is that the Atonement *is* a "must." That is the underlying and overriding doctrinal conclusion.

WAS A SACRIFICE REQUIRED?

Recognizing that an atonement was necessary in some form, the next question arises: "Why was a sacrifice required instead of some alternative way?" Alma makes it clear that the foreshadowed sacrifice was not merely the best choice; it was the only choice. Alma so records: "It is expedient that there should be a great and last sacrifice; yea, not a sacrifice of man, neither of beast, neither of any manner of fowl; for it shall not be a human sacrifice; but it must be an infinite and eternal sacrifice. Now there is not any man that can sacrifice his own blood which will atone for the sins of another. Now, if a man murdereth, behold will our law, which is just, take the life of his brother? I say unto you, Nay. But the law requireth the life of him who hath murdered; therefore there can be nothing which is short of an infinite atonement which will suffice for the sins of the world.

"Therefore, *it is expedient that there should be a great and last sacrifice,* and then shall there be, or it is expedient there should be, a stop to the shedding of blood; then shall the law of Moses be fulfilled; yea, it shall be all fulfilled, every jot and tittle, and none shall have passed away" (Alma 34:10–13; emphasis added).

There is no question that the Savior's sacrifice had great teaching implications and motivational qualities, but far more critical than either of these is the simple fact that without an infinite sacrifice, there could be no salvation. This sacrifice seems to have been the only means to satisfy those debts that are owed as a result of broken law. Perhaps Christ's suffering was the only legal tender in the universe sufficient to both pay the debt of justice and unlock the door of mercy. His sacrifice became the ransom (see Matthew 9:28), the "pay-off," the purchase price. Elder Marion G. Romney wrote: "It was . . . through acts of infinite love and mercy that he vicariously paid the debt of the broken law and satisfied the demands of justice."[5] This debt is of a two-fold nature. First is the debt owed because of Adam's transgression of the law. This is what Brigham Young was referring to when he said that the Savior "has paid the debt contracted by our first parents."[6] Second is the debt that becomes due each time a man or woman transgresses a law of God.

Brigham Young also spoke of this personal debt and the means of payment: "A divine debt has been contracted by the children, and the Father demands recompense. He says to his children on this earth, who are in sin and transgression, it is impossible for you to pay this debt. . . . Unless God provides a Savior to pay this debt it can never be paid. Can all the wisdom of the world devise means by which we can be redeemed, and return to the presence of our Father and elder brother, and dwell with holy angels and celestial beings? No; it is beyond the power and wisdom of the inhabitants of the earth that now live, or that ever did or ever will live, to prepare or create a sacrifice that will pay this divine debt. But God provided it, and his Son has paid it."[7]

Mormon taught that the Savior had "ascended into heaven . . . to claim of the Father his rights of mercy" because "he hath answered the ends of the law . . . ; wherefore he advocateth the cause of the children of men" (Moroni 7:27–28). The Savior paid the debt and therefore possessed the right to claim mercy on each debtor's behalf. In this sense, Christ championed each man's cause, provided the man had faith in him and repented.

The scriptures teach that we were "bought with a price" (1 Corinthians 6:20; 7:23) and that the Savior gave "his life a ransom for many" (Matthew 20:28; see also 1 Timothy 2:6). His generous repayment opened a new door, or as Amulek taught, it "bringeth about means unto . . . repentance" (Alma 34:15). Certainly we must pay the price of our own folly—from this there is no escape—but the Atonement presented us with an alternative payment program based on mercy, not justice alone. With the Atonement we are given a choice. Either we can pay the price of justice, which is unyielding and inflexible in its demands; or we can pay the price of repentance, as defined by the Savior. This does not mean that the repentant individual escapes all suffering; rather, he now owes his debt to a new creditor, the Atoning One, who "hath purchased [him] with his own blood" (Acts 20:28).[8]

Certainly Christ's sacrifice was necessary to satisfy the demands of justice. Perhaps another reason for his sacrifice is found in its inherent motivational powers. It may have been the maximum means to "draw all men unto [Christ]" (3 Nephi 27:14).

Amulek also gave us an insight into the purpose of the atoning sacrifice when he said, "This being the intent [i.e., purpose] of this last sacrifice, to bring about the bowels of mercy" (Alma 34:15). In other words, the magnitude of suffering was so intense, so deep, so overwhelming and unrelenting that perhaps all of the spirits of the universe, even the most hardened, may have cried out in universal accord, "It is enough." The collective spirits of God's handiwork may have been so touched, so moved by the awesome intensity of Christ's suffering that they would yield to his request to save the repentant, not because any mortal earned the right, but solely because Christ had earned the right for them. The atoning sacrifice may have been the only catalyst that could bring men to such a common accord. Again, this concept rests on the possibility that the laws of justice and mercy in the universe are dependent, at least in part, on the shared sense of fairness or equity among the members of God's kingdom.

WAS THE SAVIOR THE ONLY POSSIBLE SACRIFICIAL LAMB?

A final question addresses the issue of whether or not the Savior was the only candidate or merely the best candidate to be the sacrificial lamb. Some years ago Robert J. Matthews was discussing the question of whether or not there was an "alternative plan, another Savior, a back-up man." He tells of the interchange that took place with a group of teachers, as this topic was being explored:

"I noted that they were strongly of the opinion that if Jesus had failed, there would have been another way to accomplish salvation. They acknowledged that any other way probably would have been harder without Jesus, but, they said, man could have eventually saved himself without Jesus if Jesus had failed. . . . These teachers were saying, in effect, that Jesus Christ was a convenience but not an ultimate necessity. I countered by quoting Acts 4:12, wherein are recorded the words of Peter: 'Neither is there salvation in any other: for there is none other name under heaven given among men, whereby we must be saved.' Their retort was that Peter said this *after* the atonement and resurrection of Christ were accomplished facts, and that therefore there is *now* no other way; but if Jesus had failed to make the Atonement, they reasoned, there would have to have been and would be an alternate way."[9]

Brother Matthews said he protested their conclusions but could not think of an immediate scriptural rebuttal. Later, he said he would have drawn the following to their attention: "We find that Moses 6:52 is the earliest known reference stating that there is no other name other than Jesus Christ by which salvation is obtained. . . . The Lord tells Adam that he must 'be baptized, even in water, in the name of mine Only Begotten Son, . . . which is Jesus Christ, the only name which *shall* be given under heaven, whereby salvation shall come unto the children of men' (italics added). . . .

"Then [we have] 2 Nephi 31:21: 'There *is* none other way nor name given under heaven whereby man can be saved in the kingdom of God' (italics added).

"But the very clearest expression of this concept is given by King Benjamin, quoting the words of an angel from heaven: 'There *shall be* no other name given nor any other way nor means whereby salvation can come unto the children of men, only in and through the name of Christ' (Mosiah 3:17; italics added). . . .

"The value of these passages is that they were spoken *before* the Atonement had taken place. This gives them an additional force and focus that they might not have if they had been spoken afterwards."[10]

Brother Matthews was only giving a representative sample of supporting scriptures. More than eight hundred years before the birth of Christ, the Savior announced his singular status as the Redeeming One: "I, even I, am the Lord; and beside me there is no saviour" (Isaiah 43:11). Lehi saw six hundred years down the corridor of time when the Messiah would come: "All mankind were in a lost and in a fallen state, and ever would be save they should rely on *this* Redeemer" (1 Nephi 10:6; emphasis added). Shortly thereafter an angel of God confirmed "that all men must come unto [the Son of God], or they cannot be saved" (1 Nephi 13:40). Lehi's farewell sermon reminded his family once again "that there is no flesh that can dwell in the presence of God, save it be through the merits, and mercy, and grace of the Holy Messiah" (2 Nephi 2:8). Jacob said it about as directly as it can be said: "My soul delighteth in proving unto my people that save Christ should come all men must perish" (2 Nephi 11:6).

Nephi prophesied that the day of restoration for the Jews would come only when they "look not forward any more for another Messiah. . . . For there is save one Messiah spoken of by the prophets, and that Messiah is he who should be rejected of the Jews" (2 Nephi 25:16, 18). King Benjamin pled with his people to take upon them the name of Jesus Christ. And then he gave the reason: "There is no other name given whereby salvation cometh" (Mosiah 5:8). A few years earlier Abinadi expounded with fervent power to Noah and his wicked priests concerning the unique saving power of the one and only Holy One: "If Christ had not come into the world, speaking of things to come as though they had already come, there could have been no redemption" (Mosiah 16:6). Aaron preached the same truth to the Amalekites: "There could be no redemption for mankind save it were through the death and sufferings of Christ, and the atonement of his blood" (Alma 21:9). Amulek bore testimony of the coming Christ and then explained the need for "an infinite and eternal sacrifice," because "there is not any man that can sacrifice his own blood which will atone for the sins of another" (Alma 34:10, 11). In modern days, the Lord has confirmed his unique role as Redeemer, "for the Lord is God, and beside him there is no Savior" (D&C 76:1; see also D&C 109:4).

One might look for another redeemer; one might speculate as to other possibilities, but it will be in vain. The Savior was not just the best candidate, he was much more—he was the only candidate. The reason is straightforward: he was the only one of the Father's children who came to earth with infinitely divine qualities and thus possessed the infinite power necessary to perform the atoning act. Anyone else simply did not have the power and means to overcome physical and spiritual death.

NOTES

1. Talmage, *Essential James E. Talmage,* 148.
2. Taylor, *Mediation and Atonement,* 168.
3. Roberts, *The Truth, The Way, The Life,* 428.
4. Roberts, *The Seventy's Course in Theology,* 125.
5. Romney, "Resurrection of Jesus," 8.
6. *Journal of Discourses,* 12:69.
7. *Journal of Discourses,* 14:71, 72.
8. Contrary to the foregoing conclusion, some have said that the Atonement is not a repayment of a debt. Their argument focuses on the following scripture: "Go your ways and sin no more; but unto that soul who sinneth shall the former sins return" (D&C 82:7). Once a legal debt is paid,

they say, it is gone forever and, therefore, former sins could not possibly return if the "repayment of debt" theory were correct. In other words, if sufficient suffering had been tendered to pay the debt, then the debt is absolved forever, never to surface again.

There is in the law, however, a well-known principle referred to as a "condition subsequent." It means that a contract can be struck, but if a certain event later occurs, then the contract may be retroactively nullified. (Ballentine's law dictionary defines a condition subsequent as "a condition which follows the performance and operates to defeat or annul it upon the subsequent failure of either party to comply with the condition" [Ballentine, *Law Dictionary with Pronunciations*, 258].) For example, a creditor may have obtained a judgment against a debtor for $1,000,000. For whatever reason the creditor may agree to settle the judgment at a lesser amount, for example $200,000, provided (1) the money is paid immediately, and (2) the debtor never discloses the terms of the settlement offer. (Some lawyers may refer to the obligation of nondisclosure as a covenant rather than a condition subsequent, but in either case the contract can be drafted so that the end result is the same, namely, the lesser settlement amount is nullified and the original $1,000,000 debt is restored if the settlement terms are disclosed.)

If the debtor does in fact disclose the terms of the settlement offer, then the creditor is entitled to seek the full amount of his $1,000,000 judgment and is no longer bound by the terms of the lesser settlement. Consistent with this legal theory, the Lord could say, "I have paid your debt and you are now clean, but this contract has a condition subsequent, namely, if you later engage in the same sin, then that cleansing is retroactively nullified." In other words, Christ paid the price for our sins, but the cleansing is permanent only if we do not return to our former state. Such a legal interpretation is consistent with the scriptural proposition that Christ's suffering paid the debt created by our sins.

9. Matthews, *A Bible!*, 265–66.
10. Ibid., 266.

CHAPTER 27

APPRECIATION FOR THE ATONEMENT

—∞∞∞—

"AMAZED AT THE LOVE JESUS OFFERS ME"

As Jesus entered a certain village, he saw ten lepers standing in the distance. Their disease, considered a form of living death, required the afflicted to cry out "unclean, unclean" (Leviticus 13:45) when approaching those who were not so stricken. In like manner each of us has, to one degree or another, a form of spiritual leprosy—sins that have blotted, defaced, and eaten away at our spiritual well-being. Such a condition makes us unclean in the presence of the Holy One, and like the lepers of the ancient Israelite village, we too must stand off in the spiritual distance until the day of our cleansing. Not unlike the ten lepers, we cry out, "Jesus, Master, have mercy on us" (Luke 17:13). We know there is no hope for a chance cleansing or a self-induced healing. The only hope, the only cure, is to seek the mercy and the cleansing powers offered by the Atoning One.

The Savior exercised those healing powers upon the ten lepers and then gave the command, "Go shew yourselves unto the priests" (Luke 17:14). When the cleansing was complete, one of the lepers turned back and with a loud voice glorified God. He then fell to the Savior's feet, "giving him thanks" (Luke 17:16). He who moments before was but a shadow of life now had life in its fullest. The Savior then asked a soul-searching question of universal implications: "Were there not ten cleansed? but where are the nine?" (Luke 17:17). Are not all mortals eligible for the healing powers of the Atonement? Has not that price been paid for all? Are we among the nine who walk away healed but unmindful, perhaps even ungrateful, of the payment that made it possible? Again and again we might sing the words of the hymn, "I Stand All Amazed":

> *I marvel that he would descend from his throne divine*
> *To rescue a soul so rebellious and proud as mine. . . .*
>
> *I think of his hands pierced and bleeding to pay the debt!*
> *Such mercy, such love, and devotion can I forget?*[1]

We can never forget. The words of David should ring in our hearts again and again: "O Lord my God, I will give thanks unto thee for ever" (Psalm 30:12).

One does not speak lightly of the Atonement or casually express his appreciation. It is the most sacred and sublime event in eternity. It deserves our most intense thoughts, our most profound feelings, and our noblest deeds. One speaks of it in reverential tones; one contemplates it in awe; one learns of it in solemnity. This event stands alone, now and throughout eternity.

As Ammon recounted his success with the Lamanites, he gloried in the Lord, and then, in humble recognition of his inability to articulate it all, he declared, "I cannot say the smallest part which I feel" (Alma 26:16). In like manner, the passions of my own heart extend far beyond my verbal reservoirs. I feel as did Elder Marion G. Romney, who said, "Contemplation of the Atonement . . . moves me to the most intense gratitude and appreciation of which my soul is capable."[2] Even then I am left sorely wanting.

I have been trained by career to be a skeptic; it is inherent in the legal experience. But when it comes to the Savior, I am like a little child. I believe every written and spoken word of which he is the author. I accept every miracle "as is." I believe in every aspect of his divinity and rejoice in every drop of his mercy. I thank him again and again for his atoning sacrifice, but it is never enough—nor will it ever be. His redeeming act shall be remembered and savored "forever and ever" (D&C 133:52). I am overwhelmed, even humbled and "amazed at the love Jesus offers me."[3] I feel as did Nephi, who joyfully confessed, "My heart doth magnify his holy name" (2 Nephi 25:13).

It is hoped that this work, even with its shortcomings, may be a truthful and fitting tribute to him who deserves our all. In the course of this work, I have felt of his kindly spirit again and again. I can truthfully testify that he lives. I now add my testimony to the many who have preceded me that his sacrifice was indeed an infinite and eternal Atonement.

NOTES

1. Charles H. Gabriel, "I Stand All Amazed," in *Hymns,* no. 193.
2. Romney, "Resurrection of Jesus," 9.
3. Gabriel, "I Stand All Amazed," in *Hymns,* no. 193.

BIBLIOGRAPHY

———

Ashton, Marvin J. *The Measure of Our Hearts.* Salt Lake City, Utah: Deseret Book Company, 1991.

Ballard, M. Russell, ed. *Melvin J. Ballard: Crusader for Righteousness.* Salt Lake City, Utah: Bookcraft, 1977.

Ballentine, James A. *Law Dictionary with Pronunciations.* 2d ed. Rochester, New York: The Lawyers Co-Operative Publishing Company, 1948.

Bateman, Merrill J. "The Power to Heal from Within." *Ensign,* May 1995, 13–14.

Bennett, William J., ed. *Our Sacred Honor: Words of Advice from the Founders in Stories, Letters, Poems, and Speeches.* New York: Simon & Schuster, 1997.

Benson, Ezra Taft. "Jesus Christ: Our Savior and Redeemer." *Ensign,* June 1990, 2–6.

———. *The Teachings of Ezra Taft Benson.* Salt Lake City, Utah: Bookcraft, 1994.

———. *A Witness and a Warning.* Salt Lake City, Utah: Deseret Book Company, 1988.

Book of Jasher. Salt Lake City, Utah: J. H. Parry and Company, 1887.

Brown, Hugh B. Conference Report, April 1967, 48–51.

Church Educational System. *Charge to Religious Educators.* Salt

Lake City, Utah: The Church of Jesus Christ of Latter-day Saints, 1979.

———. "The Tabernacle: A Type for the Temples." Old Testament, Slide Set K. Salt Lake City, Utah: The Church of Jesus Christ of Latter-day Saints, 1980.

Clark, Bruce B. and Robert K. Thomas, eds. *Out of the Best Books.* 5 volumes. Salt Lake City, Utah: Deseret Book Company, 1964.

Clark, J. Reuben, Jr. Conference Report, October 1953, 83–84.

———. Conference Report, October 1955, 21–24.

———. *J. Reuben Clark Selected Papers.* Edited by David H. Yarn Jr. Provo, Utah: Brigham Young University Press, 1984.

Cook, Roy J., comp. *One Hundred and One Famous Poems.* New York: Barnes and Noble Books, 1993.

Dante. *The Divine Comedy.* Translated by Lawrence Grant White. New York: Pantheon Books, 1948.

Dickens, Charles. *A Christmas Carol.* New York: Stewart, Tabore & Chang, Inc./Creative Education, 1990.

———. *Christmas Stories.* Garden City, New York: Junior Deluxe Editions, 1955.

———. *A Tale of Two Cities.* New York: Penguin Books USA, 1980.

Dickinson, Emily. *Emily Dickinson, Selected Poems.* New York: Gramercy Books, 1993.

Donne, John. *The Complete Poetry and Selected Prose of John Donne.* Edited by Charles M. Coffin. New York: The Modern Library, 1952.

Drummond, Henry. *Natural Law in the Spiritual World.* New York: J. Pott & Co., 1887.

Emerson, Ralph Waldo. "Gifts." In *Harvard Classics.* Edited by Charles W. Eliot. New York: P. F. Collier & Son, 1937, 5:220.

Evans, Richard L. Conference Report, October 1959, 126–28.

Farrar, Frederik W. *The Life of Christ.* Portland, Oregon: Fountain Publications, 1964.

Faust, James E. "The Supernal Gift of the Atonement." *Ensign,* November 1988, 12–13.

Featherstone, Vaughn J. *The Disciple of Christ.* Salt Lake City, Utah: Deseret Book Company, 1984.

———. *A Generation of Excellence.* Salt Lake City, Utah: Bookcraft, 1975.

Fiske, John. Studies in Religion, vol. 9. In *Miscellaneous Writings.* 12 volumes. New York: Houghton, Mifflin & Co. [c. 1902].

Franklin, Benjamin. *Benjamin Franklin: His Life As He Wrote It.* Edited by Esmond Wright. Cambridge, Massachusetts: Harvard University Press, 1990.

Frost, Robert. *The Poetry of Robert Frost.* Edited by Edward Connery Lathem. New York: Henry Holt and Company, 1979.

Gandhi, Mohandas K. *Mohandas K. Gandhi Autobiography: The Story of My Experiments with Truth.* Edited by Mahadev Desai. New York: Dover Publications, 1983.

Gibbons, Francis M. *Lorenzo Snow: Spiritual Giant, Prophet of God.* Salt Lake City, Utah: Deseret Book Company, 1982.

Goethe, Johann Wolfgang von. *Goethe's Faust.* Translated by Walter Kaufmann. New York: Anchor Books, Doubleday, 1990.

"Gospel of Philip." In *Nag Hammadi Library.* James M. Robinson, general editor. San Francisco: Harper & Row Publishers, 1981.

Grant, Heber J. "A Marvelous Growth." *Juvenile Instructor,* December 1929, 696–97.

Hafen, Bruce C. *The Broken Heart.* Salt Lake City, Utah: Deseret Book Company, 1989.

Hawking, Stephen W. *A Brief History of Time.* New York: Bantam Books, 1988.

Hinckley, Bryant S. *Sermons and Missionary Services of Melvin Joseph Ballard.* Salt Lake City, Utah: Deseret Book Company, 1949.

Hinckley, Gordon B. *Teachings of Gordon B. Hinckley.* Salt Lake City, Utah: Deseret Book Company, 1997.

Holland, Jeffrey R. *Christ and the New Covenant.* Salt Lake City, Utah: Deseret Book Company, 1997.

Holzapfel, Richard Neitzel. "Eternity Sketch'd in a Vision." In *The Heavens Are Open,* 1992 Sperry Symposium on the Doctrine and Covenants and Church History. Salt Lake City, Utah: Deseret Book Company, 1993.

Hunter, Howard W. "Speeches of President Hunter While He Was the Prophet Covered Variety of Topics." *Church News,* 11 March 1995, 7.

Hymns of The Church of Jesus Christ of Latter-day Saints. Salt Lake City, Utah: The Church of Jesus Christ of Latter-day Saints, 1985.

Ingersoll, Robert G. *The Works of Robert G. Ingersoll.* 12 volumes. New York: The Ingersoll League, 1929.

Jones, E. Stanley. *Mahatma Gandhi: An Interpretation.* New York: Abingdon-Cokesbury Press, 1948.

Josephus, Flavius. *Complete Works, Antiquities of the Jews.* Translated by William Whiston. Grand Rapids, Michigan: Kregel Publications, 1978.

Journal of Discourses. 26 volumes. Liverpool, 1855–86. Reprint, Salt Lake City, 1967.

Kavanaugh, Patrick. *The Spiritual Lives of Great Composers.* Nashville, Tennessee: Sparrow Press, 1992.

Kimball, Edward L. and Andrew E. Kimball Jr. *Spencer W. Kimball.* Salt Lake City, Utah: Bookcraft, 1977.

Kimball, Spencer W. "Circles of Exaltation." Summer School Devotional Address. Department of Seminaries and Institutes of Religion, Brigham Young University, Provo, Utah, 28 June 1968.

———. *The Miracle of Forgiveness.* Salt Lake City, Utah: Bookcraft, 1991.

———. *The Teachings of President Spencer W. Kimball.* Edited by Edward L. Kimball. Salt Lake City, Utah: Bookcraft, 1988.

LDS Bible Dictionary. In Holy Bible, Authorized King James Version. Salt Lake City, Utah: The Church of Jesus Christ of Latter-day Saints, 1979.

Lee, Harold B. *Stand Ye in Holy Places.* Salt Lake City, Utah: Deseret Book Company, 1974.

Lewis, C. S. *The Grand Miracle.* Edited by Walter Hooper. New York: Ballantine Books, 1988.

———. *The Inspirational Writings of C. S. Lewis.* New York: Inspirational Press, 1987.

———. *The Joyful Christian.* New York: Simon & Schuster, 1996.

———. *Mere Christianity.* New York: Simon & Schuster, 1996.

———. *Miracles, A Preliminary Study.* New York: Macmillan, 1978.

———. *The Quotable Lewis: An Encyclopedic Selection of Quotes from the Complete Published Works of C. S. Lewis.* Edited by Wayne Martindale and Jerry Root. Wheaton, Illinois: Tyndale House Publishers, 1989.

Ludlow, Daniel H., ed. *Encyclopedia of Mormonism.* 4 volumes. New York: Macmillan, 1992.

———. *Latter-day Prophets Speak.* Salt Lake City, Utah: Bookcraft, 1977.

Lund, Gerald N. *Jesus Christ, Key to the Plan of Salvation.* Salt Lake City, Utah: Deseret Book Company, 1991.

Madsen, Truman G. *Christ and the Inner Life.* Salt Lake City, Utah: Bookcraft, 1988.

———. "The Meaning of Christ—The Truth, The Way, the Life: An Analysis of B. H. Roberts' Unpublished Masterwork." *BYU Studies,* 15 (Spring 1975): 259–92.

———. "The Olive Press." *Ensign,* December 1982, 57–62.

———. "The Temple and the Atonement." In Donald Parry, ed., *Temples of the Ancient World.* Salt Lake City, Utah: Deseret Book Company, 1994, 63–79.

Matthews, Robert J. *A Bible! A Bible!* Salt Lake City, Utah: Bookcraft, 1990.

———. *"A Plainer Translation," Joseph Smith's Translation of the Bible.* Provo, Utah: Brigham Young University Press, 1980.

———. "The Price of Redemption." Sperry Symposium, 29 January 1983, Brigham Young University, Provo, Utah.

Maxwell, Neal A. "But a Few Days." CES—An Evening with a General Authority, 10 September 1982.

————. "Enduring Well." *Ensign,* April 1997, 7–10.

————. *A More Excellent Way.* Salt Lake City, Utah: Deseret Book Company, 1969.

————. *"Not My Will, But Thine."* Salt Lake City, Utah: Bookcraft, 1988.

————. "Overcome . . . Even As I Also Overcame." *Ensign,* May 1987, 70–73.

————. *Plain and Precious Things.* Salt Lake City, Utah: Deseret Book Company, 1983.

————. "Willing to Submit." *Ensign,* May 1985, 70–73.

McConkie, Bruce R. *Mormon Doctrine.* 2d ed. Salt Lake City, Utah: Bookcraft, 1966.

————. *The Mortal Messiah.* 4 volumes. Salt Lake City, Utah: Deseret Book Company, 1987.

————. *A New Witness of the Articles of Faith.* Salt Lake City, Utah: Deseret Book Company, 1985.

————. *The Promised Messiah.* Salt Lake City, Utah: Deseret Book Company, 1978.

————. "The Purifying Power of Gethsemane." *Ensign,* May 1985, 9–11.

————. "The Seven Christs." *Ensign,* November 1982, 32–34.

————. "The Seven Deadly Heresies." In *Speeches of the Year.* Provo, Utah: Brigham Young University, 1981.

McKay, David O. Conference Report, April 1946, 111–16.

————. Conference Report, October 1952, 7–12.

————. Conference Report, October 1963, 5–9.

————. *Gospel Ideals.* Salt Lake City, Utah: Deseret News Press, 1953.

————. "Whither Shall We Go?" In *BYU Speeches,* 10 May 1961.

McKay, Llewelyn R. *Home Memories of President David O. McKay.* Salt Lake City, Utah: Deseret Book Company, 1956.

"The Millennium." *Times and Seasons* 3 (1 February 1842): 671–77.

Milton, John. *Paradise Lost and Other Poems.* New York: Penguin Books USA, 1981.

Nelson, Russell M. "The Atonement." *Ensign,* November 1996, 33–36.

Nibley, Hugh. *Approaching Zion.* Salt Lake City, Utah: Deseret Book Company; Provo, Utah: Foundation for Ancient Research and Mormon Studies, 1989.

———. *Mormonism and Early Christianity.* Salt Lake City, Utah: Deseret Book Company; Provo, Utah: Foundation for Ancient Research and Mormon Studies, 1987.

———. *Of All Things.* Compiled and edited by Gary P. Gillum. Salt Lake City, Utah: Signature Books, 1981.

———. *Old Testament and Related Studies.* Salt Lake City, Utah: Deseret Book Company; Provo, Utah: Foundation for Ancient Research and Mormon Studies, 1986.

Packer, Boyd K. *Let Not Your Heart Be Troubled.* Salt Lake City, Utah: Bookcraft, 1995.

———. *That All May Be Edified.* Salt Lake City, Utah: Bookcraft, 1982.

Phillips, B. J. "The Tennis Machine." *Time*, 30 June 1980, 56–57.

Pratt, Orson. *Orson Pratt's Works.* 2 volumes. Salt Lake City, Utah: Deseret News Press, 1945.

———. *The Seer.* Orem, Utah: Grandin Book Company, 1990.

Pratt, Parley P. *Autobiography of Parley P. Pratt.* Salt Lake City, Utah: Deseret Book Company, 1985.

———. *The Key to the Science of Theology and A Voice of Warning.* Classics in Mormon Literature series. Salt Lake City, Utah: Deseret Book Company, 1978.

Roberts, B. H. Conference Report, April 1911, 56–60.

———. *The Gospel and Man's Relationship to Deity.* Salt Lake City, Utah: George Q. Cannon & Sons Co., 1893.

———. *The "Mormon" Doctrine of Deity.* Bountiful, Utah: Horizon Publishers & Distributors, 1982.

———. *The Seventy's Course in Theology.* 5 volumes. Salt Lake City, Utah: Deseret News Press, 1911.

———. *The Truth, The Way, The Life.* Edited by John W. Welch. Provo, Utah: BYU Studies, 1996.

Robinson, Stephen E. "Believing Christ." *BYU Today,* 44 (November 1990): 26–29.

———. *Believing Christ.* Salt Lake City, Utah: Deseret Book Company, 1992.

Roget's 21st Century Thesaurus. Edited by the Princeton Language Institute. New York: Dell Publishing, 1994.

Romney, Marion G. Conference Report, October 1953, 34–36.

———. Conference Report, October 1955, 123–25.

———. "Jesus Christ, Lord of the Universe." *Improvement Era,* November 1968, 46–49.

———. "The Resurrection of Jesus." *Ensign,* May 1982, 6–9.

———. "Reverence." *Ensign,* October 1976, 2–3.

Sandburg, Carl. *Abraham Lincoln: The Prairie Years and the War Years, 1864–1865.* 3 volumes. New York: Dell Publishing Co., 1975.

Shakespeare, William. *Complete Works.* Edited by G.B. Harrison. New York: Harcourt, Brace & World, 1952.

Sill, Sterling W. Conference Report, April 1955, 116–19.

Smith, Henry A. *Matthew Cowley, Man of Faith.* Salt Lake City, Utah: Bookcraft, 1963.

Smith, Joseph. *Lectures on Faith.* Salt Lake City, Utah: Deseret Book Company, 1985.

———. *Teachings of the Prophet Joseph Smith.* Selected and arranged by Joseph Fielding Smith. Salt Lake City, Utah: Deseret Book Company, 1977.

———. *The Words of Joseph Smith.* Compiled and edited by Andrew F. Ehat and Lyndon W. Cook. Salt Lake City, Utah: Bookcraft, 1981.

Smith, Joseph F. *Gospel Doctrine.* Salt Lake City, Utah: Deseret Book Company, 1989.

Smith, Joseph F., John R. Winder, and Anthon H. Lund. "The Origin of Man." *Improvement Era,* 13 (November 1909): 75–81.

Smith, Joseph Fielding. *Answers to Gospel Questions.* 5 volumes. Salt Lake City, Utah: Deseret Book Company, 1993.

———. *Doctrines of Salvation.* Compiled by Bruce R.

McConkie. 3 volumes. Salt Lake City, Utah: Bookcraft, 1954–1956.

———. *The Signs of the Times.* Salt Lake City, Utah: Deseret Book Company, 1974.

———. *The Way to Perfection.* Salt Lake City, Utah: Genealogical Society of The Church of Jesus Christ of Latter-day Saints, 1951.

Smith, Joseph Fielding Jr. *Religious Truths Defined.* Salt Lake City, Utah: Bookcraft, 1962.

Smith, Lucy Mack. *History of Joseph Smith.* Salt Lake City, Utah: Bookcraft, 1979.

Snow, Eliza R. *Biography and Family Record of Lorenzo Snow.* Salt Lake City, Utah: Zion's Bookstore, 1975.

Snow, LeRoi C. "Devotion to Divine Inspiration." *Improvement Era,* June 1919, 653–62.

Snow, Lorenzo. *The Teachings of Lorenzo Snow.* Compiled by Clyde J. Williams. Salt Lake City, Utah: Bookcraft, 1998.

Stevenson, Joseph Grant. "The Life of Edward Stevenson." Master's thesis. Provo, Utah: Brigham Young University, 1955.

Talmage, James E. *The Essential James E. Talmage.* Edited by James P. Harris. Salt Lake City, Utah: Signature Books, 1997.

———. *Jesus the Christ.* Salt Lake City, Utah: Deseret Book Company, 1955.

———. *A Study of the Articles of Faith.* Salt Lake City, Utah: Deseret Book Company, 1955.

———. *Sunday Night Talks by Radio.* 2d ed. Salt Lake City, Utah: Deseret News Press, 1931.

Taylor, John. *The Gospel Kingdom.* Selected, arranged and edited by G. Homer Durham. Salt Lake City, Utah: Bookcraft, 1987.

———. *The Mediation and Atonement.* Salt Lake City, Utah: Deseret News Company, 1977.

———. *The Mormon,* 29 August 1857.

Tennyson, Alfred, Lord, "The Charge of the Light Brigade." In *Harvard Classics.* Edited by Charles W. Eliot. New York: Gramercy Books, 1938, 42:1006.

Untermeyer, Louis, ed. *A Treasury of Great Poems.* New York: Simon and Schuster, 1942.

Wain, John, ed. *Everyman's Book of English Verse.* London: J. M. Dent & Sons Ltd., 1981.

Wallis, Charles L., ed. *The Treasure Chest.* New York: Harper & Row, 1965.

Webster, Noah. *An American Dictionary of the English Language.* 1828. Reprint, San Francisco: Foundation for American Christian Education, 1967.

Welch, John W. *The Sermon at the Temple and the Sermon on the Mount.* Salt Lake City, Utah: Deseret Book Company, 1990.

Whitney, Orson F. *Baptism, the Birth of Water and of the Spirit.* Salt Lake City, Utah: Deseret News Press, 1927.

———. Conference Report, April 1911, 45–53.

———. *Saturday Night Thoughts.* Salt Lake City, Utah: Deseret News Press, 1921.

———. *Through Memory's Halls.* Independence, Missouri: Zion's Printing and Publishing Company, 1930.

Widtsoe, John A. *Evidences and Reconciliations.* Salt Lake City, Utah: Bookcraft, 1987.

Wilde, Oscar. *The Picture of Dorian Gray.* Chatham, Kent, England: Wordsworth Editions Limited, 1994.

Williams, Oscar, ed. *Immortal Poems of the English Language.* New York: Washington Square Press, 1952.

Young, Brigham. *The Discourses of Brigham Young.* Selected and arranged by John A. Widtsoe. Salt Lake City, Utah: Deseret Book Company, 1961.

Young, S. Dilworth. Conference session in Glendale California Stake [c. 1972].

INDEX

Aaron, 302, 322

Abel, 280

Abinadi: on redemption of mankind, 55–56, 102, 279, 323; on resurrection, 168; converts Alma, 178; on Christ as only way to salvation, 331

Abraham: preaches the gospel, 5; on word of Christ, 74; faith of, 152; understands atoning sacrifice, 163–65, 280; seeks comfort in Christ, 209; attains godhood, 245

Adam: preaches the gospel, 5; causes first physical and spiritual death, 45–46, 171; as possibly the angel who strengthened Christ, 123–24; performs ordinances, 279. *See also* Fall, the

Adam and Eve: misconceptions concerning, 13; in Garden of Eden, 31–33, 42n; mortality of, 34; are cast from God's presence, 35–36; agency of, 37–39; following the Fall, 39–41, 253. *See also* Adam; Eve; Fall, the

Adams, Abigail, 149

Advocacy, 317–19

Afflictions, 104–6, 244

Agency: of Adam and Eve, 36–37, 253; of premortal spirits, 76; continual exercising of, 106–7; of Christ, 151–53; as part of freedom through Christ, 251–52, 254; in Grand Council in heaven, 306–7

Alma the Elder, 168, 178, 182, 205

Alma the Younger: prophesies of Atonement, 3; on Christ inviting all to come unto him, 28; on man reclaimed from spiritual death, 44–45, 48; on judgment of God, 47; on being cut off from God, 56; on death of Christ, 70; on Christ suffering for all afflictions, 105; on Christ suffering as a mortal, 118; on God's time, 147; on Christ's love, 160; on resurrection, 168; on his father's conversion, 178; on not rationalizing, 180, 181; on repentance, 182, 183, 314–15; conversion of, 200; heals Zeezrom, 203; on remembrance, 289; on need for Atonement, 322; on sacrifice of Christ, 326–27

Aminadab, 199–200

Ammon, 173, 202

Ammonihah, people of, 182

Amulek: on Lord embracing all, 27; on judgment of God, 47; on Atonement, 51, 56, 322, 328; on infinite nature of Atonement, 58, 63; on procrastinating day of repentance, 80–81, 102; on resurrected bodies, 169–70; on unrepentant souls, 314, 323; on Christ as only way to salvation, 331

Angel, who strengthened Christ, 123–24

Animals, redemption of, 83–84, 86